# Ba'th v. Ba'th

# BA'TH v. BA'TH

## The Conflict between Syria and Iraq 1968–1989

Eberhard Kienle

I.B.Tauris & Co Ltd
*Publishers*
London
New York

Published in 1990 by
I.B.Tauris & Co Ltd
110 Gloucester Avenue
London NW1 8JA

175 Fifth Avenue
New York
NY 10010

In the United States and Canada distributed by
St. Martin's Press
175 Fifth Avenue
New York
NY 10010

British Library Cataloguing in Publication Data

Kienle, Eberhard
Ba'th v. Ba'th: the conflict between Syria and Iraq, 1968–1989.
– (Society and culture in the modern Middle East.)
1. Syria. Foreign relations with Iraq. 2. Iraq foreign relations with Syria
I. Title II. Series
327.56705691

ISBN 1–85043–192–2

Typeset by Selectmove Ltd, London
Printed in Great Britain by
Redwood Press Limited, Melksham, Wiltshire

# Contents

# Terminology and Transcription

Initially, and whenever misunderstandings may arise, actors are identified as precisely as possible or necessary. However, as in many instances, especially when the same actor is referred to repeatedly, such precision would only complicate the text and render it more difficult to read, shorter terms are used, such as 'Syria' and 'Iraq', for the respective regime or ruling group. When referring to political actors these terms in no case imply the responsibility of the state, country or population at large who throughout the period under review could not choose their rulers.

As a general rule, words from Arabic and Persian have been spelled as simply as possible, basically in accordance with the system chosen by the *Middle East Journal*, but without diacritics and with ayns and hamzas indicated by a prime. Moreover, if currently used, English names of countries, cities, rivers etc. are preferred to their Arabic equivalents.

# Acknowledgements

Most of those whose information, criticism, and practical help have enabled me to conceive, carry out and complete this study have to remain anonymous, because their origin or position exposes them or their families to the risk of reprisals or revenge. Unfortunately, I can only thank them collectively for their support and sympathy.

Among those whose identity I need not conceal, my foremost debt goes to Friedemann Büttner whose whole-hearted support as supervisor, in an intellectual as well as personal capacity, helped me to complete the doctoral dissertation that was the origin of this book. Submitted under the title 'The Syro-Iraqi conflict under the Ba'th regimes, 1968–1988', this thesis was examined and accepted at the Freie Universität Berlin in February 1989. Similarly, Fritz Steppat, also of the Free University, has devoted considerable time and energy to my research and has greatly contributed to it. As it stands, the present study moreover owes much to the suggestions, criticisms and comments, made at different stages, by Eugen Wirth, Peter von Sivers, Thomas Scheffler, Gerhard Weiher, Friedhelm Ernst, Hanna Batatu, Elizabeth Picard, Marion Farouk-Sluglett, Peter Sluglett, Roger Owen and Michel Seurat. While Roger played no minor role in creating the conditions under which I was able to complete this piece of work, Michel and his wife Marie, at an earlier stage with similar generosity and not least through their hospitality in Beirut, enabled me to carry out the more difficult part of my field-work.

Together with many of those already mentioned Stefan Wild, Victor el-Kik, Jean-Paul Pascual and Regina Pascual-Heinecke have also greatly facilitated my research in the Middle East itself. In this respect I am also grateful for the assistance granted by Guntram von Schenk and Birgitta Siefker-Eberle, then at the West German embassy in Damascus, by Rainer Eberle and Harald Braun, their colleagues in Beirut, and by the Auswärtige Amt in Bonn. Additional thanks go to Ofra Bengio, Itamar Rabinovich and Yohai Sella who enabled me to benefit from the newspaper archives and data bank of the Shiloah Centre in Tel-Aviv. Similarly, I am much obliged to Robert Mabro, Thomas Naff and Jürgen Fischer for information relating to Iraqi oil exports via Syria and the sharing of the Euphrates waters. Pravin Mirchandani and Javed Majeed I want to thank for improving my sometimes awkward English, Anna Enayat and Albert Hourani for their advice in transforming the thesis into the present book, Jonathan Livingstone for his editing, and Bridget Harney for her proof-reading.

However, much of this concourse and assistance would have been in vain without the moral and material support of my parents, the generous funding by the Stiftung Volkswagenwerk and the many facilities offered first by the Freie Universität and its research programme on 'Ethnicity and Society' in the Middle East, and then by the warden and fellows of St Antony's College, Oxford, and its Middle East Centre.

# Introduction

## Posing the problem

In the more recent history of the Middle East, interstate conflict has been widely regarded as synonymous with the Middle East conflict between the Arab states and Israel and increasingly also with the so-called Gulf War between Iraq and Iran. Conflicts between Arab states, except perhaps for the Nasir period, have attracted comparatively little interest, both on the part of the wider public in the West, and among historians or social scientists even in the Arab countries themselves. Nonetheless, such conflicts, more or less manifest, have been a permanent feature since the Arab states became politically independent in the aftermath of the second world war. They have also involved regimes declaredly devoted to Arab nationalism, the promotion of all-Arab interests, and the unification of the Arab world into one single state. A case in point is the conflictual relationship between the Ba'th regimes of Syria and Iraq, which, paradoxical as it may seem, is as old as their continued coexistence since 1968.

Throughout this period their relations were predominantly tense or even overtly hostile, and only rarely this overall pattern gave way to a transient *détente* of sorts or to what appeared to be instances of bilateral co-operation. Inverting Clausewitz's notorious phrase, such apparent co-operation was, however, mainly the continuation of war by other means, thus illustrating the advantages of defining conflict in terms not of visible violence but of mutually incompatible goals and interests. According to circumstances these can then give rise to different types of conflict behaviour of which acts of aggression are only one variety.[1]

The present study attempts to identify the issues that to different degrees have determined Syro-Iraqi relations since 1968 through an analysis, not only of bilateral interaction between the regimes, but also of their foreign policies at large and the internal developments in their countries. It aims to give the first comprehensive account and explanation of the major events and developments in Syro-Iraqi relations over the last two decades.

At the same time this explanation, together with the empirical evidence on which it is based, will contribute to determine more thoroughly the nature of the state in the contemporary Arab East and the changes that it has undergone since independence. More precisely, this will be a contribution to the ongoing debate on whether and to what extent the successor states to the Ottoman Empire in the Mashriq have developed into nation-states or rather remained the purely territorial states, all part of the indivisible Arab nation, which they supposedly were when created by the mandatory powers. Although to some extent this question of the emergence and existence of the nation-state can be posed for the entire Arab world, it is far more pertinent to the Mashriq than to the Maghrib.

The failure of the new states to build nations congruent with their respective territories and thus to command the prime loyalty of their nationals would coincide, at the level of interstate relations, with shifts of political allegiance to external actors. Conversely, the emergence of nation-states would imply that loyalties and references to the Arab nation be largely superseded, repelled or replaced by loyalties to the new and smaller *state-nations*. At the level of interstate relations this would inevitably lead to a sharp decrease in shifts of political allegiance across state borders.

Answering the question of the nation-state thus also means answering another, not less debated, question: whether, and how far relations between Arab actors from different countries, viewed from their own perspective, have been directed by domestic or foreign concerns, and to what extent, as a result of perceived cultural, historical-teleological and partly ethnic continuities, these actors have tended to conceive an overarching Arab polity encompassing the different Arab states. In the present case it is in fact the degree to which actors maintain or blur the distinction between internal and external affairs that will serve as the touchstone to gauge the progress made on the way to the nation-state (where the notion of *progress* does not imply any positive value judgement about this destination).

### Arab political unification and the Ba'th Party

The constitution of the Arab Ba'th Party (Hizb al-ba'th al-'arabi or Party of the Arab Renaissance), approved at its first congress in Damascus in April 1947, contained a clear commitment to the political unification of the entire Arab world. Indeed this document declares the 'struggle to gather all the Arabs in a single independent state' to be the party's main goal. This state should be coextensive with the 'Arab fatherland (*watan*) [which] is that part of the globe inhabited by the Arab nation which stretches from the Taurus Mountain, the Pocht-i-Kouh (Pusht-i-Kuh) mountains, the Gulf of Basra, the Arab Ocean, the Ethiopian mountains, the Sahara, the Atlantic Ocean, and the Mediterranean'.[2]

For Michel 'Aflaq and Salah al-Din Bitar, the founding fathers of the new party, and their supporters, some of whom they had inherited from Zaki al-Arsuzi, another albeit disabused and no longer active Arab nationalist, this seemed to be the platform from where, after years of political activity and attempts to organize support, they could now work to realize their version, or rather vision, of Arab socialism and nationalism. The constitution, which was retained when the party merged with Akram Hawrani's Arab Socialist Party (Hizb al-'arabi al-ishtiraki) in 1953 to become the Arab Socialist Ba'th Party (Hizb al-ba'th al'arabi al-ishtiraki), remains the latter's basic document to this day, in both Iraq and Syria.

Though the Ba'th remained rather insignificant in its earlier years, its development and policies seemed to reflect the commitments of its constitution. Soon local party organizations were set up in Arab countries other than Syria, in Transjordan as early as 1947, in Lebanon in 1949, in Iraq, in Saudi Arabia and in Yemen in 1952, and in Libya in 1954.[3] The year 1954 also saw the revision of the party's internal statutes and organizational form in order to reflect the growing importance of its sections outside Syria. Now for each Arab country – or, in Ba'thi parlance: *region*[4] – in which the party was implanted, a Regional Command (*Qiyada qutriyya*, usually abbreviated to RC) was set up, and above these RCs a new supreme body, the National Command (*Qiyada qawmiyya*, abbreviated to NC), was created. While the RCs were each chaired by a regional secretary, the NC and the entire party were presided over by the secretary general.[5]

Despite further changes over the years this basic structure has survived till today, with the notable difference that since 1968, to some extent since 1966, and for reasons to be elucidated in this analysis, there have been two distinct Ba'th parties one dominated by Syria and the other by Iraq.

However, in the early 1950s and early 1960s such divisive tendencies were still absent or hidden. On the contrary, the Ba'th increasingly and clearly emerged as the driving force for Arab unity. In this early period nothing yet portended the future paradox of Ba'thi rule in two countries that, instead of bringing about unity, it led to further division. Certainly, previous Arab nationalist movements had succumbed to division but conditions then seemed altogether different and far from being as promising as in the days of newly acquired independence.

The Ba'th saw in itself the culmination of the history of Arab nationalism, and considered itself to be the one movement that would finally drive home the Arabs' secular dream of political unification, and so fulfil their supreme aspirations. This claim accurately situates the party in its historical context of political thought and action, but otherwise is more a political programme than a statement of facts. For many of those embracing Arab nationalism as an ideology it did not culminate in the establishment of a state coextensive with the entire territory inhabited by Arabs; nor did Arab nationalists ever all subscribe to a definition of the Arab nation as large as the Ba'th's. And quite apart from that, not all of those defined by the Ba'th as Arabs were Arab nationalists but adopted other locally more constricted nationalisms instead.

The origins of Arab nationalism[6] can arguably be traced to the middle of the nineteenth century, especially to the *Nahda* or renaissance of Arab letters. This occurred under the more liberal conditions, first of the Egyptian occupation of Ottoman Syria and Lebanon, and then, after the Turkish *reconquista*, of the Tanzimat or Reform Period. Among Greek Orthodox Christians there was also the wish on the part of the local churches or their lower locally recruited clergy to assert their independence *vis-à-vis* encroachments from the Patriarch of Constantinople. And among Muslims projects emerged and spread to regenerate Islam through an Arab caliphate to replace the present corrupt Turkish one, as for instance the one proposed by al-Kawakibi.

However, it was not until the beginning of the twentieth century that Arab nationalism emerged as an important political force. Although the Young Turks who took power in Constantinople at this time did not immediately dismiss Ottomanism (the ethnically[7] neutral state ideology of the reformers of the empire in the 1870s), they began to formulate and then increasingly adhere to a policy of cultural and societal homogenization or *Turkization* which they considered as essential to modernize the declining and disintegrating state. In this context Arab nationalism became instrumental to the defence of Arab political interests against the cultural and inevitably political and economic threats from the new regime. Yet, many nationalists aimed at some kind of Arab autonomy within the Ottoman Empire and only gradually, largely due to the intransigence of the Young Turk government, demands for complete independence became more urgent and pressing. Certainly, the rather obscure Ligue de la patrie arabe as early as 1905, and thus before the Young Turk take-over, printed leaflets calling for the establishment of two Arab kingdoms: one in the Fertile Crescent, and the other in the Hijaz which would also assume the responsibilities of the caliphate.[8] In 1911 Talib al-Naqib, the deputy for Basra, together with 34 of his colleagues, addressed a letter to the Sharif Husayn of Mecca, declaring their support and loyalty should he choose to lead a rising against the Ottomans.[9] Yet the important Arab National Congress convened in Paris in 1913 still demanded Arab autonomy within the Ottoman Empire.[10] On the question of Arab political unification it is doubtful though not impossible that Naqib and his colleagues had any such idea in mind. They certainly offered to recognize Husayn as caliph but, as it also appears from the statements of the Ligue de la patrie arabe, the concept of the caliphate at that time no longer necessarily implied political authority beyond the defence of the Muslim faith and community;[11] even the simultaneous existence of several caliphates might have been conceivable at that time.[12] In this context the figure of Rashid Rida is significant as from early in the twentieth century onwards, and particularly in the 1920s, he argued in favour of an Islamic state which would ideally encompass all Muslim peoples. Although Muslim in name this state would possibly have been Arab in practice since for Rida a true Muslim would have to become, if not an Arab, at least a speaker of Arabic, the language of the Koran and of the guardians of the Holy Places. However, as a realist, Rida also seemed ready to accept several Muslim states linked together by simply a moral authority, possibly in the form of a caliph uninvolved in day-to-day politics.[13]

Throughout this initial period and for some decades to come Arab nationalist thought and action was confined to the Arab lands of the Ottoman Empire, and the notion of the Arab nation correspondingly excluded the Arabic-speaking people living west of the Sinai. Egypt, though formally still under Ottoman suzerainty, neither considered itself nor was considered part of the Arab nation. Under Muhammad 'Ali, a form of local nationalism had developed and Ottoman rule, whose oppressive character in Arab Asia had sparked off Arab self-assertion, was purely nominal in Egypt and thus rather welcome to counterbalance increasing Western influence.[14] Sati' al-Husri was among the first to extend the concept of the Arab nation to all Arabic-speaking countries and peoples;[15] but in the 1930s he still met only scepticism and rejection among Egyptians.[16] Egypt itself finally joined the Arab fold in the 1940s, but for reasons of power politics and not from nationalist conviction.[17] The Egyptian-promoted Arab League, founded in 1945, then for the first time gave a definition based on consensus of what could be considered as the Arab world; initially restricted to Egypt and the states of the Mashriq the League then expanded to include its present 22 members.

Egyptian nationalism was not the only *local* nationalism in Arabic-speaking countries during this period. In the Arab lands of the Ottoman Empire themselves such local nationalisms emerged, again stretching back to the *nahda*, and again largely in reaction to Turkish domination and later to the attempts at replacing Ottomanism through Turkish nationalism. The concept of an independent Syria which included Lebanon can be traced back at least as far as 1880, even though it was then still insignificant socially and politically,[18] while the idea of Lebanon had already become a strong political issue in the nineteenth century. Yet, these local or regional nationalisms like Arab nationalism owed much of their political relevance to the tendencies among the Young Turks, who towards the eve of the first world war, were beginning to favour Turkification and no longer adhering unswervingly to Ottomanism. It was at that time that the Khazins became the overt advocates of a Lebanese nation and Georges Samné the advocate of a Syrian one. Though for many of their initial protagonists these local nationalisms did not contradict Arab nationalism, these two ideologies at times were also in competition.[19]

When, after the collapse of the Ottoman Empire in 1918, Arabs of the formerly Ottoman lands for the first time since the beginning of Turkish rule had the opportunity to establish a state and government, however ephemeral, it was intended to become a kingdom explicitly limited to the area then known as Syria: that is, roughly, present Syria, Lebanon, Jordan and Palestine. This, in a way, was the logical consequence of convening a Syrian General Congress (*al-Mu'tamar al-suri al-'amm*), elected by the people of the four parts of what was then Syria or, in more modern terms, of geographical Syria. At the same time the Syrian General Congress called for an independent Iraq, and there is strong evidence that local factionalism divided Arab nationalists from Syria (in the narrow sense), Iraq and Palestine. Also, in Syria Arab nationalism in many ways seemed to be a Damascene affair with other cities still sticking to the old ideology of Ottomanism or being half-hearted converts *faute de mieux*.[20] The wish to create distinct political entities in Syria and Iraq was quite clear, even though a political and economic union was envisaged between them and the resolutions of the Syrian General Congress repeatedly referred to the existence of an Arab nation (*al-umma al-'arabiyya*).[21] In fact the existence of an Arab nation for these nationalists did not entail the creation of a state coextensive with this nation. Certainly, and in accordance with a Hashemite family scheme, one member of this family, Faysal, was elected by the Syrian General Congress constitutional king of Syria; and his brother, 'Abdallah, was elected by the less representative Iraqi Congress that simultaneously met in Damascus king of Iraq; while their father, Husayn, continued to rule the Hijaz. (In the end Faysal became king of Iraq and 'Abdallah ended up on the throne of Transjordan, later Jordan.)[22] However, the electors in both cases were well aware of the rivalries between the two brothers and the opposition of Britain and France to any kind of political entity encompassing the entire Fertile Crescent and Arab Peninsula.[23] Thus they took little risk in choosing their respective sovereigns from the same family.

It seems that due to the same factors, by the time the Syrian General Congress convened, the Hashemites themselves had renounced whatever project of an Arab unitary state they had conceived earlier. It was obvious by then that the realities of world politics would never allow the Sharif Husayn to become the king of all Arabs, as he appeared in the eyes of the West – not at all against his will – in November 1916 after his first military successes against the Ottomans in the Hijaz.[24] However, his title was ambiguous as it could mean 'King of the Arab Countries' as well as 'King of the Arab Country', thus perhaps being a synonym for 'Arabia'.[25] It may well be that Husayn first of all sought to defend the title to his emirate in the Hijaz, partly by establishing his supremacy over the Peninsula.[26] He then entered into an alliance with the Arab nationalists merely to legitimize this policy[27] or, if his ambition had really grown, to enlarge his personal or dynastic power.[28] Husayn's project had never been inspired by Arab nationalism as an ideology, even though a desire to reunite the Muslim *umma* gave it some additional impetus. Yet, his interest in an Arab caliphate need not be interpreted – necessarily – as an attempt to unite the Arab world into one state, if considered in the light of the previous remarks about the meaning of that concept at this time. The subsequent project to get Arab Asia divided up into Hashemite kingdoms of the Hijaz, Syria and Iraq was a far cry from the initial idea of a single all-encompassing Arab kingdom, especially in the light of the rivalries between Faysal and 'Abdallah.[29] These rivalries obviously did not preclude them from trying to increase their respective share in Arab territory. Faysal throughout his reign in Baghdad continued to cherish, though silently, the idea of a united Fertile Crescent[30] while 'Abdallah in Amman waited for the appropriate moment to present his plan of a Greater Syria. To both of these schemes we shall come back later, when they were actually put forth and made public.

In the period between the two world wars Arab nationalism primarily opposed the mandates imposed on the countries of the Fertile Crescent by Britain and France.[31] Arab nationalists now fought to end foreign rule and to gain independence. This implied a more local outlook, for some had to oppose the French and others the British. In this process overall Arab political unification became a secondary issue and Arab nationalist rhetoric despite continuous reference to unity increasingly referred to territorial realities created by the mandatory powers.[32] To some extent this even held for Arab nationalists in Syria, mainly in Damascus,[33] who found that geographical Syria, unlike Iraq, had been placed under two different mandates: French for its northern part, that is present Syria and Lebanon; and British for its southern part, that is Palestine and Transjordan.[34] Although this state of affairs was completely unacceptable to them, liberation obviously had to precede (re)unification. A different matter, of course, was the subsequent division of the French mandate into a Lebanese state and then of the rest of Syria further into different statelets.[35] Here the enemy was the same – unity and independence were not to be seen as having chronological order – and the imposed divisions, rather than fragmenting united the nationalists and enhanced their commitment to their cause. Although under King Faysal and then under Ghazi the Iraqi monarchy received considerable support from Arab nationalists outside Iraq and granted them material as well as moral support,[36] local nationalism gained ground, not only in Palestine where Zionist settlements had to be opposed[37] and in Lebanon[38] where Maronites seized the opportunity to rise to political prominence, but also in Syria and Iraq. This led to the rise of the Ahali movement in Iraq,[39] while in Syria the new People's Party, founded in 1925, called for the political unification of Greater Syria.[40] In the same vein Antun Sa'ada in 1932 founded his Syrian National Party (Hizb al-suri al-qawmi), often erroneously translated as Parti populaire syrien. Sa'ada's definition of the nation explicitly rejected the criterion of language and replaced it with the notion of a common interest and consciousness which he claimed united the people of Greater Syria.[41] However, what generally distinguished the local or regional nationalisms cultivated in geographical Syria from those that had currency in Iraq is that they did not accept the political divisions imposed by the mandatory powers. Lebanese nationalism or Lebanonism, mainly among Christians, is the only exception.

Had it not been for the massive Zionist immigration to Palestine which increasingly exacerbated Arab sensitivities, and the uprising of 1936–9 which definitely became the key issue of Arab politics, Arab nationalism might not have survived as a unifying ideology aimed at the creation of a political entity encompassing the entire Arab world. Thus on the background of already existing Arab solidarities, however mitigated they were, unifying factors became efficient. Apart from the immigration of European Jews to Palestine, encouraged or tolerated by Britain, it was especially the *nakba*, the defeat of the Arab armies in 1948, that highlighted the European *divide-et-impera* strategy in the Middle East and the role

of the mandatory powers in determining the political borders. It was
to a large extent the Palestine issue that brought together Arabs as
well as Arab regimes: first in the Bludan Conference in Syria in 1937
and then in a conference of members of Arab parliaments in Cairo
in 1938. The Syrian delegation to the 1938 conference proposed to
reunite Palestine and Transjordan with Syria.[42] Following this the
British government

> formally recognized the interest of other Arab countries in
> the problem of Palestine, and the existence of something
> called an Arab World, by inviting several Arab governments
> to send delegates to the Round Table Conference to be held
> in London.[43]

British policy in the Middle East then became quickly determined
by the developments of the second world war which at the same
time influenced Arab politics. The fall of France and the threats
to Britain helped further to undermine the legitimacy of the states
and borders created by these powers.

At least from the early 1940s onwards Amir 'Abdallah of
Transjordan started to promote his Greater Syria scheme. Harking
back to the resolution of the Syrian General Congress of 1920 this
project aimed at the merger of Lebanon, Palestine, Transjordan
and Syria (in the narrow sense) into one state covering the whole of
geographical Syria. In its more sophisticated version of 1942 it also
provided for cultural union with Iraq, intended to facilitate a future
confederation between the two countries.[44] At the rival Hashemite
court in Baghdad Nuri al-Sa'id launched his more ambitious but
also more serious Fertile Crescent scheme. Elaborated in 1942 and
published in the famous *Blue Book* of 1943 this called not only
for the political unification of geographical Syria but also for its
forming, together with Iraq, the core of an Arab League, which
would have far-reaching responsibilities in matters of defence and
foreign affairs. This Arab League – to be distinguished from the
one promoted by Egypt – would then have been opened up for
other states to join.[45]

However, both Hashemite schemes failed. The Greater Syria
scheme was taken seriously only by 'Abdallah himself and was
stillborn, while the Iraqi Fertile Crescent project succumbed, more
slowly, to the regional dynamics of power. Both schemes were
moreover prejudiced because their protagonists had compromised
themselves too much through their collaboration with the British[46]
and, in 'Abdallah's case, also with the Zionists.[47] It should be
added that, like Husayn's Arab kingdom of 1916, they were
projects inspired by personal or dynastic ambitions, only using
Arab nationalism for their own ends.

But 1943 also saw the birth of a more successful project: if not of an all-embracing Arab state then at least of an all-embracing political institution. In March of that year the Egyptian Prime Minister Nahhas invited the Arab governments to think about the creation of a league of sovereign states, the present Arab League, which came into being in 1945.[48] With this project Egypt, which only recently had taken a greater interest in Arab affairs, certainly pursued its own regional ambitions, especially against the Hashemites. However, these ambitions on the part of Egypt like those of its Arab adversaries were heavily influenced by events in Palestine. These events on the one hand certainly intensified Arab solidarities thus providing the opportunity to disguise hegemony projects as unity schemes, but on the other hand also compelled the different regimes to produce such schemes which would give proof of their commitment to Arab strength through unity. In the 1940s Arab unity schemes, large and small, were again fashionable and on the ascendant. And the Ba'thi one, the most far-reaching of all, has to be seen in this context, although its protagonists were not in power yet. An important exception to this tendency generally however were the communists who like Khalid Bakdash in Syria favoured several Arab states instead of one.[49]

### Syro-Iraqi relations and unity projects prior to 1968

After political independence in the aftermath of the second world war, the Ba'th did not monopolize the discourse of Arab unification or unity. Other actors devised their own projects, whether they encompassed all Arab countries or were more regionally oriented. Without dwelling too extensively on these various schemes,[50] brief reference should be made to some of those originating in Syria or Iraq, that aimed at the respective neighbouring country or otherwise affected their bilateral relations. Although Syro-Iraqi relations before 1963 do not and those before 1968 only scarcely contribute to the explanation of Syro-Iraqi relations after 1968, these earlier periods provide comparative material to assess continuities and discontinuities over time.

The increasing appeal of Arab as opposed to local or regional nationalisms – at least at the level of discourse – may be gauged from the revised concept of Greater Syria adhered to by the Syrian National Party, now rebaptized as the Syrian Social National Party.[51] Iraq was now included, and so was Cyprus in what may have been an attempt to tip the balance back in favour of Sa'ada's Greek-Orthodox co-religionists.[52] It was therefore no surprise that the two rival Hashemite schemes of Greater Syria and of Fertile Crescent unity remained in the air. 'Abdallah, who under the terms of his 1946 treaty with Britain was promoted from amir to king of Transjordan, immediately used his new independence to relaunch his Greater Syria scheme which was elevated to a principle of his government's foreign policy.[53] His Iraqi competitors moved more subtly but also more ruthlessly to promote their own Fertile Crescent project. They cultivated an important clientele among the politicians of Syria,[54] but when conspiracy failed to yield tangible results subtlety was discarded, and with the connivance of pro-Hashemite forces in Syria military attacks were twice planned, although they were not carried out.[55] A new and modified Fertile Crescent plan was issued as late as 1954 when the Iraqi government of the day put before the Arab League the project of a union between Syria, Iraq and now even Jordan as a first step towards complete union.[56]

In Syria itself 'Abdallah's plans aroused little enthusiasm, but the Iraqi solution, not least due to the substantial bribes disbursed, gained sympathy in some quarters.[57] So in March 1949 Husni al-Za'im, Syria's first military dictator after only three years of parliamentary rule, approached Baghdad with a unity scheme copied from the Fertile Crescent project.[58] The vicissitudes and ultimate failure of this project need not concern us here more than those of its subsequent versions such as the one pursued by the new People's Party (distinct from the one founded in 1925) in late 1949 after Za'im had been overthrown by Sami Hinnawi.[59]

The Iraqi side largely schemed these union or merger plans to gain the upper hand in the 'Struggle for Syria', that is in the competition for regional hegemony that opposed it to Egypt. As Patrick Seale wrote:

> the contest between Iraq and Egypt has been a striking feature of the post-war period. Each thought to contain the other on his home river-system. Each aspiring to lead the Arabs sought friends among neighbours and powerful allies farther afield. But time and again, success seemed to turn on the control of Syria: a tacit premise underlying the Arab policies of both Egypt and Iraq was that Syria held the key to the struggle for local primacy.[60]

Another factor was the ambition of the Regent, 'Abd al-Ilah, to climb on to a future Syrian throne, once Faysal II reached his majority, and thus make him redundant.[61]

In Syria unity with Iraq was mainly the interest of the People's Party whose predominantly Alepine constituency suffered economically from the Syro-Iraqi border and moreover found itself at a relative disadvantage *vis-à-vis* its bourgeois competitors from Damascus. In other cases, such as Za'im's, unity was a device to prop up unstable rule. Thus in both countries unity schemes emerged from 'particularist' interests for whom there would be a direct economic advantage or more generally considerations of power which, of course, then as much as now were translatable into economic benefit.

However, Syria as a whole was not well disposed towards Iraq. Other political actors in the country preferred close relations with Egypt or in some cases with Saudi Arabia, if only to defend their interests more effectively in internal conflicts with those who could count on support from Iraq. Iraq, of course, in turn considered its own external alliance in equally defensive terms. Syro-Iraqi relations consequently oscillated, depending on which group was in control of government in Damascus. Conflict was over Iraqi hegemony projects allied to material interests of a faction of the geographically fragmented Syrian bourgeoisie, as opposed to the latter's inner-Syrian competitors. It was exacerbated in 1955 when Iraq signed the Baghdad Pact, which was seen by Damascus as an attempt to enhance its regional position through an alliance with imperialist forces.[62] In Syria the Baghdad Pact split Iraq's supporters and further contributed to the country's *rapprochement* with Egypt.

While none of the Arab unity schemes had yet been successful, the Ba'th's efforts seemed to be more auspicious. Certainly, there had been agreements of co-operation, more or less limited or extensive, but no integration or even merger of states. The Ba'th now seemed to bring this series of failures to an end. When for the first time it achieved some representation in an Arab government, that of Syria, it attempted and temporarily succeeded in bringing about the *dépassement* of this state into a larger entity, the United Arab Republic (UAR). At this point it should be recalled that Michel 'Aflaq had served as Minister of Education from August to November 1949 under Hinnawi and then, throughout the 1940s and 1950s, had opposed union with Iraq on the grounds that it would only result in increased power for the Hashemites and Britain and consequently contradict Arab independence.[63] Among many of his contemporaries this was an entirely acceptable stance that left no stains on his Arab nationalist reputation and record (although other things did).

In June 1956, however, the Ba'th again participated in a government with, for the first time, an actual say in policy making.

Then, some twenty months after the 1954 general elections in which, with 30 out of 142 seats, it had become the third largest group in the Syrian parliament, the Ba'th obtained two key portfolios in Sabri al-'Asali's government of national unity.[64] Together with other political forces it quickly began to work for a merger of Syria with Egypt, then not only the emerging champion of anti-colonialism but also the only Arab country 'progressive' enough to be eligible as a unification partner for the Ba'th. Living up to the promise that was the NC's call for unity with Egypt of 17 April 1957, in 1958 the Ba'th leaders played a crucial role in persuading a reluctant Nasir to accept the merger of Syria and Egypt to form the United Arab Republic.[65]

The UAR failed to meet Ba'thi expectations, and when with the coup of 28 September 1961 the 'separatist regime' (*Nizam al-infisal*) came to power in Syria and put an end to the unitary experience with Egypt, some Ba'this, among them Bitar, even signed a manifesto welcoming the move. The signatories did not oppose the principle of union, but they were disappointed with the shape it had taken.[66] They, and Syrians as a whole, had been progressively excluded from decision making and Syria had effectively become an Egyptian province.[67] But for many others inside and outside the party the unitary experience had removed all illusions about the benefits and desirability of similar schemes. Within the Ba'th this group reinforced the ranks of those anti-unionists who, despite the party's programme, had never favoured merging Syria with any other country.

How committed the majority – though dwindling – of Ba'this remained in their aim of the political unification of the Arab world could again be seen, rightly or wrongly, in their vote in 1962 to expel Hawrani and his supporters from the party because, after the collapse of the UAR, they had opposed any further adventures of that kind. Despite these expulsions, however, the party maintained the name it had adopted in 1953 when merging with Hawrani's group.

While the *infisal* led to a new low in Syro-Egyptian relations, it meant normalization, even *rapprochement* in relations with Iraq. This was most visible in the three-day meeting in the border village of Albu Kamal of the new Syrian President Nazim al-Qudsi and his Iraqi counterpart 'Abd al-Karim Qasim.[68] Thus Syria's relations with Egypt and Iraq continued to follow the old pattern of the 'Struggle for Syria' when weak regimes in Damascus sought support from Cairo or Baghdad, normally inverting their predecessor's choice.

The entente came to an end when, on 8 February 1963, the crumbling Qasim regime was overthrown by a Ba'thi coup, supported by Nasirists and independent nationalists. The *infisal* regime in Syria now found itself encircled by 'radical' Arab nationalists advocating 'Arab socialism', whether the Nasirist or Ba'thist version, both of which had considerable appeal within Syria itself. And indeed, exactly a month later, on 8 March 1963, the Syrian regime fell to a coalition of Nasirist, independent nationalist and Ba'thi officers. While the Iraqi Ba'th from the outset controlled the new regime, the Syrian party still had to discard its allies in the coup, a task in which it succeeded as early as July 1963.[69] These purges led to continued Ba'thi rule in Syria, albeit of different factions, to the present day. In Iraq, ironically, non-Ba'thi groups continued to survive in the armed forces and eventually, on 18 November 1963, overthrew the Ba'th regime.[70]

Soon after the March coup in Syria the new regimes in Damascus and Baghdad started to enter into fresh negotiations with Egypt to bring about the union of the three states. Two Ba'th regimes were considered to be stronger than one, and the party leaders cherished the hope that they could achieve a larger share in power and greater guarantees than in 1958. The new unity scheme was also supported, though for reasons of their own, by Nasirists and independent nationalists in Syria and Iraq.[71] Such non-Ba'thi support, however, did not eclipse the role of the Ba'th, and its image as the driving force for Arab unity was confirmed and reinforced.

The tripartite negotiations in which 'Aflaq and Bitar took a leading part led to an agreement signed in Cairo on 17 April 1963, [72] a symbolic date as it was the anniversary of the departure of the last French soldier from Syria in 1946 and of the first public call of the Ba'th Party for Syro-Egyptian unity in 1956. More importantly, however, this new unity scheme marked the departure of Syro-Iraqi relations from the established pattern of the 'Struggle for Syria'.

When the scheme failed after a Nasirist coup attempt in Syria on 18 July 1963, Ba'thi Syria and Iraq decided to negotiate a bipartite unity scheme[73] which, for obvious reasons, incurred Egyptian wrath. But although Syria was again linked to one of the two traditional competitors for hegemony in the Arab East, the bipartite unity achieved in 1963 differed from previous such alliances in the important respect that now Damascus was quickly asserting itself as an equal partner. However, the bipartite unity scheme failed as well. The chance was irretrievably lost when the Ba'th regime in Iraq, after heavy infighting, on 18 November 1963 was overthrown by General 'Abd al-Salam 'Arif.[74] Non-Ba'thi forces had once more caused Arab unity to collapse – at least, so it seemed. The Ba'th regime in Damascus which was not affected by 'Arif's coup was now left alone, without any potential partner for unity as all other Arab regimes were either too far away or too different in their political outlooks. Consequently, it did not appear astonishing that Syria, despite continuous verbal insistence on the need for Arab unity, did not embark on any new attempt to realize it concretely.

Between November 1963 and July 1968 the major change in the triangular relationship between Syria, Iraq and Egypt was that Syria and Iraq now vied for Egypt's sympathy, and no longer Egypt and Iraq for that of Syria. Yet, Egypt's new role was not Syria's old one as under Nasir's rule it continued to pursue a consistent, 'undivided' foreign policy. Rather, a weak regime in Iraq competed for Egypt's favours against an ascendant but as yet only nascent power in Syria. In fact, the Syrian regime was on the ascendant only on the regional level where it sought to create a new dynamic in the Arab–Israeli conflict. This it attempted quite successfully by outbidding and yet supporting Egypt with the aim of pushing it towards a war with Israel. This strategy inevitably necessitated the vilification of 'Arif's regime in Iraq on which Nasir relied to contain Syrian adventurism.[75] Some Syrian Ba'this were also resentful of 'Arif's coup against the Iraqi Ba'th regime. As we shall see, however, these were, rapidly losing ground in the Syrian party and lost all their remaining power in 1966.

In sharp contradiction to the Ba'th's record as the Arab unitary force *par excellence* no merger or even *rapprochement* was attempted when in July 1968, after almost five years, the Iraqi Ba'th returned to power and there seemed once again to be two Arab countries ruled by members of the same nationalist and progressive movement. But from the very beginning of this second period of Ba'thi coexistence, Syro-Iraqi relations rapidly and sharply deteriorated. Despite transitory periods of *détente* the Ba'th regimes of the two countries have ever since been at odds, even at loggerheads; the tension was also manifested during the brief interludes of relative peace.

Nothing in July 1968 seemed to distinguish any longer the Ba'th from all its predecessors in matters of Arab unity. Like them the Ba'th now appeared as an actor verbally promoting Arab unity but actually exacerbating Arab division. Either the unitary discourse did not correspond to the actual policies or it was overtaken by their perverse consequences. Unlike in previous instances, however, now division and disunity occured between two protagonists professing the same unitary discourse.

The present study attempts to explain why Ba'thi coexistence during and after 1968 failed to bring about unity and resulted instead in conflict, even though it was, it seems, a marriage between first cousins. Did the unitary discourse, like previous though non-Ba'thi unity schemes, hide 'particularist' interests of one side that were unacceptable to the other? It has already been alluded to that strong anti-unionist – in Ba'thi parlance: regionalist – tendencies were hidden behind the Syrian party's Arab nationalist dicourse already in 1961 when some of its members came out in support of the *infisal*, and again in 1963 when actually only a declining tendency among its members was grieved by the overthrow of its Iraqi counterparts. Also, six years after the failure of the first unitary experience, the United Arab Republic – a failure which had already contributed to a greater acceptance of the existing states – the *naksa* or *hazima*, the disastrous defeat in 1967, delivered a heavy, perhaps even a fatal blow to Arab socialism, Arab nationalism, and the idea of Arab unity. These, the observers believed, were defeated with Egypt and Syria, their main advocates and representatives, who also carried the main responsibility for the unfortunate outcome of the war; though living on, Arab nationalism now merely was an empty shell.[76] Others, however, held that Arab nationalist feeling and values subsisted despite 'the national depression that covered in dark the sky of the *umma*'.[77] As we shall see, the 'regionalist' tendency of 1963, that is those giving absolute priority to Syrian interests where these are incompatible with wider Arab interests, had completely taken over by 1968; and in Iraq too similar developments had occurred within the party. This and the *hazima* may explain the absence of any unity scheme in 1968 but not necessarily the eruption of conflict. Indeed, conflict was dominated by clashes of interest – and more precisely of the 'particularist' interests of the rulers – only from March 1972 onwards. In the years 1968–72 conflict arose less from a clash of incompatible interests than from compatible interests being simultaneously expressed and defended through the same Ba'thi discourse; to be an efficient vehicle of interest this discourse, however, had to be monopolized.

If for the longer period of inter-Ba'thi conflict after 1968 the explanation is being sought in the promotion of incompatible interests through a shared unitary discourse, it should still be mentioned that to the Ba'th's previous more successful unity schemes interest other than unity for the sake of unity was not alien either. Thus the Ba'th did not completely change from a party of devout and selfless idealists to one of base egotists. The Ba'th's failure in 1968 may be easier to understand if its 'success' in 1958 is seen not only as a result of the firm and even naive belief that its leaders had in Arab unity but also of their fears that communist ascendancy and action in Syria might precipitate a right-wing take-over.[78]

### State and interstate relations in the Arab East

#### The state

When analysing the present state of the Arab world, Ba'this and most other Arab nationalists define it as one nation subdivided into several states. This view is shared, though with caveats and nuances and with different terminology, by a strong current of the social science literature dealing with the Arab world. For the Mashriq or Arab East especially, this school of thought posits the absence of nation-states, that is of states able to command the prime loyalty of their respective inhabitants. Consequently such loyalty can be extended to other 'recipients', including other states. The Arab state is primarily a territorial state, merely defined as an extractive and coercive agency exerting its domination and authority over a given geographical area.[79] In principle the regime in control of this agency can be democratic or non-democratic. However, in the present Middle Eastern context the former alternative does not seem to exist and the state mainly tends to be the *patrimonium* of rulers by their own grace.

Although by and large convincing, the assumption that the state in the Arab East is a territorial rather than a nation-state has rarely been tested empirically. As mentioned earlier, this will be one of the aims of the present analysis which, however, will be restricted to the cases of Syria and Iraq. More precisely, an attempt will be made to answer the question whether and how far these states have over time moved away from the form of a territorial state and become more of a nation-state. At this stage a nation-state will be defined very broadly as a state able to command the prime allegiance of its inhabitants by establishing among them, and then between them and itself, a common bond, based on some kind of internal homogeneity which at the same time creates a difference *vis-à-vis* the exterior. To this purpose the basic traits of the Arab version of the territorial state have to be outlined. These characteristics also supply the essentials of another hypothesis, concerning inter-Arab relations, that shall be tested as well. The degree of validity of this second hypothesis when applied to the period under consideration will determine the extent that the state has changed from a territorial to a national entity.

The claim that the Arab state is a territorial state and not a nation-state is based on the assumption that it is part of a wider Arab nation. That is to say its inhabitants perceive, though depending on circumstances, a high degree of cultural continuity with the inhabitants of neighbouring states and consider themselves part of the same community of origin or destiny. Put differently, there is a tendency, sometimes more and sometimes less salient, among the inhabitants of these states to consider themselves as members of the same nation, culturally or historically, or in terms of a common destiny. The concept of the cultural nation has been the greater influence in Arab nationalist thought, at least from the

1920s onwards when nationalist thinkers increasingly referred to
the German tradition, represented notably by Herder and Fichte.
However, as well as the concept of the cultural nation, the idea
of the nation based on common historical experience or fate as
represented by Renan, is found, for instance in Ba'thism, where
the culturally defined nation is also endowed with an 'eternal
mission' (*Umma 'arabiyya wahida dhata risala khalida*, the slogan
of the party). Both the Arab cultural nation and nation of destiny
are what may be considered as 'imagined communities',[80] whose
reality is largely that of imagination; this imagination, however, is
nontheless real and hence 'imagined communities' are key elements
of politics.

A common history of Arabs from different geographical regions
and cultural continuity between these regions must not be understood as a complete or even large-scale identity of language,
life-style, belief-system, social practice and historical experience.
Rather, it is defined in relation to certain features or markers
which the Arabs themselves regard as salient and distinctive for
their own common identity. Among these a common though varied
language and similar patterns of social organization are of major
importance.[81]

According to Barth[82] such selective reference by the agents
themselves to cultural features they consider to be distinct (in
a broad conception these include religion) is the basis on which
ethnic boundaries are drawn; the sum total of cultural differences
is irrelevant for their delineation. These ethnic boundaries divide
human society into us-versus-them groups, termed ethnic groups,
which structure social interaction, often by separating those eligible
for marriage from those who are not. Barth argues that ethnic
boundaries are essentially *vertical* divisions of society, based
on qualitative differences in terms of identity, as opposed to
the *horizontal* ones of class or wealth, based on quantitative
differences in power or income. Yet, class differences may create
us-versus-them groups with distinct basic identities and without
intermarriage. Thus not all ethnic boundaries need to be vertical,
and in the same way not all vertical boundaries need to be ethnic:
vertical divisions of society may also be based on kinship or
clientelistic structures. While ethnic ties are of a different nature
than kinship ties they may, however, coincide with one another
since, at least in the Middle Eastern context, relatives by kin
generally tend to share the same ethnic identity and marriage tends
to be ethnically endogamous. The question is further complicated
by the quite common phenomenon of invented genealogies.

In the Arab world, however, the perceived overall continuity
in cultural terms does not necessarily create an equally extended

ethnic group that would encompass all those sharing the relevant
cultural traits. Cultural continuity is rather the *potential* foundation
of such ethnic continuity. In terms of social interaction cultural
continuity, especially over such a wide and diverse area, certainly
produces 'imagined communities'[83] but not necessarily actual
communities. The same seems to apply to imagined communities
based on the perception of a shared history and destiny. Whether
certain cultural continuities or differences finally become relevant
for the formation of ethnic groups and boundaries seems to be
largely circumstantial and to depend on their efficiency in the
competition for resources.[84] The same observation applies to
historical-teleological criteria, which may either be included in
this broad concept of culture or – following the distinction between
Herder's and Renan's concept of the nation – be considered as a
second set of features on which ethnic groups and boundaries can be
built. This instrumentalist approach to ethnicity[85] means that actors
can switch between ethnic identities, depending on the benefits
they may yield. For instance an 'Alawi may conceive of himself
both as an Arab, and as a member of a particular 'Alawi tribal
confederation.[86] Even when such change initially is 'superficial'
and effected merely for self-presentation *vis-à-vis* others, it may
come to be considered as genuine by the actors themselves. It
may also be 'sincere' from the outset, bringing to the fore this or
that – possibly latent – aspect of a multiple identity. It may then
be institutionalized and perpetuated, develop its own dynamic and
perhaps even become counter-productive in the competition for
resources. Ethnicity thus remains an ascriptive category, though
one subject to transformation over time. Such transformations are
certainly easiest where not too many kinship ties have to be severed
(conversely kinship can always be artificially created by invented
genealogies). Ethnic criteria may not only be reinforced, but also
overridden by other loyalties that may partly vindicate primordialist
– as opposed to instrumentalist – approaches to the issue, provided
they are properly understood.[87]

The mismatch between the imagined and the real may well reside
in the many, partly criss-crossing, cultural cleavages and differences
that run through the Arab world beneath this overarching but often
minimal cultural continuity. This cultural diversity of the Middle
East – whereby cultural is again understood in the same broad
sense as above – has facilitated the emergence of numerous distinct
ethnic identities, some of them quite persistent over time, others
more ephemeral and short-lived. If the groups thus emerging are
relatively small in size they are socially more effective than the
imagined Arab community. However, as already noted, this does
not mean that the latter is less real, though at a different level.

Although some of these other ethnic identities are socially more effective than the Arab nation, in their political efficacy they are generally all stronger than loyalties to the state. They are often more successful in commanding political allegiance than the state which finds itself sandwiched between them. The state, in fact, seems to be too small and yet too large. While not containing the entire Arab nation it normally houses several ethnic entities or parts of such entities. Not only is it divided into different groups which are formed according to partly overlapping criteria like religion (e.g. Druze, 'Alawi, Sunni), region (e.g. coast versus mountain (*Ahl al-sahil* versus *Ahl al-jabal*, or Aleppo versus Damascus), or mode of subsistence (i.e. bedouin, peasant and urban), but also these groups live in several countries simultaneously: 'Alawis in Syria and Lebanon; Druze in both countries and in Israel; Greek Orthodox in several; and Sunnis in all Arab countries. Apart from ethnic challenges from within, the state is thus confronted with ethnic cross-border solidarities not only at the Arab level but also at the level of such additional identities. The matter becomes yet more complicated as some of these cultural and thus at least potentially ethnic boundaries also encompass non-Arab populations, as in the case of the Sunnis, Twelver-Shi'is or Isma'ilis. So far, however, it seems that these bonds between Arabs and non-Arabs have not been of great political consequence, certainly less than the last variety of ethnic division: the presence of non-Arab populations in Arab countries, such as the Berbers in Algeria or the Kurds in Syria and Iraq.

By contrast, states and their borders have no societal reality, or only an imposed one, not always accepted by their inhabitants. There is no complete correspondence between state and society. Firstly, because the state can be described as composed of several societies, to the point that society as such becomes 'undiscoverable' as Michel Seurat claimed for the Syrian case.[88] Secondly, because these societies often brim over the state's borders and extend beyond them. In more harmonious cases such internally divided states can also be seen as 'plural societies.' But at any rate these conditions vindicate the warning, given by Touraine[89] and reiterated for Syria by Seurat,[90] that a territorially defined population need not *ipso facto* constitute a society, the latter concept implying a direct correspondence of the population with an institutional framework and a *champ d'historicité*.

The failure – if such failure should be demonstrable – of Arab states to become nation-states seems to be connected to the great degree of autonomy of their respective societies (the term society being understood within the limits of the above caveats). Though this autonomy of the state (that is the capacity of the regime to maximize its penetration of and domination over society while minimizing the impact of the society on itself) is hardly disputable, its origins and later causes have given rise to considerable debate. Wittfogel in his *Oriental Despotism* gave a masterly description of the phenomenon,[91] but hardly convinces when explaining it through the assumed imperatives of 'hydraulic society'; often in fact the enormous and economically vital irrigation schemes characterizing such societies do not seem to have been constructed by a central authority, and even where this was actually the case this authority might have been set up and supervised by the individuals or collectivities benefiting from the irrigation scheme.[92] The same applies to Katouzian's attempt at another ecological explanation, this time based on the conditions of 'aridisolatic society' that he claimed prevailed in Iran.[93]

One relevant factor is that in the Mashriq the state or government has generally been imposed from outside on a given territory, frequently, though not always, inhabited by a heterogeneous population. While this does not necessarily distinguish these states from their counterparts in Europe, the latter in the course of the great capitalist transformations of the last centuries became nations – internally homogenized and distinct from their neighbours. The exogenous state-building powers in the Middle East were mainly the Ottoman and European conquerors of the Arab lands who often, in disregard of local ties and interests, established provinces, colonies, protectorates or mandates which then became independent states.[94] But on occasion they were Arab rulers and dynasties whose military power enabled them to carve out emirates or kingdoms for themselves.[95] Sometimes like Ibn Sa'ud they did so on their own; sometimes they did so with the acquiescence of European powers, as for instance 'Abdallah did when he established himself in Transjordan. Most had to accommodate themselves with the European powers, but not all were initially their creatures.

Despite political independence after the second world war the state in a number of Arab countries remained – or chose to remain – externally dependent in order to maintain its internal autonomy. Hashemite Iraq and Jordan illustrate this quite well. More important, however, though partly connected to the traditional autonomy of government *vis-à-vis* society, private property has always been weak, precarious and permanently under the threat of arbitrary confiscation. Consequently, the development of productive forces remained modest and by contrast with Western Europe no strong, dominating bourgeoisie emerged that would have economically united a certain geographical area, taken over the state and then been challenged by its proletariat – to whom it finally might have given some sort of participation in the affairs of the state. Nor did government itself pursue a policy of capitalist investment, economic growth and active creation of resources; instead it relied on the exploitation of available, more or less 'natural' resources. The absence of this very process may also explain the absence – if verifiable – of nation-states, in the sense used here, since the relatively undynamic and simple economy (if compared to nineteenth- and twentieth-century Europe) did not demand cultural and societal homogenization in order to function, nor did it need to facilitate complex communication [96] and enhance popular mobilization[97] in order to increase productivity.

*Anciens régimes* depending on increasingly precarious external support and weak bourgeoisies were no match for the rising Arab 'socialist' and nationalist groups like the Free Officers movements or the Ba'th that in the 1950s and 1960s took over the state in Egypt, Iraq and Syria and increased its autonomy by expropriation, nationalization and a dominant public sector.

More recently the rising external resources of these states and thus their growing external dependence have further increased their degree of autonomy *vis-à-vis* their own societies resulting more and more in internal despotism.[98] While 'hydraulic society' perhaps never existed, 'hydrocarbon society'[99] certainly does. Revenue from oil brought material benefit not only for the producer countries but also indirectly to the non-producers who received growing amounts of financial assistance. Thus the rentier state has become the dominant feature, the only difference being between its direct control over oil resources and the 'induced' sub-type[100] dependent on the oil wealth of others.

Hence the modern state in the Middle East more often than not weighs heavily on society, even crushes it. This state is not the instrument of one or more economically dominant classes. Nor is state action explainable in the terms of an antagonistic stalemate between such classes that enabled the state to emerge as an independent actor reminiscent of Bonapartism. These explanations do not apply because in most countries there is no economically dominant class,[101] though there are classes with some economic and political leverage[102] such as the *infitah* bourgeoisie in post-1970 Syria. Instead the state itself is economically dominant,[103] especially in oil countries like Iraq, and thus its autonomy is not solely based on its military might. Egypt seems to be the only exception at the time of writing, others being supplied only from more distant periods: for example the three years of bourgeois democracy in early independent Syria (1946–9) or Lebanon before internal war broke out in 1975. Finally, it would also be erroneous to define these regimes as the representatives of the *petite bourgeoisie* or the peasantry from whom many of their representatives originated.[104] This explanation may partially hold for certain periods and places, such as Syria between 1963 and 1966, but generally the social origin of the rulers should not be confused with rule by their class of origin. This issue, however, will be raised again below.

Prevailing over society – as far as society exists – the autonomous state does not allow for any form of actual political participation which would in fact deprive it of its autonomy.[105] This state corresponds to the meaning of the Arabic term *dawla* designating a regime sovereignly exerting power over a given territory. The absence of participation by the population, however, results in an absence of legitimacy for the state, except in the case of so-called traditional societies or polities (a description which no longer adequately reflects the Syrian and Iraqi reality). This problem of legitimacy is exacerbated if the state is unable to cater for the material demands, even needs, of its inhabitants as is increasingly the case in some countries at present. In the absence of legitimacy it is then difficult for the state to command and obtain the prime allegiance of its inhabitants and thus to become a nation-state.

The autonomous state, instead of expressing developments at the level of society and being subject to change from 'below' in its totally unscrupulous versions like in Syria or Iraq, shapes, forms, reforms and transforms society at its whim and in an authoritarian patrimonial manner from 'above'. This includes the creation and destruction of social and even economically influential classes as again illustrated by the emergence of the *infitah* bourgeoisie in Syria or its lesser sibling in Iraq.[106] This creation of classes, however, is always paralleled by strategies to prevent them from becoming classes-for-themselves.[107] Yet, the general tendency of the modern state in the Mashriq is to attempt the destruction of society and its replacement by mass organizations that have no dynamic of their own.[108] This illustrates the most extreme version of what Touraine designates as the *État intégrateur*.[109]

If successful the destruction of all social structures or of what may be termed civil society would allow the state to atomize and mobilize its population to a degree of almost complete obedience, overcome the need for real political participation and thus solve the crisis of legitimacy.[110] However, in its initial stage such a policy of desocietization further reduces the state's legitimacy. This even more so as the Arab state hardly disposes of adequate means to implement such a policy successfully. Hence rather than mobilization the result is incomplete desocietization with some form of opposition, however inefficient, or apathy – the kind of empty-eyed apathy so common among Syrians obliged to demonstrate on the anniversaries of their regime.[111] With such apathy it is of course difficult to foster belief in a nation-skeleton – a nation made of bones without flesh – that some Arab regimes try to inculcate into their subjects' minds.[112] It remains true that although shared and outwardly distinctive experience or cultural traits help to create solidarities and loyalty to a group and its ruling agents, in the absence of total mobilization such loyalty can only be consolidated and guaranteed by participation. In other terms: the nation-state will have to be the state representing the nation defined as its inhabitants in contrast to a state representing a sovereign external to the so defined nation. It will have to represent not one – '*L'État, c'est moi*' – or a few, but all, without of course restricting this term to a yet exclusive third estate as it did the Abbé Sieyes and the *Assemblée nationale* of 1789.

At this stage the agents in control of these autonomous states should be briefly identified. If they do not represent a class or constellation of classes, that is horizontal layers or sectors, they might possibly represent ethnically, that is mainly 'vertically', defined segments of society. There is much talk about 'Alawi rule in Syria and Sunni rule in Iraq, but tempting though it is to adopt this view, it is nonetheless incorrect. Nor would it be more correct to infer from the frequent presence of military officers at the helm of these states that the army as such is in control. As it will appear more clearly below, after the *naksa* or *hazima*, the Arab defeat in the Six-Day War of 1967, ruling groups and their challengers, at any rate in Syria and in Iraq, increasingly tended to be organized as *jama'at* (sing., *jama'a*) – as gangs or cliques.[113] These draw their strength and cohesion from one or several kinds of informal ties which in the eyes of their members command and generate personal loyalty: kinship, camaraderie and intimate friendship, but also religious, regional or local factors.[114]

The glue of power thus seems to be made from '*asabiyya* in all its varieties as described by Ibn Khaldun.[115] Michel Seurat, though somewhat polemically, even claimed that 'the modern state in the Mashriq, where it actually exists and not only as an idea, is an '*asabiyya* that successfully established itself.'[116]

These factions then extend their basis in and grip over society by means of clientelistic networks which are often based on ethnic ties and lead to the large-scale clientelization of ethnic groups and their mobilization. These ethnic groups, however, are not in power, they merely form a *glacis de protection* for the ruling group.[117] Quite similar is the function of certain classes: a prop and support for the regime rather than the reverse, [118] although occasionally a class attains a higher degree of emancipation. Generally the clientelistic networks entertained and cultivated by the regime disrupt solidarity at the class level as they offer selective access to resources.[119] Consequently the dangers of class power recede.

## Inter-state relations

In the preceding pages the hypothesis has been described according to which the modern state in the Mashriq is a non-nation-state unable to command the prime loyalty of its inhabitants. This state of affairs is aggravated, perhaps even produced, by a lack of internal legitimacy due to a lack of participation which in turn results from the state's autonomy *vis-à-vis* society. If this is so then this type of state, especially under the conditions of cultural, historical-teleological or even ethnic and kinship ties with neighbouring countries, incites many of its inhabitants to shift their political allegiance to external actors whom they consider to be better representatives of their cause.

This obviously gives an entirely different quality to the relations between the regimes of these countries and their political actors in general. Such shifts in political allegiance to external actors indicate that the classical distinction between internal and external or home and foreign affairs is blurred. In other terms: by chosing external actors as their representatives, that is for the very roles normally considered to be the absolute privilege of internal actors, those who make this choice extend the notion of their interior beyond the borders of their state of origin or abode. As long as political actors from within a given Arab state give their political allegiance frequently and extensively to external actors, this state has not become a nation-state. Every attempt to unite Arab countries and to create one instead of several interiors confirms this.

In the final analysis extending the realm of one's internal affairs boils down to a question of mobilizing resources. A given actor's subjective interior thus can be defined as the area – geographical or interactional – where he or she considers it legitimate to mobilize and to invest resources essential for his or her policies; *investing* in this sense implies the expectation of some return. Political allegiance is the most sensitive of such investments. It is always aimed at mobilizing for the benefit of those who invest it, those others in whom they invest it. In principle, it should be stressed, such mobilization and investment is not necessarily tied to the types of cross-border continuities that exist between Arab countries. Other types of continuities and interdependencies may well serve the same purpose.

This definition is wide enough to be valid for non-Arab actors as well, who often feel entitled to relevant resources from beyond their state borders or invest them there.

The possibility for Arab actors to mobilize or spontaneously obtain support from each other's countries presents the individual actor with advantages as well as disadvantages, and even threats. On the one hand external support paves the way to increased benefit, and possibly to domination which in itself is convertible into benefit. On the other hand, however, a loss of internal support may menace a regime's survival and ultimately lead to its collapse. In this context, even the active quest for external support may in the end serve not the purpose of domination but that of self-defence. Indeed, the regimes' 'tendency to interfere in the internal affairs of neighbouring states' serves 'the interests either of building up local sets of supporters who would influence policy decisions or of preventing reciprocal attempts to stir up hostile activities against themselves at home'.[120]

The shifting sands of political support compel regimes – if they want to ensure their survival, benefit, or domination – not only to repress forces within their countries that are sympathetic to external actors but also to influence positively the fluxes of allegiance. In this their aim must be to win a maximum of external support but to lose a minimum of internal support to external actors. To obtain this support it is essential for an actor to outbid and outdo fellow actors in precisely those values, qualities and goals that they share most with him or her. On the basis of this logic it is naturally imperative to appear as the most ardent defender of the Arab cause and even to represent Arab legitimacy incarnate. Yet, despite these necessary measures of self-defence, the ease with which support can be mobilized 'abroad' may also facilitate bids for leadership and all kinds of Napoleonic designs that are far from being defensive. Both the defensive and the expansionist use of cross-border continuities and solidarities in the Arab world are illustrated though not yet conceptualized by the two classics of scholarship on inter-Arab relations, Patrick Seale's *Struggle for Syria*[121] and Malcolm Kerr's *Arab Cold War*,[122] which deal with earlier periods than does the present analysis.

The extension by political actors of their interior beyond the borders of their 'own' states is an issue that to different degrees and in different ways has concerned a great number of writers. The idea of a non-distinction between internal and external affairs is present for instance in the vast literature on dependency and centre –periphery relations,[123] or though often implicitly or by allusion, in that on transnational society and transnational politics.[124] Most thoroughly and explicitly it was so far acknowledged by Rosenau in his concept of the 'penetrated political system'[125]. However, Rosenau later watered down this concept to a mere sub-type of linkage processes[126] which actually depend on the dichotomy between internal and external politics, as no linkage could exist if these two 'systems'[127] thus linked were to coincide. In any case, however, nowhere has the interior been defined as here in terms of a reservoir of resources which the respective actor considers as particularly relevant.

As the various Arab actors by relying on ethnic mobilization tend to regard the same area – that is the Arab world or parts of it, like for instance the Mashriq or Fertile Crescent – as their interior, there is something like an overarching Arab polity encompassing, though to different degrees, the several Arab states.[128]

The notion of an overarching Arab polity should, however, not be confused with that of an Arab regional system or sub-system, which is based on mainly quantitative criteria such as the frequency of certain interactions and which continues to view these interactions as belonging to the realm of foreign policy, that is as interactions between external powers.[129] Only these concepts of an Arab regional system which explain inter-Arab conflicts and alliances in terms of the search for anti-hegemonic equilibria within this system,[130] come close to the present notion of an overarching Arab polity. These concepts, by positing an inbuilt common concern of all actors about their relative power, presuppose a shared responsibility for a given region and thus the extension of each participant's interior over the entire region. This region, then, in the last analysis is conceived as a segmentary society whose members, unlike in the classics of anthropological writings, are not tribes or sections of tribes[131] but states.

Although the *naksa* or *hazima*, the Arab defeat in the Six-Day War of 1967, greatly delegitimized Arab socialism, nationalism, and unity projects, its affects on the acceptance of the existing states were ambiguous. On the one hand the failure of co-operation in the war led to greater pragmatism and to a greater valorization of the individual states and their own capacities.[132] On the other hand the defeat ushered in and, in conjunction with other factors, caused, the multi-sided crisis that has affected Arab society throughout the 1970s and 1980s. It thus contributed to the rise of Islamist movements[133] which sometimes maintained the blur between internal and external affairs on the grounds of religious or seemingly religious cross-border ties. And although it is more difficult to establish a causative or contributory link between the *hazima* and tendencies towards political self-affirmation among religious minorities, these tendencies became clear only in the late 1960s. More generally, the shattering experience of the defeat reinforced tendencies towards loyalties other than 'civic', particularly *vis-à-vis* smaller societal units, down to families or factions and cliques (*jama'at*).[134]

Where such a *jama'a* takes power, monopolizes it, and exercises it through clienteles based on ethnic or kinship ties, quite naturally vertical divisions within 'society' deepen. However, as the societal segments resulting from these divisions often extend into other countries of the region – the Druzes for instance live in Lebanon, Syria and Israel, and many Syrian families have a Lebanese branch or the other way round – cross-border alliances are reinforced on the part of those actors. The result is continued or enhanced non-distinction between internal and external affairs and the perpetuation of the overarching Arab polity. Again using Khaldunian terminology Michel Seurat claimed that:

> In the Mashriq politics is conceived and carried out at the level of the entire region. And within what thus could be defined as a *global Arab political system* the different *'asabiyyat* are able to give proof of their abilities to move about and manoeuvre.[135]

To determine the degree of fusion between internal and external affairs, and the efficacy of the overarching Arab polity since 1968, is the third aim of the present study, based on the analysis of Syro-Iraqi relations.

The results of these three enquiries can be briefly sketched as follows. Conflict between Ba'thi Syria and Iraq was initially caused by the need of the Ba'thi rulers of Syria to rally their Ba'thi supporters, civilian and military alike, many of whom, for different reasons, could be tempted to shift their allegiance to the new Ba'th regime in Baghdad. After these dangers had receded bilateral relations passed through a calmer phase, nonetheless interrupted by serious narrow conflicts of interest.[136] This calm, however, progressively gave way to a competition for regional influence, which from 1975 on has dominated Syro-Iraqi relations despite and even during the short-lived *rapprochement* of 1978–9. This means that in the early period bilateral relations were heavily affected by real as well as suspected shifts of political allegiance across the common border, confirming the thesis of large-scale non-distinction between internal and external affairs. The narrow conflicts of interest of the second period and the struggle for regional power seem to indicate the emergence of a nation-state, but although this is not to be denied completely, the antagonists continued to pursue their interests by taking advantage of cross-border ties and continuities. Moreover, in Syria the receding threat from shifting allegiances to immediate regime survival is due to possibly fragile developments that need not imply successful nation-building. Throughout the following three chapters this argument will as far as possible be underpinned by factual evidence, but it has to remain somewhat speculative as far as the ultimate motifs of the main characters are concerned. Where the absence of cabinet minutes or similar documents could not be compensated by insider interviews information had to be interpreted in what appeared to be the most consistent way.

## Sources

The present analysis is based on both written and oral sources. The oral sources are sixty-four interviews with thirty persons, carried out in Syria, Lebanon, Jordan, France, Great Britain and West Germany in the years 1984–7. As these figures show, some interlocutors could be interviewed several times. All interviews were conducted on an informal basis, some lasting up to seven hours. These interlocutors can roughly be divided into three categories. The first of these categories, and the smallest in number, comprises well-informed local observers, such as journalists or lawyers, but also eyewitnesses to certain relevant events. A second group is made up of persons who worked or still work for either of the regimes, whether just for particular tasks or on a regular basis as higher civil servants, officers and the like. The third and last group consists of former or present leading members of the regimes or of oppositional forces linked to the respective neighbouring regime.

As the identity of many of these interlocutors cannot be revealed without exposing them to the risk of reprisals, no names or hints as to their identity will be given in the text. I am of course, aware of the fact that such secrecy reduces the reader's ability to verify information and thus affects the credibility of the argument presented here, but under the circumstances the only alternative would have been to omit or neglect certain information.

With regard to written material, this analysis is mainly based on primary sources, though not on documents from archives which in countries like Syria and Iraq are unavailable to researchers. The material referred to here as primary sources are media reports and comments, including surveys of broadcasts such as the *Summary of World Broadcasts for the Middle East and Africa* published by the British Broadcasting Corporation (*BBC/SWB*), and the *Daily Report, Middle East and Africa* issued by the Foreign Broadcasting Information Service in Washington, DC (*FBIS/DR*).

Reports and comments appearing in the official media of the two countries can be assimilated to official statements. Alternatively they may be seen as an intermediate category of semi-official sources. Although in some periods the media in Syria had some room for manoeuvre, it is difficult in the present context not to regard these potentially semi-official sources as mouthpieces of the respective regimes. This, of course, is not to discount certain differences in tone that exist between accounts in the media and statements directly issued by the governments, mainly because they consider it useful to present certain information or points of view as less official.

Moreover, this analysis draws on a number of political auto-biographies and polemical writings by politically active individuals. Finally, the work is also based on existing academic literature which includes extremely rich and enlightening studies on a number of aspects of Syrian and Iraqi politics, but is highly disappointing in the specific area of Syro-Iraqi relations. There are a number of well-researched and thoughtful exceptions which, however, deal with certain issues, aspects or periods only: a few articles about the short-lived *rapprochement* in 1978–9,[137] a study of the Euphrates issue,[138] and various paragraphs or remarks in publications dealing with wider topics such as Syrian or Iraqi politics or foreign policies.[139] The paucity and poverty of research on Syro-Iraqi relations in the Ba'th period is best illustrated by the absence of a monograph – a gap that cannot be filled by the brief existing overviews of the issue that are slightly flawed and superficial at best[140] and incorrect and mistaken at worst.[141] Most other publications express opinions rather than presenting the results of thorough research and though not always wrong in their assumptions hardly ever ground them on anything more solid than pure impressions and some scattered evidence.[142]

# 1

# The Consolidation Conflict, 1968–1972

## *Ba'thi dichotomy and regime stability*

In these early years of Ba'thi coexistence[1] the main source of bilateral tension was the need on the part of the ruling factions in Damascus to defend their legitimacy in the eyes of their most immediate supporters. Yet, their hostile attitude towards Iraq was more than just an attempt to reduce internal strife through a more or less arbitrarily chosen external conflict; the very existence of the Ba'th regime in Baghdad was a major source of instablity for Syria's rulers. The faction that dominated the Ba'th regime in Damascus had been increasingly at odds with some of its supporters, some of whom now were, or seemed to be inclined to shift their allegiance to the new rulers in Baghdad. Such shifts of allegiance among members of the apparatus were dangerous, for any conspiracy at that level might easily have brought down the regime. Conversely, the Iraqi Ba'th was not threatened by such defections, as for different reasons the Syrian regime hardly exerted any attraction for Iraqi Ba'this.

To prevent members of its own apparatus from changing sides, the Syrian regime embarked on a propaganda war to deny any Ba'thi legitimacy to its counterpart in Iraq. To this the Iraqi side responded mainly in self-defence, even when it later sought actively to destabilize the Syrian regime. Although it then used the communicating vessels of Ba'thi legitimacy to pull the carpet from under its counterpart's feet, the aim was essentially to get rid of a neighbour that had become too much of a nuisance. Moreover, a divided Ba'th could not possibly claim to unite the Arab world and thus both sides might lose support even among those who did not prefer the version in the neighbouring country. Though still at a modest level the two regimes also competed for influence in and support from the region. This competition mainly expressed itself in a dispute over Arab legitimacy, which also helped the regimes to enhance their internal legitimacy among those who could not be mobilized through Ba'thi arguments.

Apart from the war of words the conflict in this period mainly expressed itself in the persecution, especially by the Syrian regime, of Ba'this sympathetic to the other side, and in non-co-operation in sensitive matters such as military affairs. However, in economic and technical matters co-operation thrived, since it posed no threat to the regimes, but rather benefited them both.

## The origins of Ba'thi dichotomy

The cleavage that in the period of Ba'thi coexistence separated the rulers of Syria from some of their supporters and from their counterparts in Iraq can be traced back to 1958, although it did not come to the fore till 1966. In these early days it was purely an inner-party affair, opposing on the one hand the Ba'th's 'historical leadership' around Michel 'Aflaq and Salah al-Din Bitar who together with their supporters controlled the party's highest body, the National Command (NC), and, on the other hand, younger party members of a different social and societal background who often had a different understanding of what Ba'thism should stand for. In these days also the cleavage was mainly between Syrian Ba'this. After 1963, when the Iraqi party was reorganized by appointees of the 'historical leadership' in the National Command, the Iraqi party in general and Syrian supporters of the party leadership in Damascus were ranged against Syrian dissenters. It was not until 1966 when the Syrian dissenters had succeeded in their coup against the old guard that the party organizations in the two countries were each controlled by one of the competing factions, thus opposing Syrian to Iraqi Ba'this.[2]

The immediate cause of contention in 1958 was the high-handed decision of the National Command to dissolve the Arab Socialist Ba'th Party in Syria (but in no other Arab state) to comply with Gamal'Abd al-Nasir's demand that all parties be dissolved in the newly created United Arab Republic (UAR) uniting Syria and Egypt. The 'historical leadership' around 'Aflaq was ready to pay this price as under the circumstances it appeared the most reliable way of defending their concept of 'Arab socialism' and thus their interests. Deeply resenting the National Command's autocratic behaviour, many of those who opposed such a far-reaching unity scheme remained secretly organized and soon became known as the *qutriyyun* or 'regionalists'. The supporters of the National Command, who believed the realization of Arab unity to be the foremost aim of the party, were henceforth referred to as the *qawmiyyun* or 'nationalists'. Most consequential for the future of the party, however, was the opposition of a few young Ba'thi officers whom the UAR government had transferred to Egypt in order to forestall possible plots against the union. In 1959 five of them founded the secret Ba'thi Military Committee (MC). All five belonged to religious minorities: Muhammad 'Umran, Salah Jadid and Hafiz al-Asad were 'Alawis, 'Abd al-Karim al-Jundi and Ahmad al-Mir were Isma'ilis. When later the Military Committee was expanded nine of its fifteen members still belonged to minorities.[3] Only six belonged to the Sunni majority and, unlike the old guard and its supporters, most of them were not of urban origin but, together with the *qutriyyun*, came from an often modest rural background.

Neither the *qutriyyun* nor the officers shared the party leaders' commitment to Arab unity.[4] In the poverty-stricken rural ares they mostly hailed from, more immediate problems such as land reform, medical care, or the building of schools had to be tackled first. Moreover, those who belonged to Muslim minorities had joined the Ba'th mainly because of its secularism and were suspicious of Sunni domination of any unified Arab state. Therefore, the *qutriyyun* and many officers tended to stress the last of the three Ba'thi watchwords: socialism.[5] And for many of them socialism, though still limited in scope, was nonetheless more than the synonym for social justice that it was for the *qawmiyyun*.

When, half a year after the collapse of the UAR, the Ba'th's Fifth National Congress decided to reconstitute the Syrian party organization, membership remained limited. But inner-party division increased, again opposing the followers of the old guard to the *qutriyyun* who drew ever closer to the officers. The rift became more conspicuous after 8 March 1963 when the *infisal* (or 'separatist') regime was overthrown by an alliance of Nasirist, independent nationalist and Ba'thi officers and the latter, while purging their allies from the coup, invited the *qawmiyyun*, nominally still in charge of the party leadership, to join the newly created National Revolutionary Command Council (NRCC) and the new government. The invitation, however, was purely tactical, in order to broaden the new regime's base and to purge the extreme left within the party. In the new unity scheme with Egypt and Iraq which the old guard then hastily began to negotiate, none of the Ba'thi officers actively participated. Clearly the 'Alawis and members of other minorities did not find Arab unity more attractive now than they had in 1958. They certainly did not blame Nasir and 'Arif for foiling the new project.

In the following years much formal power was vested with the old guard but most actual power lay with the officers of the Military Committee, the existence of which was ignored by the civilian

party leaders till 1965. Thus Syria was ruled by a dual regime,
and much see-sawing went on between the two centres of power,
increasingly exacerbating their conflict. Finally, on 23 February
1966, the officers, most prominent among them the 'Alawis around
Salah Jadid and Hafiz al-Asad, as well as a Druze faction led by
Salim Hatum, took over. Supported by the civilian regionalists
they overthrew the last Bitar government together with its ally,
the National Command, which was also based in Damascus. Salah
Jadid became the discreet strongman of the new regime which
stressed its commitment to 'scientific socialism' and class struggle,
improved Syria's relations with the Soviet Union, continued the
policy of nationalization already initiated in 1963, and created
new industries and infrastructures. These policies were not only
intended to serve the interests of the workers and peasants as the
regime claimed; they were also intended to reinforce the position
of the state and its leaders by firmly establishing their grip on the
economy. Consequently, Jadid and his allies, the *qutriyyun*, soon
lost part of the support they had enjoyed among these classes, and
increasingly had to rely on party militants and on the Popular Army.
Those known to be *qawmiyyun* were expelled from the party. Some
of them were arrested or deported from the country while others
went underground.

The movement of 23 February soon disintegrated as new infighting culminated in the confrontation of Salah Jadid and Hafiz
al-Asad. With the army on his side and additional support from
business quarters in March 1969 Asad greatly enhanced his position
and on 16 November 1970 completely took over. His 'Corrective
Movement' (*al-Haraka al-tashihiyya*) thus brought to an end the
'radical' period of Syrian Ba'thism and ushered in the new era of
*infitah* or economic liberalization.

In Iraq the Ba'th Party had to be reorganized and rebuilt after
the débâcle of November 1963. As party elections were impossible,
Michel 'Aflaq in his capacity as Secretary General of the National
Command in early 1964 designated Saddam Husayn initially known
as Saddam Husayn al-Takriti, as Secretary of the new Iraqi Regional
Command and Ahmad Hasan al-Bakr as head of its military
branch.[6] Bakr and his relative Husayn were ideologically close to
'Aflaq, and basically advocated the same pro-middle-class policies,
although partly more radical stances were adopted to curb the
influence of the Iraqi Communist Party. When in 1966 the National
Command, residing in Damascus, was overthrown by the Syrian
officers, Bakr, Husayn and their fellow Ba'this in Iraq, among
them Hardan al-Takriti and Salih Mahdi 'Ammash, remained, at
least verbally, loyal to the 'legitimate' party leadership. Some two
years later, on 17 July 1968, they took part in the overthrow of the

'Arif regime and a fortnight later, on 30 July, rid themselves of their allies in the first coup, thus becoming the sole rulers of Iraq.[7] Soon afterwards Syrian Ba'this exiled in 1966 travelled or moved to Iraq, and in late 1970 'Aflaq himself settled in Baghdad.

### The forces of destablization, suspected and real

The post-1963 developments in Syria produced opposition among three partially overlapping categories of civilian and military Ba'this. To many of these the Iraqi party offered, either in their own eyes or in those of the Syrian rulers, exactly what they missed in the Syrian party. The Jadid regime moreover had to be afraid of the however qualitatively different Iraqi connections of a fourth group, the faction of Hafiz al-Asad, by which eventually it was overthrown in November 1970.

First of all, the Iraqi party attracted all those in the Syrian party who, after the coup of 23 February 1966, for personal or ideological reasons remained loyal to the old National Command. Despite numerous purges a secret organization of *qawmiyyun* survived, even within the Syrian party itself. It was set up immediately after the February coup by Munif al-Razzaz[8] in order to re-establish the authority of the 'legitimate' party leadership. There is no doubt that it pursued this aim seriously for Razzaz immediately entrusted the Druze General Fahd al-Sha'ir with the tasks of setting up the military branch of the organization and preparing a *coup d'état* to overthrow the new Jadid regime.[9] Although the plot was discovered, there was no guarantee against similar threats in the future, all the less after July 1968 when the *qawmiyyun* could hope for support from Baghdad. This support eventually reduced their independence and transformed their organization into the pro-Iraqi Ba'th in Syria.

Contacts between Syrian Ba'thi exiles and the new Iraqi regime began soon after it came to power. As early as August 1968 Salah al-Din Bitar among others travelled to Iraq while from Lebanon, Amin al-Hafiz, Shibli al-'Aysami and Ilyas Farah together addressed a congratulatory telegram to Bakr. Soon al-Hafiz and several others were reported to have settled in Baghdad. Yet the spread of Iraqi influence among Syrian Ba'thi exiles and *qawmiyyun* was hampered till late 1970, mainly because Michel 'Aflaq was not as receptive as the Iraqi leaders may have hoped. 'Aflaq delayed his first visit to Iraq until 25 May 1969 and, reportedly, made his residence in Baghdad dependent on conditions the Iraqi regime found difficult to accept.[10] As long as Michel 'Aflaq, representing legitimacy incarnate, restricted his relations to short visits to Baghdad[11] – as he did until mid-November 1970[12] – many followers of the 'historical leadership' hesitated to lend their support to the Iraqi Ba'th.

The second category attracted to the Iraqi party were Sunni and other non-'Alawi members of the Syrian Ba'th, many of whom had grown increasingly resentful of 'Alawi officers monopolizing power in the army, party and country. After the March 1963 coup, control of the armed forces and thus ultimately of the party and country was quickly assumed by the Isma'ili, Druze and particularly 'Alawi officers,[13] who since 1958 had dominated the Ba'th's military organization, through the Military Committee.[14] Though some Sunnis retained seemingly important functions they were but figureheads excluded from key positions. When after 23 February 1966 the Ba'thi officers of 'Alawi origin began to push aside the Ba'thi officers of Druze extraction, resentment against the former also emerged among their previous supporters and allies.[15] Some Druze officers then joined the clandestine pro-'Aflaq organization in Syria while others, more numerous, formed their own organization under the leadership of Salim Hatum.[16]

In spring and summer 1966 the two secret organizations – the one loyal to the old NC, the other led by Salim Hatum – decided to co-operate in order to bring down the Jadid regime. Some of the plotters went ahead with the plan even after the regime had come to know of it, but they eventually failed.[17] Large-scale purges in the Syrian armed forces followed, mainly affecting Druze officers.[18] Yet, Druze officers and officials remained in both army and party, and thus after 1968 there was always the possibility of their conniving with Iraq. The same, of course, applied to Sunni officers, who today still account for a sizeable part of the Syrian officer corps, although they are for the most part excluded from key posts.

The third group for which the Iraqi party offered a Ba'thi shelter were the numerous members of the Syrian party who held their rulers responsible for the *naksa* or *hazima*, the disastrous defeat in the Arab–Israeli war of June 1967. The Iraqi Ba'th had come to power after that war, and was the only 'revolutionary regime' in the Arab world not compromised by the defeat. In its Proclamation No.1 it had even called for 'establishing the responsibilities of the defeat' – a demand that, though quickly watered down, must have been alarming to the Syrian side, which certainly had a lion's share of the 'responsibilities'. It was plain that the Syrian regime had been ill-prepared for the war[19] and it was also plain that despite repeated warnings by Syrian and Egyptian officials[20] it had precipitated it through deliberate provocations against Israel. These provocations at the same time were attempts to outbid Nasir and thus finally made the Egyptian president abandon his cautious and reticent attitude towards a war. Obviously Syria's attempts to precipitate the war were no less meant to enhance its own regional standing *vis-à-vis* Egypt than to liberate Palestine.

However, the greatest threat to the Jadid regime came from Asad and his supporters. Unlike the other groups of discontented Ba'this, Asad commanded great and growing support, especially in the army and air force. In his irresistible ascent he deliberately sought Iraqi support and thus a *rapprochement* with Baghdad, which, however, remained tactical and limited. The Iraqi regime in turn welcomed the advent in Syria of less antagonistic forces. In addition to Iraqi support such *rapprochement* assured Asad of sympathy throughout the Arab world, as it was taken as another indication of his willingness to normalize Syria's relations with the other Arab states. It also won him friends among all those in Syria who wanted to end the isolation of their country provoked by Jadid's radical stances. Most important among these were the followers of Muhammad 'Umran. 'Umran continued to command significant support among 'Alawi officers, even after 23 February 1966 when he had to take refuge in Lebanon. Jadid and his faction had reduced the Ba'thi goal of unifying the Arab nation into one state to that of mere unity of action of Arab progressives, and in accordance with their regionalist outlook they had sought to implement their version of Arab socialism 'in one country'. But the 'Umrani officers, hostile to socialist and communist ideas, continued to consider Syria as part of a larger Arab entity and hoped to bring about, if not political unification, some form of closer co-operation *between* the Arab states. To a limited extent, 'Umran and his supporters were close to positions of the *qawmiyyun*.[21] A notorious anti-communist and advocate of economic liberalization, Asad was in a good position to obtain the support of the 'Umranis. His rather conciliatory attitude towards other Arab regimes won him additional sympathy, although his ultimate aim was not the greatest possible integration of the Arab world but the greatest benefits for Syria (as to 'Umran–Asad relations, see p. 44). In a way Asad was himself a regionalist and certainly an 'Alawi 'separatist', but unlike Jadid he did not appear as such.[22] Thus at the Fourth Regional Congress held in early October 1968, as well as at the extraordinary meeting of the same congress convened in March 1969, Asad openly called for reconciliation and even reunification with the Iraqi party.[23] In private he reportedly promised the Iraqi leaders he would recognize the authority of the 'historical leadership'. In any case, his contacts with the Iraqi regime were frequent and intensive. So reportedly, from March 1969, the Iraqi Foreign Minister 'Abd al-Karim al-Shaykhli came regularly to Damascus, about every two weeks for several days, where he had an office in Asad's Defence Ministry.

The first three categories of dissident Ba'this posed all the more a threat to the Syrian regime as, apart from those sympathising with the *qutriyyun*, many Sunni Syrians – far more than Iraqis – felt, thought and acted as Arabs, rather than inhabitants of a certain country or, in Ba'thi parlance, region. Consequently they were more inclined than Iraqis to be loyal to Arab actors from outside their state borders.[24]

Conversely, there was no such strong proclivity among Iraqis, Ba'this and non-Ba'this alike, to identify with Arab interests at large. They were therefore less ready to give their support to Arab actors from beyond the borders of their own country. Possibly vertical cleavages in Iraqi society whether between Kurds and Arabs, or Shi'is, Sunnis and Christians, or even people from different regions and cities, were far deeper than in Syria. This led to Iraqis being unwilling to consider non-Iraqis, who were even more 'different', at least in their local origin, as eligible to enjoy their confidence.

In any case, the Iraqi Ba'th Party had long ceased to be a genuinely 'pan-Arab' party. Its leaders after 1963, Ahmad Hasan al-Bakr and Saddam Husayn, although designated by the pre-1966 National Command, led a party whose actual outlook was less Arab nationalist than Iraqi nationalist. The term *qutriyyun* has never been applied to the Iraqi party of this time, nor have Iraqi Ba'this ever referred to themselves as such, but it certainly applies to them no less than it applies to the Syrian *qutriyyun*.[25]

Nevertheless, this commitment to Iraqi interests does not necessarily preclude a certain attachment to wider Arab interests – a remark that is equally true for the Syrian *qutriyyun*. Nor does it preclude Arab nationalist rhetoric, which is an extremely valuable instrument for mobilizing Arab resources, including political support for Iraqi interests and, ultimately, the egotistic purposes of the Ba'thi rulers. However, what it does preclude is the complete non-distinction between inside and outside, between Iraqi and Arab, or Syrian and Arab, that characterizes the convinced and practising Arab nationalists of the type represented by Michel 'Aflaq.

Apart from this more precise distinction between internal and external affairs, and thus between internal and external actors, none of the inner-party opposition groups in the Iraqi Ba'th at that time had any affinities with the dominant faction of the Syrian Ba'th. Most importantly, Hardan al-Takriti, dismissed in October 1970, and Salih Mahdi 'Ammash, dismissed in September 1971, the strongest competitors of Bakr and Saddam Husayn, had no 'Syrian connection'.[26]

## The dispute over Ba'thi legitimacy

Tension between Syria and Iraq increased from the first July coup in 1968. From its very beginning it expressed itself in an argument over Ba'thi legitimacy, which over the second half of the year and especially in early 1969 became the dominant propagandist feature of the conflict. However, in contrast to the future course of events, the argument was first sustained by the Syrian side only, not yet by openly challenging its Ba'thi neighbour but by pointedly ignoring its Ba'thi character.

On the morrow of the 17 July coup in Iraq, *al-Ba'th*, the official mouthpiece of the Syrian party, in the lower left quarter of its front page carried a small report entitled 'Radio Baghdad announces military coup in Iraq'. More than the size, the contents and the terms reveal the Syrian *malaise*. After rather extensively dwelling on technicalities such as the imposition of a curfew and on the hours during which it was enforced the article only briefly reported the appointment of Ahmad Hasan al-Bakr and Hardan al-Takriti as President of the Republic and Chief-of-Staff, respectively. Significantly, their membership of the Iraqi Ba'th was passed over in silence and the party was not mentioned at all. Instead the event was referred to as a 'military coup' (*inqilab' askari*)[27] – a term implicity excluding the participation of any sincere Ba'thi, since no party organ ever fully endorsed such practice and usually never missed an opportunity to condemn it. After the initial announcement of the coup the Syrian media fell silent.[28] While there was no confirmation of alleged troop concentrations,[29] internal security was reinforced, and reportedly congratulatory telegrams sent to the new rulers in Baghdad were seized.[30] In one instance an anonymous Syrian Ba'th leader was quoted as saying the authors of the 17 July 'coup' had earlier been expelled from the Ba'th for their 'deviation' from party principles, their 'infamous plots' to overthrow the Ba'th regime in Syria, and their 'infamous connections' with imperialism and reaction.[31] From Syrian soil, however, no such recriminations were yet pronounced. Even Prime Minister Zu'ayyin in his important speech at the inauguration of the new port at Tartus on 27 July, though denouncing the Syrian Ba'thi exiles in Lebanon, only discreetly hinted at Iraq when he said, 'The enemy has every hope that a new series of coups will break out in the Arab world.'[32]

The Syrian embarrassment was even more conspicuous after the second July coup in Baghdad which left the Iraqi Ba'th in exclusive control of government. *Al-Ba'th* in just two paragraphs told its readers that the Iraqi president had formed a new government replacing the previous one presided over by 'Abd al-Razzaq al-Nayif, and that Salih Mahdi 'Ammash and Hardan al-Takriti had been appointed Minister of the Interior and Minister of Defence, respectively. Neither the name of the president and supreme commander (Ahmad Hasan al-Bakr), nor his or 'Ammash's and Takriti's affiliation to the Ba'th were mentioned.[33] And again silence was resumed.[34]

But silence could not last, and the initial restraint gave way to open and ever more frequent and violent accusations. Towards the end of 1968 Syrian propaganda had embarked on a vitriolic campaign against the Ba'th regime in Baghdad. On 18 November President Nur al-Din al-Atasi delivered an important speech commemorating the 'overthrow of the Ba'th revolution' five years earlier in Iraq, whereas the new Ba'th regime in Baghdad had deliberately chosen not to commemorate this event any more. Atasi explicitly claimed sole Ba'thi legitimacy for the Syrian side, and described the 1968 'revolution' as just another coup, in no way distinct from 'Arif's coup on 18 November 1963.[35] By January 1969, when Asad's pressure on Jadid had increased substantially, Jadid's propaganda war against Iraq was in full swing.

By contrast, Iraqi statements after the July coup and even towards the close of the year were conciliatory. For instance, Bakr stated that the Syrian and Iraqi Ba'th parties had no differences over principles but just over views, saying 'They are Ba'this, and we are Ba'this.[36] However, the Iraqi rulers did not hide their contacts with Syrian Ba'thi exiles in Lebanon, who had been overthrown by the movement of 23 February 1966.[37] They also supported Lebanon against economic sanctions adopted by Syria to force the government in Beirut to restrict dissident activities. This was done partly to defend the regime's own claim to Ba'thi legitimacy but also to maintain Iraqi trade through Lebanese ports. Yet, careful not to escalate the affair, the Iraqi Foreign Minister 'Abd al-Karim al-Shaykhli stated that 'there is nothing to prevent co-operation between us' – 'us' meaning Iraq and Syria.[38]

The violence and frequency of Syro-Iraqi propaganda exchanges intensified from about the beginning of 1969 as Asad's first and limited coup against Jadid approached. Nonetheless, Iraq often ignored Syrian charges, which until Asad's second coup, the 'Corrective Movement', of 16 November 1970 occurred on a daily basis. Although continued immediately after Asad's take-over, they nonetheless diminished under his rule. Accusations on both sides continued to turn around the question of Ba'thi legitimacy, often accompanied by an argument over Arab legitimacy, till they subsided in early 1972.

Responsibility for Syrian attacks on Iraq prior to this date lay with the Jadid faction, whereas Asad after the Fourth Regional Congress in October 1968 openly called for the normalization of relations with the Iraqi Ba'th.[39] Although the Iraqi party, too, was divided, the three major factions of 'Ammash, Hardan al-Takriti and Bakr/Husayn hardly differed in their common hostility towards the Jadid faction and their relative preference for Asad.

In the dispute over Ba'thi legitimacy Jadid and his propaganda apparatus described the Iraqi regime in terms which implicitly, but nonetheless clearly, denied its Ba'thi character. Standard phrases included 'clique (tum'a) of 17 July',[40] 'plotting rightist clique',[41] 'Barkr's suspect coup,[42] or 'Iraq's dominant faction'.[43] In one case the Iraqi Ba'th was surprisingly called an 'Arab nationalist gang',[44] the emphasis presumably being on 'gang'. Though never qualified as 'Ba'thi', the recurrent insistence that the Syrian Ba'th was the 'true Ba'th' (al-Ba'th al-haqiqi) implied that the other regime was also somehow Ba'thi in character. More explicit were statements calling for a 'Ba'th regime' to 'replace Iraq's present reactionary regime' (nizam raji),[45] or describing the latter as the continuation of 'Arif's regime and in fact plotting against the Ba'th.[46] Perhaps the most elaborate way of insinuating the continuity with the 'Arif regime was blaming the new rulers in Baghdad for the 'Iraqi inactivity' in the 1967 war with Israel.[47] Quite ingeniously many of these statements, especially the more important ones, were made on the anniversaries of either the first Ba'thi 'revolution' (thawra) in Iraq on 8 February 1963 or its overthrow on 18 November 1963.

That the Iraqi party was Ba'thi only in name could, of course, also be seen from the fact that again and again it persecuted, arrested and tortured 'party strugglers'. Much was made of the assassination of the Ba'thi officer 'Abd al-Karim Mustafa Nasrat. Nasrat, a key figure of the 8 February 1963 coup in Iraq and a close friend of the Syrian Chief of National Security 'Abd al-Karim al-Jundi who in turn was a staunch supporter of Jadid, was murdered in his Baghdad home on 27 January 1969. A communiqué released by the National Command of the Syrian Ba'th Party stated that

> hundreds of party strugglers and other progressive forces in Iraq have been subjected to arrest, torture and assassination since July 1968. This campaign has affected students, workers and other citizens. The latest and most treacherous crime in this series has been the assassination of Comrade Staff-Colonel 'Abd al-Karim Mustafa Nasrat. This abominable crime clearly points to the turncoat plotters who have shed the blood of many honest, progressive people to serve their imperialist masters and the owners of the monopolist oil companies.[48]

Thus again the regime's hierarchy, far from leaving the propaganda campaign to the media, did not hesitate to put forth heavy accusations itself.

After Asad's coup in November 1970 the question of Ba'thi legitimacy continued to play an important part in Syrian propaganda for more than a year till it subsided, and with it most of the war of words, in early 1972. Although Asad had previously called for an improvement in relations with Baghdad his attitude quickly changed as he set out to consolidate his own position. The very first communiqué released on 16 November 1970 by the new Regional and National Commands denounced the rightist ideology governing our people in Iraq'.[49] Subsequently, however, such accusations were mainly left to the media; for instance *al-Ba'th* wrote:

> the agent rightist clique has returned to conspire, under the guise of the party, against Iraq's revolutionary forces and to launch terrorist campaigns of liquidation against the elite of the progressive citizens.[50]

At about the beginning of 1969, after the initial period of restraint, the Iraqi regime took up the challenge and sought also to deny the Syrian side any Ba'thi legitimacy. In Iraqi parlance, too, the term 'true Ba'th' now frequently recurred[51] to distinguish the guardians of truth residing in Baghdad from the 'opportunists, the most dangerous of all enemies'[52] in Damascus. Consequently, the Syrian regime had to be replaced by a 'truly Ba'thi one'.[53] Ahmad Hasan al-Bakr who had once admitted that the Syrian rulers were Ba'this as well,[54] now changed his mind and declared that there was no Ba'th Party except the Iraqi one, and that the Syrian rulers formed a 'military junta'.[55]

On another occasion it was claimed that

> the Socialist Arab Ba'th Party's National Command has described the renegade movement of 23rd February 1966 in the Syrian region as one linked with the renegade movement of 18th November 1963 in Iraq and with the criminal secession of 28th September 1961 . . . The statement says: The claim of the renegade movement of 23rd February to the Ba'th and the Ba'th slogans was a major part of the plan designed to destroy the original historical movement . . . The transformation of the 5th June setback into a victory over the enemy cannot be achieved until the mentality and methods that accompanied the movements of 28th September, 18th November and 23rd February are rooted out.[56]

Dismissing the movement of 23 February as a 'renegade movement' (*harakat* or *hukm al-ridda*) and thus opposing it to the 'original historic movement' (*haraka tarikhiyya asila*) in Iraq then and later was a standard feature of Iraqi propaganda.

After the coup of November 1970 in Syria, Baghdad more

often ignored the new rulers' continuous, though slowly abating, insistence on Ba'thi legitimacy. And when voicing its criticism vis-à-vis Syria it again acknowledged the existence there of a Ba'th Party. Even Saddam Husayn did so when he declared:

> Our relations with Syria are good but, as far as the Syrian Ba'th Party is concerned, the case is different. None of the crises this party went through after 1963 revealed a change in its mentality. As to us, we refuse to admit that tanks, guns or fighter planes can replace normal party methods.[57]

This softer line is also illustrated by a rather friendly congratulatory telegram that Bakr sent to Asad after his election as president of Syria in March 1971.[58] Perhaps this more lenient attitude also in part resulted from the fact that 'Aflaq shortly after Asad's take-over finally settled in Baghdad, thereby conferring additional legitimacy to the Iraqi Ba'th.[59] Even so, till early 1972 the issue of Ba'thi legitimacy progressively disappeared from Iraqi statements as much as it did from Syrian ones. With it the war of words subsided for a while, giving way to a markedly quieter atmosphere.

That the dispute over Ba'thi legitimacy was started by the Jadid faction in Syria at the very moment when Ba'thi officers took over in Iraq, and that it intensified with the infighting within the Syrian regime in early 1969, indicates that the purpose of this dispute was to rally Syrian Ba'this, especially in the apparatus, around the instigators of the argument. This is further confirmed by the fact that the Asad faction, after its successful coup on 16 November 1970, quickly forgot its previous sympathies for Baghdad. Indeed this faction, which due to its contacts with the Iraqi regime had been able to muster some support among Syrian qawmiyyun, now had to check the pro-Iraqi pull it had partly created itself and make it clear that it did not intend to become Baghdad's junior partner.

Yet, more significantly, the dispute over Ba'thi legitimacy subsided with the economic liberalization or infitah initiated as early as 1971, which positively disposed the apparatus towards the ruling group. Also, the assassination of Muhammad 'Umran removed Asad's last potential competitor of consequence from within the armed forces to whom members of the apparatus might have shifted their allegiance.

The infitah quickly resulted in an economic boom reflected in the rapid growth of the gross national product (GNP) by some 9 per cent from 1970 to 1971 and to more than 6 per cent from 1971 to 1972.[60] However, the new economic possibilities that now began to be offered to the private sector in Syria as well as to private business from abroad all depended on authorizations which could only be obtained from regime agencies. Those who controlled these

agencies or had some influence over them could now, by their simple
capacity to block private projects, demand ever higher commissions
and percentages from the applicants. This applied for instance to
the import licences private companies and entrepreneurs could
obtain from 1971 for certain commodities, mainly raw materials
and capital goods. But it also applied to the increasing reliance
of the government, in development and infrastructural projects,
on co-operation with private firms, at home and from abroad,
to whom the specific terms of this co-operation generally opened
enormous possibilities of defrauding the government.[61] This quite
naturally led to an increase in corruption among an apparatus that
disposed of public money, was not accountable to public audit,
and indeed was even encouraged to make its own profit to bind it
closer to the regime.[62] Such benefits from economic liberalization
became far more important over the subsequent years, notably in
1974 and 1975 when oil drilling licences were granted to foreign
companies and the private sector was authorized to import luxury
goods and to sign loan agreements with foreign investors for private
development projects.[63] Of course, economic growth in Iraq was
even faster and Iraq's GNP per capita exceeded that of Syria by
more than 20 per cent,[64] so that members of the Syrian apparatus
could have regarded Baghdad as a yet more profitable source of
income. Yet, technicalities made disbursements from Iraq rather
hazardous and only a potential revenue, while those from Damascus
were real and immediate. Moreover, Iraq for its own reasons had to
be economical in its spending policies (see the conclusion).

Although with the *infitah* Asad also won sympathy among the
followers of Muhammed 'Umran, many of them continued to
remain loyal to their leader. According to some sources many
supporters of 'Umran only resolved to participate in Asad's coup
after they had obtained assurances that 'Umran would become
prime minister.[65] Partly disgruntled, partly harbouring continued
hope, the 'Umrani Officers resigned themselves to Asad's rule only
when 'Umran was assassinated on 4 March 1972 in exile in Tripoli
in the north of Lebanon.

The aim which Iraq pursued in this conflict is reflected in the
timing of its reply to Syrian propaganda. That Iraq denied the
Ba'thi legitimacy of the Syrian regime only when the latter's
internal divisions had clearly emerged, but thereafter denied it
vehemently, points to an Iraqi interest in replacing Jadid by Asad.
Apart from that, Iraq obviously had to deny the Ba'thi legitimacy
of its Syrian counterpart if it did not want to risk its own legitimacy
and position being endangered. The abandonment of the argument
at about the same time that Syrian propaganda subsided indicates
that Iraq ceased to insist on the issue when it no longer had to

defend itself and when it realized that the Syrian regime now had succeeded in establishing control over its own apparatus. Although Iraq in these early years was poorer than after the 1973 rise in oil prices it was wealthier than Syria. Thus from a material point of view as well there was no need to rally its apparatus by insisting on Ba'thi legitimacy.[66]

Secondary motives in the argument over Ba'thi legitimacy were differences over what Ba'thism should stand for and personal hostilities. However, although the authors of the coup of 23 February in Syria advocated a different version of Ba'thism than that of the *qawmiyyun*, and a few of them, like Jadid, seemed to have some ideological motivation, their main objective was simply to take power.[67] The stronger emphasis on socialism presumably served largely to mobilize supporters who could not be reached with more moderate arguments.[68] The Iraqi Ba'th, for its part, had no actual programme at all, and indulged in complete ideological vagueness.[69] As far as ideological differences had a bearing on the conflict this was largely due to the preferences of the Syrian *qawmiyyun* for the rulers in Iraq which threatened to erode the basis of the Syrian regime.

In any case, the Jadid as well as the Bakr regime favoured a dominant public sector as well as the overall regulation and planning of economic activities. Neither of the two, however, intended to nationalize small and medium-sized firms. The underprivileged classes received a minimum of social services and security, but more substantial improvements were restricted to those working in the government and public sector. Despite all the revolutionary rhetoric, the policies actually implemented were made to suit the interests of the lower middle classes.[70] In Syria then, Asad's *infitah* policy increasingly favoured private enterprise and the emergence of a new bourgeoisie, even if it was largely dependent on the state. Although no similar measures had yet been taken in Iraq, the private sector there also continued to prosper, especially with the country's rising oil revenues.

Ba'thism in Iraq and Syria certainly diverged at the verbal level: whereas the Iraqi party continued to stick to the traditional Ba'thi discourse and vocabulary, Jadid and his supporters borrowed Marxist-Leninist terms and concepts.[71] Both sides, however, claimed to recognize the Constitution of the Ba'th Party, passed by its first congress in Damascus in 1947,[72] as the theoretical basis of their political practice.

Perhaps not less important were personal hostilities between leading members of the Syrian and Iraqi regimes. Under the prevailing circumstances political opponents quickly became merciless enemies as power either was taken completely and 'for ever' or immediately lost, the losers purged, imprisoned, humiliated or even executed. The authors of the 23 February movement had been resentful of 'Aflaq and Bitar ever since the two had decided to dissolve the party in 1958; even worse, Bitar in 1961 signed the famous manifesto justifying the *infisal*, and thus was considered a most unreliable opportunist.[73]

Animosities against 'Aflaq and his friends would not have played any noteworthy role, had Bakr not been so readily assimilated to the 'old guard'. Bakr, who had also been expelled from the National Command on 23 February 1966, was considered as 'Aflaq's creature and accomplice. Hafiz al-Asad also disliked Bakr for his 'betrayal of the Ba'th' when, after 'Arif's take-over, he had continued to serve as Iraqi prime minister.[74] Asad not only disliked but apparently even hated, Saddam Husayn.[75]

Conversely, Bakr is said to have been extremely resentful of Salah Jadid who in 1966 kicked him out of the National Command and who had used the party for 'sectarian purposes'[76]. Aflaq's personal grievances against other Ba'this, especially those of 23 February 1966, were many, but had no important bearing on Syro-Iraqi relations after 1968; they merely had to be somehow accommodated by the Iraqi leaders when they wanted the grand old man to move to Baghdad.

### Corollaries of the dispute over Ba'thi legitimacy

#### Restriction on contacts

Non-verbal events also indicate that the conflict in this early period served the successive dominant factions in Syria to consolidate their rule while the Iraqi side, though only temporarily and also in self-defence, used it to destabilize the Syrian regimes.

Jadid and his faction sought almost desperately to prevent contacts and communication between members of the Syrian apparatus, civilian as well as military, and the Iraqi regime. However, Jadid lacked support in the military and in the police and could only rely on 'Abd al-Karim al-Jundi, the then chief of National Security. Jundi, a staunch supporter of Jadid, was responsible for many but not all the arrests of pro-Iraqi or supposedly pro-Iraqi Ba'this and officers in Syria.[77] Moreover, after Jundi's death, while besieged by Asad's troops in March 1969, his agency came under the authority of Asad who in his capacity as Minister of Defence already controlled the secret services of the army and air force.

Despite its confidential top-level contacts with Baghdad, the Asad faction tried to limit contacts at the lower levels as much as possible, and testimonies abound of Ba'this arrested by Asad's forces for actual or alleged collaboration with Iraq.[78] So the Air Force Intelligence (*Mukhabarat al-quwat al-jawiyya*), commanded by Muhammad al-Khuli, a close confidant of Asad, carried out the two waves of arrests of April and June 1970; many of the victims were Ba'this.[79] Asad in early 1971 released a number of persons previously arrested for pro-Iraqi activities, but others, mainly Ba'this, remained in prison or were newly arrested on the same charges. Responsibility for the arrests that took place immediately after the July coups in 1968 is harder to determine.[80] Some of those arrested were released after the Fourth Regional Congress held in October 1968. Others remained imprisoned and some of those released were reimprisoned sooner or later.[81]

After Asad's complete take-over on 16 November 1970, his earlier *rapprochement* with Iraq clearly appeared a tactical move. Apart from persistent propaganda attacks, the previously established communication links with Baghdad were now also severed,[82] and, of course, no party unification was negotiated. Certainly also 'Aflaq's move to Baghdad in late 1970 contributed to Asad's decision to continue to restrict Iraqi contacts with the Syrian apparatus as much as possible. As 'Aflaq's presence in Iraq greatly enhanced Baghdad's Ba'thi legitimacy, the Asad regime as early as January 1971 brought his case before its own State Security Court which on 3 August 1971 convicted him – *in absentia* – of trying to overthrow the Syrian regime with Iraqi aid (see p. 55).

Throughout the period, before as well as after Asad's take-over, the Syrian regime tried to limit general contacts between the two countries. No Iraqi newspaper could be found in Syria, not even in the offices of *al-Thawra*, an official Damascus paper. Travellers to Iraq were questioned after their return. Further, although diplomatic relations were 'normal', the staff of the Iraqi embassy in Damascus were completely isolated and 'nobody dared to talk to them'.[83] Only on the symbolic date of 22 February 1971 was the first, however modest, agreement reached to promote communication between the people of the two countries. According to this agreement reciprocal visits by trade unionists were to be encouraged and a grant scheme set up to facilitate such visits.

Though less frequently, Iraqi secret services were also reported to have arrested pro-Syrian Ba'this, as for instance shortly after the promulgation of Iraq's first Ba'thi constitution in September 1968[84] or in the first half of September 1969.[85] If Syrian accusations were correct, the assassination of Colonel Nasrat in late January 1969 was part of the same policy. Obviously no restrictions applied to top-level contacts, for example between Bakr's and Asad's personal envoys. In 1970 exiled supporters of the Syrian ex-president Amin al-Hafiz were even removed from party positions in Iraq because they opposed the *rapprochement* with Asad.[86]

## Mutual subversion

Certainly from late 1968 on, but perhaps already earlier, Iraq actively supported oppositional factions and groups in Syria with the aim of weakening or overthrowing the increasingly cumbersome Jadid regime. As the *qawmiyyun* in Syria were too weak, Baghdad entered an alliance with Hafiz al-Asad and his fellow officers who for their own reasons sought to put an end to Jadid's rule. To a lesser extent the Iraqi Ba'th also supported Akram Hawrani, the charismatic veteran socialist from Hama, who partly recruited his support from the same social groups as the Ba'th. Hawrani could also mobilize 'progressives' and thus threaten the Jadid regime from the left. As a progressive, for instance, he and a few other members of this party, then called the Arab Democratic Socialist Party, were invited to the anniversary ceremonies for the Iraqi 'revolutions' of 1958 and 1968 held on 14 July 1969. When their attendance was confirmed the Damascus rulers, who had previously banned Hawrani's party in Syria, decided to boycott the festivities.[87]

Conversely, the Jadid regime could not command much support in Iraq. Its own organization there was modest, and no important group of inner-party opponents had pro-Syrian sympathies. In fact, only Jalal al-Talabani's breakaway faction from the Kurdish Democratic Party (KDP) could be relied on.[88] The KDP itself, led by Mulla Mustafa Barzani, still kept its distance with Syria.[89]

Baghdad's desire to topple the Jadid regime was certainly motivated in the first instance by the need to rid themselves of an obnoxious neighbour whose attacks threatened to erode their own Ba'thi as well as wider Arab legitimacy. The Iraqi leaders might well have liked to extend their sphere of influence but they knew that, although they could possibly provoke the fall of Jadid, they would not have the means to control and keep in check his successor. The Jadid regime presumably even more than the Bakr regime would have liked to overthrow its Ba'thi neighbour, but in its case the realization to such a plan belonged entirely to the realm of wishful thinking.

## The intractability of Ba'thi dichotomy

In those early years, at least theoretically, there was yet another way to solve the problem and forestall the dangers of shifting political support. Instead of rallying support through bilateral conflict the Ba'thi dichotomy could instead have been overcome by peacefully uniting the parties. The possibility of simply coexisting only emerged later, when as in the course of the Syrian *infitah* allegiance could be obtained through material benefit instead of ideological force of conviction.

In part the unification of the two parties did not occur because there was no actual need to unite the two countries. Iraq would certainly have obtained free access to the Mediterranean, but presumably preferred to remain or become the exclusive owner of its oil resources. For Syria the co-ownership of these oil resources would certainly have been advantageous, but was not imperative. More importantly, however, it was factionalism that made the ruling groups reluctant to merge. In both countries power was and still is monopolized and exerted by ruling groups whose founding members gathered and then continued to co-opt newcomers on the basis of specific, though partly changing, informal criteria. The critical features required vary from group to group and those indispensable in Syria are incompatible with those in demand in Iraq. Contrary to a commonly held view membership of a certain religious 'community' – 'Alawi in Syria and Sunni in Iraq – does not rank highest among these criteria. Presumably religion like other ethnic (see the definition in the introduction, pp. 18ff.) or regional criteria remains yet too general and widely encompassing to produce brothers in arms. The 'elites' and 'counter-elites' recruit themselves from individuals fulfilling far more specific conditions. They either belong to certain families, kinship or tribal groups, or are linked by neighbourly and close local ties, or they have lived together through crucial periods of their lives, including early political socialization or studying together at the military academy. The only condition is that something like a Khaldunian *'asabiyya*[90] emerges, whether it is based on blood ties or an experience such as the joint traversing of a desert. Sharing a number of salient traits may enhance this *esprit de corps*, and indeed members of one group seem to have more than one thing in common. Theoretically, however, there may also be alternative ways to become eligible for membership, when only one or more of these conditions have to be fulfilled.

Since the kinship and tribal groups from which these 'elites' or *jama'at* recruit themselves are not generally divided by religious boundaries it is in a sense correct to consider Syria as being ruled by 'Alawis and Iraq by Sunnis. This, however, does not mean that Syria is ruled by *the* 'Alawis and Iraq by *the* Arab Sunnis. The criteria determining eligibility for co-optation into the factions around Asad,[91] Bakr/Saddam Husayn,[92] Jadid[93] and their wider clienteles have been examined elsewhere and need not be dealt with in detail here. The Asad family, it may be recalled, belongs to the Kalbiyyun, one of the four major 'Alawi tribal confederations while a sizeable proportion of their closest supporters come from the al-Nmailatiyya section of the al-Matawira confederation, co-operation between the two groups not always being completely smooth. The Asad faction, of course, extends beyond these narrow tribal bonds through ties of marriage and business. In Iraq a great number of key posts in the apparatus are filled with officers and officials hailing from Takrit in the 'Sunni triangle', the native town of Bakr, Husayn and other influential members of the ruling group. Many 'Takritis' are linked to each other through family or kinship ties of some sort. So Khayrallah al-Tulfah, the former Defence Minister, as well as Hasan al-Majid, head of General Security and Party Security until at least 1987, were cousins of Saddam Husayn. Tulfah was moreover the son-in-law and cousin of Bakr.

However, neither the specific criteria for membership in these factions and clienteles, nor the specific difference existing between them, can account for their reluctance to merge. As in the case of religious differences they certainly overdetermine this reluctance, but they do not cause it. If certain kinship origins or other salient features are in most cases essential for co-optation into a faction or even a clientele, neither the faction nor clientele ever encompass all those sharing these origins or traits. Large membership would reduce the amount of benefit each member could draw from the association and is thus avoided. Consequently several competing factions or clienteles could recruit themselves according to the same criteria and exist and thrive in this same milieu.

The salient differences between the ruling groups thus appear to be less important determinants of their reluctance to merge parties and armies than the simple fact they belonged to different factions or clienteles. These depend on the state for their reproduction, and would lose the only instrument ensuring their political survival if they merged their apparatus with that of a neighbour and thus lost absolute control over it. Renunciation of this control would introduce an element of uncertainty into previously secure political spheres and institutions, and the breach could easily be exploited by one associate to enhance his own position at the expense of his partner and even to expel him – if only out of the fear that the other might do the same first. The situation very much resembles the difficult coexistence of the two independent Ba'th regimes, but with the difference that in separate state apparatuses subversion is somewhat more difficult.

For the 'Alawi rulers of Syria these general perils of a merger with another faction were topped by another risk. Having discovered and increasingly imagining themselves as a community,[94] many of them were not inclined to make Syria part of a larger Arab state with an even larger Sunni majority.[95] Although in numerical terms Arab Sunnis were a minority in Iraq with its large Kurdish Sunni population and an Arab Shi'i majority, they were politically and economically dominant. Moreover, as the Twelver-Shi'a to which Iraq's Shi'i population belong did not recognize Syria's small but politically dominant 'Alawi minority as genuinely Shi'i, the 'Alawis could not hope to bolster their position with much Shi'i support.[96]

### The dispute over Arab legitimacy

As already indicated, the two sides not only competed for Ba'thi legitimacy but also disputed each other's right and capacity to represent the Arab cause and Arab interests at large, in other words their respective Arab legitimacy. However, till Asad's take-over each side did this in its own way, with Syria insisting more than Iraq on the progressive character of its Arab legitimacy. Under Asad, however, Syria softened its line and stressed its general Arab legitimacy.

One of the key charges levelled by the Jadid regime against its Iraqi counterparts was of conspiring against the revolution in the Arab world, either in general or against specific parts of it. According to Syrian propaganda, this plot to thwart the revolution had already succeeded in Iraq, from where similar attempts were now being made to thwart it in Syria as well. This type of argument is illustrated by the earlier quoted comment on the seventh anniversary of the 'Arif coup that appeared in the Syrian al-Ba'th,[97] and recurred frequently before Asad's take-over.

The plot in which Iraq allegedly took part was also directed against the liberation of Palestine: 'As for the right-wing regime in Iraq, it serves the conspirational settlement in a manner fully calculated in imperialist oil circles, despite its verbal attempt to appear as one of the positive aspects of the Arab nation. The Iraqi regime continues to keep the Iraqi army and people away from the true battle.'[98]

Other statements pointed more explicitly to the connection between Iraqi leaders' hostility to 'revolution' and their connivance with imperialism:

The forces of imperialism tried . . . to exploit . . . the vestiges of the right wing [after the movement of 23 February 1966] . . . culminating in the 17 July 1968 coup in Iraq to distort the Party's name in the area and using the coup's dubious logic and cheap methods to infiltrate the ranks of the Party's strugglers in the Arab homeland to undermine the revolution in Arab Syria.'[99]

Denouncing the distinctive mark and main sin of the Iraqi regime – collusion with imperialism – these statements at the same time served to underpin the Syrian claim to sole Ba'th legitimacy.

Considering the Syrian explanation of alleged Iraqi misdeeds and crimes against the revolution or the Arab cause it is not surprising that the rulers in Baghdad were continuously accused of 'suspect contacts'[100] and, of course, 'collusion with imperialism'[101] when their stances in Arab affairs were criticized. In other cases the Iraqi regime was called an 'agent regime' (nizam 'amil) or 'agent clique' (tum'at al-'umala)[102] committing 'treacherous crimes'[103] and 'waging campaigns' against citizens with 'nationalist and patriotic attitudes'.[104] Iraq's conflicts with the Kurds and with Iran were accordingly described as side-shows deliberately created to avoid responsibility in the Arab–Israeli conflict.[105] An official statement on the occasion of the sixth anniversary of the Iraqi 'February revolution' well illustrates the language resorted to when it qualifies the Iraqi leaders as 'defeatist plotters, assassins of valiant progressives for the benefit of imperialism and its oil companies.'[106] Such imputations, however, did not prevent Syria from assuring Iraq of support in its dispute with Iran; still ruled by the shah, Iran was not yet eligible as an ally of the 'revolutionary' regime in Syria, which consequently exploited the affair as far as possible to prove its Arab legitimacy by defending also the 'rights' of its antagonist.[107]

The quest on the part of both sides for Arab legitimacy expressed itself also in policy decisions. So in the summer of 1970 both sides, individually and separately, rejected the Rogers initiative which had been accepted by Egypt and Jordan and called for an Israeli-Arab cease-fire and the subsequent resumption of the Jarring mission. Further away, Iraq denounced the initiative in extremely harsh terms while Syria, anxious to remain on good terms with Egypt, merely rejected it. Both regimes again disagreed with other Arab states, as well as with each other, when in September President Nasir invited the Arab kings and heads of state to Cairo to put an end to the fighting between Jordanian and Palestinian troops. Syria's President Atasi went to Cairo but did not formally attend the talks and did not sign the final declaration. Iraq, for its part, again outdid Syria by maintaining a complete boycott.

The argument over Arab legitimacy explicitly referred to these and other events. However, they merely served as convenient pretexts and did not actually cause this argument. So when after endless preparations and postponements the Jordanian, Iraqi and Syrian regimes on 18 September 1968 finally agreed to establish a Joint Eastern Command to confront Israel (see p. 58), Syria soon accused Iraq of 'evading' its 'national responsibilities'.[108] And when the Joint Eastern Command collapsed less than two years later, Iraq on the one side, and Syria and Jordan – supported by Egypt – on the other, blamed each other for the outcome of their mutual obstructionism. In September 1970 the arguments centred on stances adopted during the Jordanian 'civil war', each side blaming its opponent for passively watching King Husayn and the forces of 'reaction' annihilating the Palestinian resistance and 'revolution'.[109] Under Asad the newly established 'Federation of Arab Republics' formed by Egypt, Libya and Syria (see pp. 57) offered the Syrian side the opportunity to distinguish between those who took Arab unity seriously and the other who merely 'brandished slogans'.[110]

The argument over the 'civil war' in Jordan illustrates the 'progressive' connotation of Arab legitimacy in Syrian propaganda. When criticizing Iraqi stands in Arab affairs Jadid's propaganda machine regularly condemned the 'reactionary' and 'rightist' attitudes of the Iraqi regime[111] and charged it with the betrayal of the lower part of the global class society. Recurrently also, the 'plotting rightist military clique' in Baghdad was accused of waging a 'hysterical campaign of intimidation and arrests against the toiling masses and select strugglers in Iraq'.[112] From March 1969 the Jadid faction no longer contented itself with joyful hints at the Iraqi 'gang's' imminent downfall[113] but now actively called on the Iraqi people to 'rise in order to defend . . . their . . . liberation and to unite . . . in a progressive front which will be able to confront the enemies of the people'.[114] For some time the Asad regime continued this argument in a slightly more moderate form when it recommended setting up a 'Progressive National Front' in Iraq comparable to the one already more or less agreed to in Syria. Such a front alone, it was argued, could oppose the 'rightist' (*yamini*) and 'fascist' (*fashisti* or *fashi*) regime in Baghdad, which, as in previous times, was blamed for arresting Ba'this as well as other nationalist and progressive militants.[115]

When insisting on its Arab legitimacy Iraq rarely claimed it was more progressive than Syria. One of the rare instances that it did so was Baghdad's well-timed claim to represent the 'genuine left' (*al-yasar al-haqiqi*) after the Syrian government in May 1970 for the first time offered guarantees to foreign capital and investment.[116]

Rather, the Iraqi leaders fully exploited their country's remoteness from Israel to stress their commitment to the Arab cause. Iraq's outright rejection of any kind of negotiation with Israel, even if it was only to agree a cease-fire as proposed in the Rogers plan, as well as its repeated call for a military solution to the conflict, clearly illustrate this radicalism. After initial pledges of co-operation with all Arab regimes[117] Iraq instead increasingly opposed them all, even the 'progressive' ones, in words and deeds.[118]

Concerning Syria, Iraq would first insist on its 'defeatism' in the struggle against Israel, claiming for instance that: 'We will not let ourselves be dragged into arguments by those whose aim . . . is to cover their military discomfiture . . . by having surrendered the Golan fortress to Israel without putting up any resistance.'[119] How serious a defender of Arab interests and rights the Iraqi Ba'th claimed to be readily appeared in its promise in July 1968 to establish the responsibilities of the disaster in 1967.[120] Syria was also denounced for sabotaging the activities of *fida'iyun*, even of persecuting them,[121] and obstructing the functioning of the Joint Eastern Command.[122]

Quite naturally, the eventual collapse of the Eastern Command was blamed on Jordan, Egypt and Syria, which had not rejected the Rogers initiative or not done so with sufficient insistence.[123] But although the Iraqi point of view was presented peremptorily, the charges were mainly couched in technical language, refraining from too many insults or from alleging collusion with imperialism. This line was generally maintained after the change of regime in Syria, except concerning the Federation of Arab Republics. Saddam Husayn called its Tripoli Charter the first step towards the 'crime' of recognizing Israel,[124] and *al-Thawra* later condemned the Proclamation of Damascus 'which undermines the basis of Arab revolution and throttles the Palestine resistance, the two principal obstacles to imperialist plots'.[125]

Perhaps the most astute technique used by both sides to emphasize their Arab legitimacy was to denounce plots allegedly aimed at overthrowing their own regime which, of course, was presented as the Arab revolution incarnate and thus as the main obstacle to imperialist objectives in the Middle East. The Iraqi regime between July 1968 and early summer 1970 denounced at least thirteen such plots, with either the United States, Britain or Iran, though never Syria, having a hand in them.[126]

Conversely, the Syrian regime missed no opportunity to accuse the Iraqi side and Syrian exiles of plotting to overthrow the

'Ba'thi revolution' in Syria.[127] In 1969, for instance, first Amin al-Hafiz already in exile in Baghdad,[128] then other Ba'thi exiles in Lebanon,[129] and finally the Iraqi regime itself,[130] were accused of similar conspiracies. Not long after Asad's take-over 350 Ba'this of the 'rightist clique', including 'Aflaq (who shortly before had definitely moved to Baghdad), were indicted for conniving with Iraq in an attempt to overthrow the Syrian Ba'th regime. Ninety-nine defendants were convicted, several death sentences were passed, including for Michel 'Alfaq, Amin al-Hafiz and Shibli al-'Aysami, who were tried *in absentia*. On 22 November 1971, however, Asad commuted the death sentences and completely remitted 'Aflaq's sentence (see p. 47).[131]

The dispute over Arab legitimacy was partly addressed to the Ba'thi audience in order to underpin claims to Ba'thi legitimacy. As in the later periods, though, it was certainly also addressed to non-Ba'thi audiences, inside and outside the two countries, whose support enhanced the general inner-state as well as regional position of the regimes, if not their chances of short-term survival. However, as Syria and Iraq had chosen the same method of drumming up and retaining support, they necessarily had to outbid each other. Clearly also the Ba'thi competitor, commensurate with the high degree of Arab legitimacy with which it was credited among a wider public, had to be accused more virulently than other Arab regimes.

Internally Arab legitimacy was particularly important for the rulers of Syria, not only to make the crushing defeat of 1967 more acceptable but also because many Ba'thi and non-Ba'thi Syrians, but not the *qutriyyun*, still felt that their 'artificial' and 'borderless' state,[132] the cradle of Arab nationalism, had no *raison d'être*, except to be the instigator of Arab unity, thus surpassing its own amputed and fragmented existence. Moreover, the emphasis on Arab legitimacy in Syrian propaganda was not unconnected with the narrow societal basis of the Jadid and later the Asad regime: it had to be proved that 'Alawis, too, were valiant Arabs.[133]

Baghdad found itself under similar constraints, although in Iraq Arab legitimacy was relevant mainly because of its anti-imperialist dimension. The Iraqi Ba'th could hardly afford to be less anti-imperialist than its predecessors, Qasim and the 'Arifs. As long as the Ba'th had not dealt a blow to imperialism as severe as Qasim's Law No. 80,[134] nationalizing all unexploited oilfields it had to prove its anti-imperialist credentials through diatribes and the verbal outbidding of other 'nationalist' and 'progressive' forces. Any alliance with other Arab regimes would have compromised this policy; moreover it would have recognized the losers of the 1967 war as acceptable interlocutors. Apart from that, the war

against the Kurds necessitated the mobilization of the country's
Arab population, all the more so as it demanded heavy human
and economic sacrifices.[135] At the same time these policies of
verbal radicalism in Arab affairs conferred on their protagonists
a position of strength in relation to other Arab regimes which with
the prevailing circumstances they could not have acquired in an
alliance with those regimes. Apart from enticing radicals from all
over the Arab world with their capacity to pressurize third actors,
these policies also enhanced their protagonists' bargaining positions
in direct dealings with other Arab regimes. By simply widening the
gap separating one's own policies from those of fellow Arab states,
the latter could be induced to make concessions out of a concern to
secure at least a minimum consensus in Arab affairs, or to prevent
the subversion of their own policies.

In the case of both the Jadid and the Iraqi regime, radicalism,
apart from its internal function seems to have aimed at being a
nuisance to the more moderate and conservative Arab regimes in
order to extort material assistance. Syria, after the *naksa*, badly
needed financial support to ease economic strains, and it obtained
significant reconstruction aid at the Khartoum summit in late
August 1967, although, and perhaps also because, its delegation
refused to sign the final resolution and instead walked out of
the conference. This policy, it should be stressed, was entirely
compatible with the regime's 'regionalist' philosophy since there
is no contradiction between seeking resources from abroad and
investing them at home. Moreover, the *qutriyyun* like any other
Arab actor had to operate in the milieu of the overarching Arab
polity and thus alleviate internal loss of support through external
Arab support. Finally, from this early date both sides intended,
through their radicalism, to impose themselves as obligatory interlocutors in any attempt to settle the Arab–Israeli dispute and thus
to get access to additional resources from the great powers. While
Iraq abandoned this policy of 'negative Arab leadership' only slowly and over a period stretching roughly from 1971 to 1974,[136]
the Syrian stands were quickly modified when Asad took power
on 16 November 1970, and a carrot was added to the stick in the
new regime's dealings with fellow Arab states. This reorientation,
however, had only limited repercussions on the regional competition with Iraq, because courting the moderates did not make Asad
abandon his canvassing for radical support, and because the final
aim, maximizing regional influence, remained the same.

Yet, the Asad regime had realized that Jadid's previous policy
did not help Syria to gain access to sufficient outside resources,
either Arab or non-Arab. By offering some degree of co-operation
to the wealthy conservative regimes these services could be charged

for and, more importantly, well-timed doses of radicalism could be used to remind the paymasters, by illustrating the contrast, how much more comfortable it was for them to pay and thus be left in peace.

Obtaining resources from the oil countries also entailed a more 'realistic' attitude on the part of Syria in the Arab–Israeli conflict. This realism and Syria's new policy of economic liberalization in general appeared as early as 27 November 1970 when Asad announced Syria would join the Federation of Arab Republics, a project already launched by Egypt, Libya and Sudan. This move brought to an end the country's isolation, and produced a *rapprochement* with Egypt, which Asad had constantly advocated in the days of Jadid. Moreover, joining this project allowed Asad to demonstrate his concern for Arab co-operation and even unity. Even though Syria was not the instigator it could, as the only other front-line state, still play a paramount role in this federation. And moreover Mu'ammar al-Qadhdhafi rewarded Syria financially for the valorization of Libya in the federation.[137] The Federation was officially set up by Egypt, Libya and Syria on 17 April 1971 while Sudan postponed its entry due to internal unrest. Later access to this federation was denied to Iraq, which Syria as well as Egypt wanted to keep as isolated as possible.

The swift changes in Syrian foreign policy immediately after Asad's take-over were well described by the late Malcolm Kerr:

> In December [1970] Asad paid visits to Sudan, Egypt and Libya. Normal telephone service with Jordan was restored. A previous ban on flights of Saudi Airlines was lifted. Asad received a prominent Lebanese Christian politician and assured him of his respect for Lebanese independence. In January 1971 a group of Syrians arrested many months previously on charges of working for the Iraqi regime were released. Steps were taken toward resumption of diplomatic relations with Tunisia and Morocco. The American-owned Trans-Arabian Pipeline Company was finally permitted to repair a portion of its line in Syria that had been damaged in previous May (in exchange, to be sure, for a promise from the company of increased payments). Asad visited Moscow in February, and hinted in the communiqué that was issued that Syria would not obstruct resolution 242.[138]

By making simultaneous overtures to the United States and the Soviet Union, fully playing the card of its strategic importance, Syria also succeeded in inducing them to outbid each other. This policy clearly appears in the agreement on economic co-operation with the Soviet Union, signed on 14 February 1972 at a time when the *infitah* and thus the opening of the Syrian economy to the West was gaining momentum.

## Other features

### Military non-co-operation

On this background of conflict it is not surprising that Syria and Iraq avoided military co-operation.[139] But in this particular conflict, the Syrian side more than in other conflicts had to be concerned about contacts between members of the apparatuses, contacts which would inevitably have intensified in the event of military co-operation. The Jadid faction considered military non-co-operation as essential for its survival, and Asad co-operated with Iraq militarily only as long as he still had to oppose Jadid and only to a very limited extent. Syrian reticence was manifest in the endless rows over the organization of the Joint Eastern Command which was supposed to exert overall authority over all Jordanian, Syrian and Iraqi troops on the Jordanian and Syrian front. Closely linked to this was the question of stationing Iraqi troops in Syria, which, apart from all the organizational disputes, created difficulties in itself. When the Command was finally established on 18 September 1968 the Syrian regime immediately demanded that Iraqi troops be stationed in Syria; but this demand was made at a time when the Syrian side could be certain that the new Iraqi regime, still shaky internally and already threatened by the shah of Iran, was unable to send any troops.[140] Only in March 1969, when Hafiz al-Asad, then widely thought to be close to the Iraqi Ba'th, prepared for his first show-down with Jadid, were a few hundred[141] (according to other sources 5,000–6,000)[142] Iraqi troops stationed near Dar'a (Dera) at the Jordanian border to secure and protect supplies for Iraqi troops in Jordan. On 30 July 1969, the two governments exchanged the instruments of ratification of the Syro-Iraqi defence agreement Asad and 'Arif had signed in May 1968. Nonetheless, Asad consented to no more than the token co-operation that was necessary to keep the temporary tactical alliance with Iraq going.

Iraq, for its part, probably saw the dangers of military co-operation in its political consequences. When Egypt and Jordan had expressly accepted the Rogers plan and Syria could be suspected of having done so privately, any further Iraqi participation in the Eastern Command would have endorsed their 'defeatism' and compromised the credibility of Iraq's own radical stances which excluded any negotiation with Israel. When in August 1970 the Joint Eastern Command was divided into separate

Northern (Syrian) and Eastern (Jordanian) commands, excluding Iraq from any formal responsibility, Baghdad verbally opposed the move but was probably not unhappy about this outcome. The Iraqi departure from the 'battlefield' was, of course, beneficial to Syrian propaganda as well since it excluded Iraq from the select club of 'confrontation states'.

*Economic and technical co-operation*

At least economic and technical co-operation thrived. Of the numerous negotiations between the two countries, interestingly enough, only two served to settle existing or potential differences: the economic sanctions against Lebanon that Syria adopted to curb the activities of Syrian Ba'thi exiles (see p. 40) and that had repercussions on Iraq as well; and the partition of the Euphrates waters discussed in May 1971. Like the sanctions against Lebanon the second issue, too, posed no serious difficulty in the early period, and nothing yet indicated the dramatic turn it would take in the mid-seventies.

Apart from the talks on the sanctions and the Euphrates issue all other negotiations or agreements served not to settle differences but to further co-operation between the two sides. This spirit of co-operation is illustrated by discussions such as those of 21 August to 10 September 1968 on oil; the agreement of 21 March 1969 to act against contraband activities; the agreement of 11 May on economic co-operation, which included Egypt; of 22 September on civil aviation; of 7 January 1970 on the co-operation between the official news agencies INA and SANA; of 23 November on ending previous trade restrictions; of 28 March 1971 on building a new pipeline from the North Rumayla oilfields in southern Iraq to Tartus in Syria; of three days later on building a railway line linking Baghdad to the Dayr al-Zawr–Aleppo line; and of 31 May 1971 to improve telecommunications, including Jordan. Certainly, the pipeline from North Rumayla, more or less alongside the existing pipeline originating in Kirkuk, never materialized. Iraq even considered building this second line to a Turkish port, but this episode, though partly anticipating a later conflict, only cast a small shadow on the overall positive developments in economic and technical co-operation.

Even diplomatic relations were fully restored when in August 1968 the Bakr regime again sent an Iraqi ambassador to Syria, after ten months of lower-level representation.[143] This was of course a largely symbolic but nonetheless important development, even though Iraqi diplomats were regarded with utmost suspicion in Syria. Co-operation in economic and technical matters as well as diplomatic relations certainly improved because it offered material advantages to both sides; or, rather, because non-co-operation would have damaged the interests of each side without, however, affecting the adversary sufficiently heavily to prevail upon him in the main conflicts of the period.

# 2

# From Regime Consolidation to Regional Competition, 1972–1975

*Acute issues and underlying antagonisms*

This period, from March 1972 to March 1975, resembled the calm between two storms. The conflict dominating the previous period had largely subsided, and the one that would dominate the years after 1975 was still only nascent, although throughout the period the past and future conflicts were both present in the background, and the emerging conflict quickly gained momentum after the Arab–Israeli war of October 1973.

As the Syrian regime had largely succeeded in consolidating itself *vis-à-vis* its apparatus, there was no longer any need, and as far as Iraq was concerned no longer any tempation, to maintain or rekindle the dispute over Ba'thi legitimacy. On the other hand, conditions were not yet ripe for full-scale competition over regional influence. Though during and after the October War Syria embarked on a more ambitious policy, Iraq, despite its rapidly growing oil revenue, was still impeded by its conflict with the Kurds and with Iran. After the October War tension gradually rose again as Iraq used Syria's acceptance of the cease-fire to question its Arab legitimacy and to counter its quest for regional influence. However, rather than stepping up the argument, Syria insisted on its own achievements in the war without mentioning those of Iraq, and illustrated its own Arab legitimacy through extensive media coverage of the war of attrition fought on Mount Hermon. As in the previous period, both sides needed Arab legitimacy to enhance their internal position.

Nevertheless the period of relative calm prior to the October War was shaken twice by acute crises which left their imprint on bilateral relations, although the one was only transient and the other was cut short by the war. Both concerned the export of Iraqi crude oil via Syria. The first of these pipeline rows was completely, and the second one largely, unconnected to the main conflicts of the earlier and later periods. While the first, which simmered from June 1972 to January 1973, concerned the amount of royalties to be paid by Iraq for the use of the trans-Syrian pipeline, the second errupted when Iraq decided in the late summer of 1973 to build new pipelines bypassing Syria and thus eventually depriving it of its revenue from royalties.

## Regional ambitions

Regional ambitions in these years appeared more clearly in the policies pursued by Syria. While the Iraqi regime was still very much occupied with the internal consolidation of its position, particularly in the face of growing Kurdish unrest, the Syrian regime faced no such difficulties and could devote its energy to its regional designs. Though it had gained control of its apparatus later than the Iraqi regime, it had been able to consolidate its position in the country more rapidly, securing acceptance on both fronts largely through the policy of economic liberalization or *infitah*.

The Syrian regime enhanced its regional position mainly by waging, together with Egypt, the October War in 1973. Though the benefits had to be shared with Egypt, which moreover fought more successfully, the war increased Syria's political prestige and influence and thus facilitated its access to resources, including political support.[1] In contrast Iraq, despite its important contribution, obtained little or nothing from this war as both Syria and Egypt, each for reasons of its own, pushed it out; from the outset it had been a game that they had wanted to play without Iraq.

In addition the temporary *rapprochement* with Iran after May 1974 seems to have been intended to enhance Syria's position in the region, though the move may more specifically have been directed against Iraq, then close to war with its eastern neighbour. Improved relations with Iran increased Syria's manoeuvrability due to the shah's close relations with the USA and Iran's military strength in the Gulf; moreover, an Iranian credit of some US $150 million for reconstruction after the October War[2] made the *rapprochement* profitable even in the short term. Though Saudi Arabia and the other Arab riparians of the Gulf may have been apprehensive about Syria moving closer to Iran, there could be little objection to the move in the aftermath of the October War. In the policy of combined pressure and co-operation *vis-à-vis* the Arab Gulf countries, Iran was only one of the sticks that could be wielded; others were increased co-operation with the Soviet Union (an alliance all the wealthy conservative regimes considered particularly frightful and distasteful), and excessive violence against Israel leading in turn to heavy Israeli retaliation. The last could prove more delegitimizing for the financiers of the war than for those who had the aura of heroic fighters on the battlefield.

A stick and carrot policy also continued to be used against other actors, mainly against the United States. The October War itself was waged according to this logic, to pressurize the United States into the role of broker, not to defeat Israel. Syria certainly later bailed out of the 'peace process', not because of objections in principle, but only because of the scope and extent of the concessions required. For the period from 1972 to 1975 the pressures and overtures are clearly parallel features. Anti-American rhetoric in the media now supplied the background for co-operation as articulated in the disengagement agreement with Israel signed on 31 May 1974, which included guarantees to end all *fida'i* activities across the Syro-Israeli border;[3] in the state visit to Syria by the president of the United States, Richard Nixon, of 15–16 June 1974;[4] and in the subsequent resumption of diplomatic relations between the two states. Propaganda against American policies in the Middle East under these conditions could admittedly be regarded as a smoke-screen hiding actual collaboration, particularly as sometimes, for instance during the Nixon visit, it receded significantly. But the Syrian policy of pressure against the United States is demonstrated in the simultaneous co-operation with the Soviet Union with which, in February 1972, a treaty of economic co-operation had been concluded,[5] and from where Damascus received important military aid.

At the same time, of course, Nixon's visit may well have served to remind the Soviet Union that it had no other ally in the region after the break with Egypt and the increasing rift with Iraq.

Iraq to some extent also sought to mobilize external material (financial, weaponry) and political resources for its own purposes but still on a far more modest scale and through a different policy. Iraq continued to put pressure on other Arab actors by emphasizing its radicalism in matters pertaining to the defence of the Arab cause, although it slowly started to imitate the Syrian example and to combine this policy with overtures to conservative regimes like Saudi Arabia and to the West. Iraqi toughness is well illustrated by the refusal to accept the cease-fire which ended the October War in 1973; the subsequent refusal to attend the Algiers summit where this cease-fire was to be endorsed (see below); the continued rejection of UN resolutions 242 and 338; the rejection of the Golan disengagement agreement of 31 May 1974; and the refusal to attend the meeting of the front-line states in Cairo from 3 to 4 January 1975. Yet these 'principled' stands were progressively paralleled by overtures to the West, as in the endorsement in 1974 of the concept of a Palestinian state comprising only the West Bank and the Gaza Strip.[6]

At this point it may be objected that, with the increase in oil prices after the October War in 1973, Iraq was less compelled than Syria to bargain over resources and influence which to some extent it now obtained by the mere fact of being an oil country. However, to play a role in the politics of the region Iraq had to mobilize not only a certain absolute amount of resources but also a certain relative part of the overall resources available in the region (in the last resort, of course, a certain relative part of resources available globally) and which, following the increase in oil prices, had increased as much as Iraq's own resources. Consequently, Baghdad had to continue to struggle for access to these additional resources.

In the end Iraq's shift to a policy of pressure-cum-overtures could only exacerbate the regional competition with Syria as both sides now not only fought for the same long-term goal, but also attempted to achieve it by the same means – that is by seeking support from the same audience or constituency. Now both sides attempted to win over the conservatives and 'moderates', especially among the Arab regimes, while in the early seventies Iraq had still sought to enhance its regional role mainly by mobilizing the so-called radicals. Although the Syrian regime, despite the reorientation under Asad (see pp. 56ff.) had never abandoned this 'radical' constituency, there was only a partial overlap between the forces from which the two sides tried to draw their support. The increasing overlap resulting from Iraq's attempt to mobilize support from more 'moderate' forces did not produce an entirely novel situation, as in the late sixties both sides had temporarily competed for the same, then 'radical', audience.

Once the propaganda war centring around Ba'thi legitimacy had died down in late 1971 and early 1972, mutual accusations also ceased to be the necessary and essential ingredients of all speeches and communiqués. Nonetheless, neither side completely ceased to incriminate its neighbour, partly along the main lines already chosen in the previous period, but now differently emphasized, and partly with new arguments. And although accusations increased and decreased according to the policies pursued by the incriminated party, they also had life of their own, independent of specific political developments. They became a permanent feature of Syro-Iraqi relations, articulating the mitigated antagonism over Ba'thi legitimacy and the nascent struggle over regional influence.

Yet, in this period, unilateral and mutual accusations were far less frequent and violent than in the periods before and after. They intensified during the pipeline crises, and at least as far as Iraqi propaganda is concerned gradually after the October War; they became extremely violent only during the second pipeline crisis. In several instances the antagonistic parties even described their relations as normal, correct or good. More than that, after Bakr and the then Iraqi Foreign Minister Murtada 'Abd al-Baqi al-Hadithi had openly called for the uniting of Egypt, Syria and Iraq, the two sides on 26 March 1972 even published a joint communiqué, thus concluding talks devoted to this matter held in Damascus by Saddam Husayn and President Asad. Although these talks never had any chance of success, the issuing of a joint communiqué, even if it was only to agree to disagree, was a novelty indicating an improvement in bilateral relations. During this second period neither side insisted strongly on the question of Ba'thi legitimacy, and the notion was hardly ever used except on the anniversaries of certain events in the party's history. The main issue of the reduced propaganda battle concerned Arab legitimacy. Syria almost exclusively relied on this theme whereas Iraq to some extent also accused its neighbour of harming specifically Iraqi interests; Syria, in contrast, never defended its own interests without declaring them to be Arab ones. Only Iraq claimed to be the victim of subversion attempts by its neighbour, though both sides were presumably involved in such activities. Economic and technical co-operation – except in matters of oil exports through Syria – was developed while diplomatic relations remained normal for most of the period. In contrast, co-operation at the party and military level – except for the 1973 war – remained as non-existent as ever.

As the conflict during this period intensified or receded chiefly according to the two rows of the trans-Syrian pipeline and the one over the October War, it appears useful to discuss these disputes before turning to the propaganda warfare and other articulations of the conflict. This is all the more important, since after the October War bilateral interactions generally remained more violent than they had been before, except for peaks reached during the two pipeline disputes.

### The pipeline rows

Of the two pipeline disputes the first concerned the amount of royalties to be paid by Iraqi for oil exports via Syria and was exclusively motivated by considerations of short-term material advantage. The second dispute, slightly more complicated, arose when in reaction Iraq decided to build alternative pipelines enabling it to discontinue oil exports via Syria. While in this case Syria was again concerned about immediate economic advantages, Iraq was motivated by the long-term desire to ensure its economic and political independence; in addition, the wish to curb Syria's regional ambitions may have played a minor role inasmuch as Iraq was ready to incur small losses in order to create relatively bigger ones for Syria.

### Syria's demand for higher royalties

The first pipeline dispute began soon after the nationalization of the Iraq Petroleum Company (IPC) by the Iraqi government on 1 June 1972.[7] Syria retaliated and within a few hours had expropriated the company's installations situated on Syrian soil, most importantly the trans-Syrian pipeline. Damascus apparently considered the moment opportune to try to repeat the experience of December 1966–March 1967, when the Jadid regime had pressured the IPC into accepting higher royalties.[8] Certainly not without these prospects in mind Syria encouraged the Iraqi plans, as it reportedly did during the visit Saddam Husayn paid to Damascus from 21 to 26 March 1972.[9] Another motive was probably the need to catch up with Iraq as much as possible in matters of Arab and anti-imperialist legitimacy.

However, the Iraqis must have been well aware that the Syrians were not easy negotiation partners. This had been demonstrated not only in the 1966–7 row over the trans-Syrian pipeline, but also by the course another joint Syro-Iraqi project had taken. To maximize the flow of oil from the north Rumayla oilfields in southern Iraq (owned by the Iraqi government, not the IPC), the Iraqis had planned in the late 1960s to compensate for insufficient shipping facilities in the Gulf by building a pipeline to the Syrian port of Tartus. In June 1970 Syria and Iraq had agreed in principle to build such a pipeline. But Syria reportedly soon insisted on owning half the installations while Iraq wanted to retain majority control,[10] and the project disappeared with the IPC nationalization and the subsequent row over a pipeline that at least had the advantage of already existing. Interestingly, Iraq had already covertly threatened to build an alternative pipeline through Turkey, which was discussed in January 1970 during a visit by the Iraqi Vice President 'Ammash to Ankara.[11]

Unlike the IPC in 1966–7 the Iraqi regime could not survive a prolonged loss of revenue from oil production.[12] Indeed the final straw in the decision to nationalize the IPC was the loss in royalty remittances resulting from production cuts the company had decided in March and April 1972. According to the company these cuts were economically motivated, but presumably they also served to pressurize the government into rescinding Law No. 80, promulgated in the days of Qasim, which confined the IPC's activities to the oil fields it was already exploiting, as well as consecutive anti-monopolistic measures.[13] To understand the Iraqi decision in 1972 it must be known that in 1970, before production cuts by the IPC, 64.8 per cent of the government's annual revenue came from the IPC and its subsidiary companies, the Basra Petroleum Company (BPC) and the Mosul Petroleum Company (MPC).[14] Of the overall oil production of 83.5 million tons in 1971,[15] some 60 million were produced by the Kirkuk fields.[16] These and some 1 million tons a year from Mosul had to be exported via Syria. Despite a slightly better price obtained for the Basra crude, the royalties for IPC outputs exported via Syria thus amounted to some 60 per cent of the Iraqi regime's average total annual revenue in 1971.

Although from March 1972 production in Kirkuk was cut by about 44 per cent[17] and royalties to the government dropped correspondingly, some 60 per cent of its expected and budgeted revenue continued to depend on the production of Kirkuk, and on the functioning of the trans-Syrian pipeline. This dependence was hardly reduced after 7 April 1972 when the north Rumayla oilfields near Basra with an outlet to the Gulf started to operate.[18]

After the nationalization of the IPC financial difficulties increased dramatically, due to acute marketing problems.[19] Despite a French stand-by credit of an undisclosed amount[20] (French interests were exempt from the nationalization) the 'Iraqis [stood] with their backs to the wall of an empty treasury'.[21] And although the Soviet Union guaranteed to 'absorb surplus nationalized oil',[22] and a few barter deals and other contracts could be concluded,[23] this situation continued till the spring of 1973. By then Iraq had apparently become more successful in marketing its oil,[24] in part because it had settled its outstanding conflict with the IPC in London.[25] However, in the immediate aftermath of the nationalization the financial situation of Iraq was very shaky indeed, and the government found it necessary to adopt new austerity measures, in addition to those already implemented, to prepare for the nationalization.[26] In this situation a complete interruption of production in Kirkuk or of trans-Syrian pipeline exports would have been disastrous.

After numerous talks, on 13 October 1972 Syria publicly requested that Iraq pay transit dues for the period starting with the nationalization of the IPC on 1 June.[27] On 15 October an Iraqi spokesman replied saying that Iraq had offered several times to pay the rate previously paid by the IPC but that Syria had demanded twice this amount.[28]

The quarrel continued until in early January 1973 the Syrians unilaterally passed a law fixing the new amount of the transit dues at US $0.50 per barrel loaded at Banyas with the port services included, and at US $0.44 per barrel pumped to the Lebanese port of Tripoli. Each barrel going to the Syrian refinery in Homs was charged at US $0.32. The law was to take effect retroactively on 1 June 1972. Compared to the 24–5 cents per barrel plus 7 cents of operating costs, paid by the IPC before that date, the new transit dues were roughly doubled. On 7 January the law was submitted to President Asad, but he did not sign it,[29] allowing one last chance for a negotiated settlement.

Syrian pressure paid off, and the Iraqi side, trying to salvage what it could, was soon ready to sign an agreement. Under this agreement, concluded in Damascus on 18 January 1973, Iraq agreed to pay Syria US $0.41 per barrel of crude oil shipped from Banyas and US $0.30 per barrel sent to Tripoli. However, Iraq had to guarantee to pump a minimum of some 88 million barrels a year.[30] Otherwise, even in case of *force majeure,* it had to pay Syria US $13 million annually.[31] Thus the Iraqis at least obtained a small concession from the Syrians which at the time, however, was vital to them.[32] The agreement was applied retroactively, from 1 June 1972, and was valid for 15 years, except for the financial provisions which were to expire on 31 December 1975.[33] Apart from the amount of transit dues the financial provisions also stipulated that payment had to be made in hard currency, that Syria would be able to purchase some 30,000 barrels a day [34] for its Homs refinery at a price of US $2.45 per barrel for the rest of 1972, progressively mounting to US $2.75 in 1975. Syria, for its part promised to maintain the pipeline without additional charges.[35]

Considering that the Syrian regime in 1971 received about US $40 million of royalties from the pipeline,[36] representing 9.02 per cent of its total domestic revenue of US $443.14 million in that year,[37] the demand for higher royalties in 1972–3 was doubtlessly intended to increase this revenue. The doubling of royalties would have greatly enhanced the Syrian regime's financial possibilities, without involving any additional investments or expense, especially in view of its regional ambitions and the new war planned against Israel.

*Iraqi projects for alternative pipelines and their realization*

Iraq was not ready to play the Syrian game. During the royalties dispute projects were pushed ahead to reduce dependency on Syria in oil exports. The idea of an additional outlet through Turkey for oil from the northern oilfields, already debated in 1966–7, was now given renewed attention.[38]

On 1 May 1973 Iraq and Turkey signed a protocol to construct a pipeline and to fix the royalties at some US $0.35 per barrel. This was to be a flat transit fee valid for twenty years and only subject to alteration in the event of a devaluation of the American dollar.[39] Considering the length of the new line and the partially mountainous area it was to traverse, this price was quite favourable to Iraq compared to the royalties demanded by Syria. Already two months earlier, on 8 January, the Iraqi RCC had set up a committee chaired by Saddam Husayn himself to examine the project of a 'strategic pipeline' linking the northern oilfields to the Gulf.[40] But despite these two projects Iraq planned to continue oil exports via Syria. Five months after the agreement of 18 January, on 12 June 1973 Iraq granted an interest-free loan of US $15 million to Syria in order to renew the pipeline's pumps, thereby increasing its capacity from 1.2 million to 1.4 million barrels a day and consequently Syrian revenue by some US $30 million per year. The loan was to be repaid through deductions from the transit dues payable by Iraq.[41]

Whether by magic or coincidence, on 27 August 1973, the very day this Iraqi-Syrian agreement was to take effect, Iraq and Turkey signed the accord for the construction of the pipeline from Kirkuk to Dörtyol.[42] This line was planned for an initial capacity of 25 million tons a year or 500,000 barrels a day,[43] somewhat more than one-third of the then total capacity of the northern oilfields of approximately 1.4 million barrels a day. The first shipments of Iraqi crude left Dörtyol in June 1977.[44]

Work on the strategic pipeline was started in late 1973 and completed two years later, and the opening ceremony was held on 27 December 1975.[45] Interestingly, some of the main contracts for the construction of this line were placed during the October war (on 19 October) with a Japanese consortium, and (on 22 October) with ENI in Italy.[46] This line was built for a capacity of 800,000–850,000 barrels a day or 40 million tons a year to be reached three months after its completion, in March 1976.[47] According to some sources it was, at a later stage, to carry as much as 48–50 million tons a year, roughly 1 million barrels a day [48] (for details of this pipeline and its functioning, see p. 112).

As early as 1973 Syria had therefore to face the fact that in the

long run its policy over Iraqi royalties had failed, and that within
a few years Iraq would be able to export the bulk of its production
from the northern oilfields through other pipelines. It is therefore
not surprising that the Syrian regime chose the date on which the
Iraq-Turkish agreement was signed to start a violent propaganda
campaign against Baghdad (see p. 76.), which may also have
been helpful in diverting attention from the preparations for the
October War.

### The October War

The October War led to a lasting deterioration in Syro-Iraqi
relations, foreshadowing the post-1975 period. On the surface
this resulted chiefly from Syria's acceptance of the cease-fire with
Israel without consulting Baghdad. Depending on the version
one prefers to accept, the preparation for the war was a further
source of discontent, for either the Iraqis or the Syrians. Iraq had
nevertheless quickly dispatched troops to the Golan where the
Syrians, after initial successes, had soon lost the initiative to the
Israelis. Iraqi troops then stopped the advance of Israeli troops,
but despite rather than because of Syrian assistance. The real
problem, however, was that in spite of all losses Syria's regional
stature had grown through this war, while at the same time the
cease-fire between Syria and Israel offered Iraq the opportunity to
attack its Arab legitimacy and thus this new position.

Though the Iraqi absence at the beginning of the war was
undisputed, it was explained differently by Damascus and Baghdad. According to Syria Iraq had been invited to participate in
the war against Israel first in November 1972 and again in July
1973. President Bakr, however, had only wished Egypt and Syria
success, but expressed his fear that they would be defeated. Finally,
before the outbreak of hostilities the Iraqi ambassador to Syria had
been informed again but Iraqi troops were dispatched only after a
high-ranking Syrian official was sent to Baghdad.[49]

In contrast Iraq accused Syria and Egypt of having deliberately
excluded it from the preparations for the war and concealed from
it the date and hour for which the initial attack was scheduled.
Later, the official report on the October War affirmed that Iraq
had submitted proposals for a 'war of liberation', but that none of
the other sides had taken an interest in this proposal.[50]

Nonetheless, some Iraqi statements preceding the war, as well as
acute threats to the security of the country, give some credence to
the Syrian thesis. Pointing to Iranian threats, the Iraqi al-Thawra
of 26 February 1973 had made it plain that Iraq would dispatch
troops to the 'Northern Front', that is the Golan, only if it was

given concrete assurances that the Arabs would actually go to war and did not only intend to make a show of force.[51] Even the official Iraqi statement after the cease-fire contained some ambiguities (see p. 79).

Iraqi fears regarding Iran were certainly not unjustified. Since the advent of the Ba'th regime in Baghdad, tension with Iran had been mounting.[52] Soon after July 1968 a propaganda war developed, and Tehran increased its support for the Iraqi Kurds,[53] who in March 1969 succeeded in staging a bold attack on the Kirkuk oil refinery and continued to fight the Baghdad regime till March 1975 (see p. 87).[54]

Iraqi-Iranian relations took a definite turn for the worse in February 1969 when Tehran demanded the abrogation of the Saadabad Treaty of 1937 which had fixed the common border on the east bank of the Shatt al-'arab. Instead Iran demanded that the border should be drawn along the *thalweg*, that is, where the river is deepest, thus leaving half of the navigable deep water channel under Iranian control. When Iraq, instead of accepting the renegotiation of a new treaty, tried to impose new measures to illustrate its sovereignty over the entire Shatt al-'arab, Iran on 19 April unilaterally denounced the Saadabad treaty and withdraw its recognition of the Iraqi right to co-ordinate and supervise shipping in these waters.[55] Troops were concentrated on the common border,[56] and Iran may have been involved in the unsuccessful coup staged on 30 June 1973 by the Iraqi Intelligence Chief Nadhim Kzar.[57] After more than three years of continuous tension Iraq broke off diplomatic relations with Iran when in November 1971 the forces of Tehran occupied the Gulf islands of Abu Musa and Greater and Lesser Tunb which belonged to the emirates of Sharjah and Ras al-Khaymah.[58] Over 1972 and 1973, Iranian pressure on Iraq continued and even increased, partly directly, [59] partly by way of Iranian support for Iraqi Kurds,[60] whose relations with the central government in Baghdad constantly deteriorated.[61]

The Iraqi government had lost control over parts of Kurdistan[62] and frequent border incidents opposed it to Iran.[63] Consequently throughout the early 1970s a sizeable part of the Iraqi army was bogged down along the eastern borders and in the northern areas.[64] Open war with the Kurds finally broke out in early 1974 and lasted till Iran, in the Algiers agreement of March 1975, withdrew its support for the Kurds.[65]

Both versions, the Syrian and the Iraqi, would seem to be at least partially correct. The Iraqi regime indeed had no great interest in an additional conflict at that time, while Syria tried to isolate Iraq in this most crucial test of Arab legitimacy. In addition, the Asad regime may have been afraid of being overthrown or at least of being put under pressure if it allowed Iraqi forces to enter the country, particularly as the two regimes had just started to exchange vitriolic attacks over the Iraqi-Turkish pipeline project. The Syrian rulers were perhaps further encouraged not to associate Iraq with the war effort as they could be sure that Iraq, for reasons of its own Arab legitimacy, would – as it finally did – bring succour if things got bad. However, if all went well Iraqi assistance could be declined and it could be demonstrated that Iraq did not belong to the confrontation states.

The October or Ramadan War started on 6 October 1973 between 1.30 and 1.50 p.m.[66] with an Egyptian attack across the Suez Canal. When almost simultaneously, at 2 p.m., the first attack was launched from Syrian soil,[67] no Iraqi troops were present on the 'northern front'.[68] Reportedly, the Iraqi President Ahmad Hasan al-Bakr rang the Syrian President Hafiz al-Asad as soon as he learned of the offensive in order to arrange for Iraqi troops to be sent to the Golan.[69] Although Asad declined the offer, Bakr put the Iraqi Third Armoured Division on alert.[70] The Syrian attitude radically changed on 8 October when the Israelis, after initial setbacks, succeeded in regaining the initiative and advanced even further into Syria than they had in 1967. Asad now sent a high-ranking envoy to Baghdad to ask for assistance, and immediately, on 9 October, an Iraqi staff general came to Damascus where 'the Syrians asked for as many tanks as possible, as quickly as possible.'[71] On the same day the first Iraqi contingents arrived in Syria.[72] On the following days additional units crossed the border and arrived in the Golan on 11 October.[73] On 22 October some 22,000 Iraqi troops were reported to have taken part in the war on the Golan.[74] To send so many troops Iraq felt it necessary to reduce tensions with Iran and asked for the resumption of diplomatic relations. This happened on 15 October.

A few days after the outbreak of hostilities disarray seemed complete in Syria:

> Colonel Imami arrived in Damascus at about 1900 hours to find he was not expected and neither instructions nor information were available. He was simply told to 'go forward and fight', the direction of the front being vaguely pointed out to him . . . The Iraqis had only the maps they brought with them; none were issued by the Syrians. They were given no codes, call signals, radio frequencies.[75]

In the second half of the war the Israelis momentarily came close to taking the road between Damascus and the border, thus bringing Damascus within their shelling range. Only the arrival of Iraqi and then Jordanian troops prevented this.[76] Syrian war communiqués however remained persistently silent as to the role of the Iraqi 'Salah al-Din' expeditionary force.[77]

When the cease-fire between Syria and Israel was concluded on 19 October, Iraq claimed it had not been consulted; the communiqué then issued jointly by the Revolutionary Command Council (RCC), Regional Command of the Ba'th Party (RC) and National Command of the Ba'th Party (NC) could not have been clearer in affirming this: 'However, as we had heard the news of the outbreak of fighting over the radios, we also heard the news of the cease-fire over the radios' (see also p. 79).[78] Syria, for its part, pretended that it had consulted Iraq, but never actually denied Iraqi charges on this matter.[79]

Soon after the cease-fire, in the last days of October Iraqi troops withdrew from the front and from Syria altogether. The regime in Baghdad sought in this way to express its disagreement with the cease-fire, and in some statements quite explicitly established a link between the two events. The Syrian regime, despite everything, apparently hoped the Iraqis would stay on, but was disappointed in this.

### Between co-operation and subversion

The pipeline disputes and the emerging competition for regional influence and, to a minor extent, the residual need to consolidate the regimes, especially in Syria, were expressed in different ways, but most of all through propaganda.

### Syrian propaganda

In Syrian propaganda before and between the two pipeline rows, the new and, despite its initial pungency, smoother line adopted after Asad's take-over in November 1970 was continued and became even smoother. The frequency of accusations greatly diminished, as did their 'volume'. And the use of rather moderate terms, the most salient change immediately after Asad's coup, became still more conspicuous. By contrast to the Jadid period, Iraq was only on rare occasions portrayed as an 'agent of imperialism' deliberately betraying Arab interests; Iraq was still portrayed as a force that damaged Arab interests, but no longer deliberately so.

Even when tension increased during the two pipeline disputes, accusations hardly ever took the shape of insults. Iraq was no longer charged with assassination attempts, successful or unsuccessful, or terrorist actions against Syrians at home or abroad (but see p. 85). Nor was it accused of attempting to overthrow the Syrian regime or resorting to military threats or action. Moreover the propaganda campaign, even in the two periods of heavier dispute, was mainly confined to comments by the media and, in some cases, by Iraqi exiles living in Syria.

Indeed, Asad and other top leaders or agencies of the regime often tried in their declarations to ignore the differences with Iraq; this new restraint was also to be seen in declarations made to commemorate important state and regime anniversaries. Speeches delivered on these occasions usually deal with the general policy choices of the regime which to a small degree are also reflected in the communiqués released by the Regional or National Commands of the Ba'th Party. In the preceding period no such opportunity was missed to incriminate the Iraqi regime which, of course, often replied in kind. Asad in his speech announcing the formation of the Progressive National Front on 7 March 1972, the eve of the anniversary of the 'March revolution', did not waste a single word on Syro-Iraqi relations.[80] Nor did he raise the issue in a second speech on the day of the anniversary itself, although bilateral tension could be inferred from his omission of Iraq when enumerating those Arab countries already liberated from the yoke of imperialism.[81]

Now leading figures or bodies of the regime remained discreet and silent about Syro-Iraqi relations even at times of crisis, and continued to be so after the October War when relations, even after the actual dispute over the cease-fire had died down, remained more strained than before. The silence was extremely striking in the autumn of 1973.

In much the same vein the comminiqué issued by the National Command on 15 November 1973,[82] less than three months after Iraq and Turkey had agreed to build a new oil pipe line bypassing Syria and in the midst of post-war tension, feigned that relations with Iraq were not worth a single word. Similar silence marked later interviews and statements by Asad,[83] the National Command[84] and the Regional Command.[85] In a few instances high-ranking Syrians even spoke positively of Syro-Iraqi relations or their prospects, as Asad himself did in two interviews granted to al-Anwar in Beirut[86] and to al-Ray al-'amm in Kuwait.[87]

Only rarely, and not very overtly, did the theme of Ba'thi legitimacy appear in Syrian statements. For example Asad in his address on the party anniversary in 1972 said hardly more than that in 1966 the party had 'rid itself forever of the rigid rightist mentality' prevailing till then.[88] In a party statement of 22 February 1973 commemorating both the foundation of the United Arab Republic in 1958 and the Movement of 23 February in 1966, the latter was mentioned so briefly and in such veiled terms that it was difficult to read into it even an implicit reference to Ba'thi legitimacy.[89]

Some evidence suggests that even in the propaganda specifically addressed to party members the theme of Ba'thi legitimacy had become peripheral. On 25 October 1972 the Beirut daily *al-Hayat* published a document presented as an internal circular of the Syrian Ba'th Party.[90] Dated 27 March 1972 the alleged circular justifies the refusal of the Syrian hierarchy to admit Iraq as a member to the newly founded Federation of Arab Republics.[91] Although the Syrian and shortly afterwards the Egyptian regime issued joint communiqués with the itinerant Saddam Husayn they opposed a clear *fin de non-recevoir* to the Iraqi proposal. According to the circular the Iraqi proposal aimed at reducing the isolation of the rulers in Baghdad, internally, regionally, and globally. Although this isolation was partly linked to their lack of Ba'thi legitimacy, the matter was referred to rather indirectly, and considered as grave only because: 'The present regime in Iraq belongs to the right-wing group which took power in the coup of 17 July 1968 and which our party in its rectifying movement of 23 February 1966 had denounced as a rightist group.'

By contrast, the lack of Arab legitimacy as a cause of the isolation of the Iraqi regime was presented far more emphatically:

> Right from the initial coup this regime has tried to use terrorism in order to consolidate its rule and to extend its domination. It did not shrink back from extinguishing the national parties, striking the patriotic forces and destroying the popular organizations by massacres, terror, prison torture, and assassination attempts which, as everybody knows, continue to mark the policy of this fascist regime whose distinguishing marks in the Arab world and in the world at large have become its methods of oppression and terrorism.
>
> This regime has fled the confrontation and withdrawn its forces from the Eastern front. It has invented sideshows and pretexts to excuse the shirking of its responsibilities *vis-à-vis* the Arab people and homeland and to dissimulate its . . . shameful positions which are exemplarily illustrated by its policy towards the Palestinian resistance in September 1970.[92]

The issue of Ba'thi legitimacy would not have provided convincing reason to refuse Iraq's membership among a group of states in which non-Ba'thi regimes were the majority. However, it might have been expected that the Syrian Ba'th would seize the opportunity and raise the issue. However, the issue was no longer an issue since the *infitah* policy enabled the Syrian regime to

provide enough material advantages to generate or enhance loyalty
on the part of the apparatus. These stabilizing effects of the *infitah*,
already perceptible at the end of the previous period, were now
more obvious, partly because the initial measures began to yield
fruit, and partly because new and more far-reaching measures were
adopted.[93]

Arab legitimacy was also the main theme of Syrian propaganda
directed at a wider audience (the 'public'). Interestingly, this theme
was also resorted to when purely Syrian interests were at stake.
So when Iraq objected to higher royalties in the pipeline dispute
Damascus accused it of creating a 'secondary battle' that diverted
Arab energies from the 'main battle' against the 'enemy'.[94]

The same strategy was adopted when in the late summer of 1973
the tables were turned and, aware of its new weakness, Syria
relentlessly raged against the Iraqi-Turkish pipeline project. Now
the Iraqi leaders were accused of having

> embarked on this project at a moment when the imperialist-
> Zionist plots against the Arab nation have reached their apex
> and when attempts are made to deprive the Arabs of the
> oil weapon and to impose the Zionist occupation as a *fait
> accompli*. The Iraqi regime has not only deprived the masses
> of their weapon but even put it into the hands of their Zionist
> and imperialist enemies at the very moment when they need
> it more than ever to win the decisive battle.[95]

The argument over the trans-Turkish pipeline came to an abrupt
end with the October War after which it recurred only sporadically.
The main dividing issue then was the cease-fire concluded by Syria
and rejected by Iraq. However, verbal violence was less intense than
in the previous two crises. Iraqi critiques remained rather lenient,
and Syria too, in its responses, kept a rather low profile. Instead
of entering into an argument over the cease-fire, Syria in a more
general way stated and restated its position on the Arab–Israeli
conflict. This restraint may well have been motivated by Syria's
extreme vulnerability after the Iraqi withdrawal from the front and
continued attempts – or at least continued hope – to make the Iraqis
reverse their decision to withdraw.

After the October War Damascus usually tried to ignore Iraqi
propaganda which tended to undermine Syria's Arab legitimacy by
reference to its acceptance of the cease-fire. Instead Syria insisted
more on its own merits in the October War and on the new age
that had been brought about by this war, which had been so
bravely fought by the Syrian and Egyptian armies. Although it
was sometimes admitted that the war had been fought by 'the
Arab armed forces on the Syrian and Egyptian fronts', no explicit

reference was made to Iraqi or Jordanian participation. Damascus thus compared Syrian action in the war with Iraqi talk about its end. And, benefiting from the fact that the war took place on Syrian territory, Damascus presented it as a Syrian war.[96]

Minor accusations were made against the Iraqi regime for its ruthless internal repression, and the arrest, imprisonment without trial, torture and murder of its opponents.[97] These charges, however, were always closely linked to accusations relating to Iraq's stance on Arab affairs, as Syrian propaganda always identified the persecuted as 'progressives' and especially as 'nationalists'.

However, already before the October War in 1973 Baghdad's Arab illegitimacy was attached to a new and quite original argument. The Iraqi regime now was sometimes referred to as a 'tribal regime', a 'fascist tribal regime' or as 'the Takriti regime'.[98] Takrit in the 'Sunni triangle' of northern Iraq was the home town of Ahmad Hasan al-Bakr, Saddam Husayn – originally Saddam Husayn al-Takriti – and most of the members of the ruling group. Many of these key figures were moreover linked among themselves by tribal and family ties.[99] To insist on the restricted societal basis of the Iraqi regime and its alleged tribal character was to insinuate that it could not represent the interests and cause of a wider group, such as the Iraqis or the Arabs in general.

The emergence of Iraqi stands in Arab affairs as the main theme in Syrian propaganda marks a difference *vis-à-vis* the preceding period of 1968–72. However, as in the previous period this type of accusation and critique was not to any significant degree caused by actual disagreement over how to defend the Arab cause or by individual decisions made in this respect. To a great extent this also applies to the time after the October War. Once again the Syrians and the Iraqis continued to seek top place as the defenders of Arab legitimacy in order to enhance their respective internal legitimacy and their own regional position. And by seeking this supremacy the two sides inevitably collided again.

While the importance of the emphasis on Arab legitimacy for the regime's regional ambitions can be gauged from the previous outline of these ambitions, the relevance this argument had for the regime's internal legitimacy still has to be illustrated. The need for the rulers of Syria to appear as straightforward defenders of Arab rights in order to increase internal legitimacy lost little of its urgency after 1972.

In Syria the beginning of 1973 was marked by the opposition of some Muslim quarters to the new constitution, which did not now explicitly require that the president be a Muslim. This omission led to demonstrations and riots in late February 1973, first in Hama, then in Damascus and other cities. The agitation subsided only when the regime accepted the inclusion of an article stipulating that Islam be the required religion of the head of state.

Having lost ground in terms of Islamic legitimacy, it was dangerous to lose in terms of Arab legitimacy as well, and this all the more as 'Alawis more than others had to prove their commitment to such values. Seen in this context the reference to the Iraqi regime as a 'tribal regime' not only seemed to reduce the attractions the latter might exert over potential supporters in other Arab countries, but also to divert attention from the similar deficiency of the Syrian regime.[100]

During the two pipeline crises the theme of Arab legitimacy served the further purpose of justifying Syrian financial claims. The demand for higher royalties in 1972–3 could, if at all, only be justified by referring to Syria's obligations as the front-line state *par excellence*. And in September 1973 the only chance of mobilizing Arab support against Iraq's plans to create additional outlets for its Kirkuk oil was to insist on the potentially negative consequences of these for Arab interests.

## Iraqi propaganda

As with Syrian propaganda, with Iraqi propaganda a certain continuity linked this second period to the end of the first. This continuity also articulated itself in the same way, namely in the receding frequency and 'volume' of accusations and in a growing tendency to refrain from insults or violent expressions. This tendency, till early 1974, led the Iraqi side to replace accusations with explanations of why it disagreed with Syrian policies, even though already before that date and unlike in Syria key figures of the regime took an active part in the exposure of bilateral differences. Nonetheless, the overall attitude was marked by considerable restraint, maintained to some extent even during the pipeline crisis in 1972, and – to a lesser extent – the weeks preceding the October War when Syria raged against the Iraqi-Turkish pipeline project. Only after the October War and especially from late 1973 and early 1974 onwards did Iraqi propaganda become more aggressive.

Although Iraqi restraint did not always imply silence on the part of the hierarchy, here again a distinction has to be made between the time before and the time after the October War. Until the end of the war Iraqi leaders, too, frequently tried to conceal their grievances, as for instance illustrated by the speech of Zayd Haydar of the Iraqi National Command on the party anniversary in 1972,[101] or the speeches delivered by President Bakr in 1972 to celebrate the 'revolutions' of July 1958 and 1968[102] which completely ignored strains in the relations with Syria. Thus Saddam Husayn in his press conference on 19 July 1973 even said that relations were 'normal between us and Syria and we strive to develop them in the services of the Arab struggle'.[103]

When on other occasions they did mention differences with Syria, rather than accuse it, they preferred to explain their own position.[104] The bone of contention was in most cases Arab legitimacy, illustrated mainly by the alleged difference that existed between the positions of the two sides on the Arab–Israeli conflict.

This explanatory approach was not immediately abandoned after the end of the October War as is evident in the joint communiqué issued by the Iraqi RC, NC and RCC presenting the Iraqi stand on the cease-fire:

> Compatriots, masses of the Arab nation: On 6 October 1973, we heard the news of the outbreak of fighting against the Zionist enemy over the radios. Immediately . . . a decision was made to participate in the battle with all the military, economic and political capabilities of Iraq.
>
> When we made the decision to comprehensively participate in the battle, we were not unmindful of the delicate assessments we had announced and declared to the masses and at official Arab meetings. This decision of ours emanated from the fact that the outbreak of fighting against the Zionist enemy – despite our assessments of the manifestations that preceded the outbreak of fighting and the horizons charted for it – required Iraq's effective and comprehensive participation in the fighting. We have not kept it a secret, then, that there are Arab sides and international circumstances seeking to reach a so-called peaceful settlement in one way or another. Moreover, we took this possibility into consideration and decided to enter the battle, hoping to contribute as much as we could . . . However, as we had heard the news of the outbreak of fighting over the radios, we also heard the news of the cease-fire over the radios. Following the approval by the Egyptian and Syrian governments of the Security Council cease-fire resolution – the resolution we rejected because, according to our view, it does not secure the rights of our nation in its usurped land, particularly the rights of the Palestine Arab people to their land, we found that the task of our armed forces there raised delicate and serious military and security matters.

Therefore, it has been decided to withdraw our armed
forces stationed at the two fronts to return to perform their
national duty of protecting the homeland's independence,
building the new revolutionary society and preparing themselves to fulfill their pan-Arab duty when the situation
arises.[105]

Only from about early 1974 did high-ranking regime members and
agencies start to actually accuse the Syrian side rather than merely
express disagreement. It is perhaps significant that none of these
interventions preceded the secret meeting between Asad and Bakr,
and presumably Saddam Husayn, that allegedly took place at the
beginning of January 1974 (see below), although more generally
they were connected to Iraq's new oil wealth following the war
and concomitantly increasing regional ambition, as well as to the
almost simultaneously deteriorating situation in Kurdistan. In a
clear reference to Syria and Egypt, President Bakr now denounced
the 'defeatist Arab countries' whose leaders 'for personal interests
extinguished the flame of fighting and with infamous settlements
crushed the heroism that had marked the battle'.[106]
    Also the Iraqi media became more outspoken and aggressive
from late 1973 onwards. Before that date they had observed
considerable restraint, even at times of crisis when either Iraqi
interests were threatened or when Syria – in the second pipeline
row – used extremely strong language. As in statements made by
the key figures themselves, the dominant theme in the media was
always, before and after late 1973, the one of Arab legitimacy.
Up to late 1973 Iraqi newspapers had rarely described Syria as
'defeatist' or 'capitulationist' as they did now after Syria stated that
under certain circumstances it would accept UN Security Council
resolution 242, thus implicitly recognizing the State of Israel.[107]
More typical of previous Iraqi propaganda is an example occurring
in early January 1973, when, after seven months of protracted
conflict over the royalties for the trans-Syrian pipeline, Syria was
still confronted with mostly 'technical' arguments and explanations
of the Iraqi position, devoid of harsh language or insults.[108] Nor had
Iraqi propaganda become significantly more violent and aggressive
in the immediate aftermath of Syria's decision to accept the
cease-fire in October 1973 and the Israeli-Egyptian agreement
of Kilometre 101 on the Cairo–Suez road. Certainly Iraq had
rejected the cease-fire and in its statements advocated a military
solution to the conflict with Israel instead of the political solution
which it claimed was pursued by Syria. But the media had rather
minced their words when they accused Syria and Egypt of having

expressed their readiness to recognize Israel, but not of actually recognizing it by signing the cease-fire.[109] Syria and Egypt then were hardly accused, never insulted, only criticized. However, without abandoning the explanatory approach, statements and press reports increasingly began to 'warn of the bad consequences of seeking capitulationist plans'.[110] These plans, according to Iraq, were synonymous with political solutions, and were schemed in the United States, so it was a fatal error to distinguish between the two, putting the blame on Israel while trying to get support from the United States.[111]

Nonetheless, towards the end of November, at the time of the Algiers summit, Iraqi propaganda agents began to sharpen their knives. The summit was not attended by Iraq, which considered it as a step towards a political settlement. Iraq was even more opposed to the Geneva Conference that opened on 21 December, although it continued to confine itself to verbal warnings as it had done a few days earlier when Kissinger, on his new shuttle mission, first paid a visit to Damascus. Though Syria did not attend the Geneva Conference, Iraqi propaganda now strongly attacked it for its attitude to the 'Zionist enemy'. Syria's attitude was deemed worse than that of Egypt which had participated in the conference, since it was more deceitful, waiting for Egypt to blaze the trail.[112]

Catching up with political developments new arguments were added: the cease-fire had not brought the Syrians closer to the political settlement they expected.[113] Moreover this policy now was said not only to serve but to be inspired by the imperialists, though its Arab implementers were not yet termed imperialist agents. So in the report on the October War adopted by the Eighth Regional Congress in January 1974 and released on 13 June 1974 one could read:

> For some time already the party leadership expected that the Egyptian and Syrian regimes, guided by some foreign and Arab quarters, would possibly resort to military action against Israel in order to overcome the stalemate in the region and to promote the implementation of the peace settlement.[114]

Iraqi criticism subsequently became even harsher and more violent. Syria was now denounced as a treacherous ally of forces hostile to the Arabs and as a renegade deserting the Arabs' cause. So Iraq raged against Syrian defeatism after Asad, according to *Newsweek*, did not exclude the possibility that Syria might sign a peace treaty with Israel, provided Syria got back the Golan and a Palestinian state was established:[115]

Agreeing to negotiate with the Zionist enemy and to conclude
a peace treaty reduces the Arabs' national cause to its
territorial dimensions and thus puts the future of the Arab
homeland into the hands of American imperialism, and this
just for the sake of remaining in power . . . We denounce the
Syrian regime, which is composed of a clique of renegades
who care more for their own interests than for those of the
party and the Arab nation, and which is the promoter and
instrument of a conspiracy aiming at surrender and scheming
to liquidate the national cause of the Arabs.[116]

The reason for the increasingly quarrelsome attitude of the Iraqi
media and the party hierarchy is that the differences over the ending
of the October War, and over the sequels resulting from Syria's
way of ending it, were the first issues in which Iraq could pretend
to be the more determined advocate of the Arab cause. If Iraq
restrained its criticism until the Bakr–Asad meeting in early 1974,
it presumably did so not because it put much hope in this encounter
but just in order not to forfeit a last chance to rally Syria to its own
position. This was, as it was in Syria, relevant internally as well as
regionally. But to use Arab legitimacy at the regional level had
suddenly become more attractive in the aftermath of the October
War. It was during this time that the Iraqi leaders for the first time
realized their potential strength. If the oil weapon perhaps did not
prove successful in winning the war against Israel it at least proved
successful in economically strengthening the producer countries.
Iraq considered this strength as a stepping-stone to increase its own
political influence but also to contain similar Syrian ambitions that
had become obvious with the October War. But it was only after
the failure of the Bakr–Asad meeting that the Iraqi propaganda
machine came into full swing.

Iraq's growing insistence on Arab legitimacy finally also served as
a rallying theme in the mobilization of Iraqi Arabs in the Kurdish
war of 1974–5. It did so in two ways: by emphasizing the ethnic
difference between the Kurds and the Arabs, and by opposing the
anti-imperialist connotation of Arab legitimacy to the pro-Western
declaration of the Kurdish leader Barzani.

Perhaps with the Kurds in mind Iraqi propaganda sometimes
also claimed Syria damaged specifically Iraqi interests. This kind
of reproach distinguishes Iraqi from Syrian propaganda where the
defence of Syrian interests was always presented as the defence
of wider Arab interests. Mostly Iraq blamed Syria for harming its
economic well-being and development or at least for trying to do
so, as for example when Iraq complained that Syria's claim for
higher royalties in 1972–3 would leave Iraq with less revenue

from the exportation of its oil than before the nationalization of the IPC.[117] Occasionally, however, Iraq claimed that Syria attempted to subvert the Iraqi government. Such charges mainly alleged Syrian support for Kurdish resistance groups which of course were identified as criminal gangs and the like.[118]

## From Ba'thi to Arab legitimacy

At the same time the theme of Ba'thi legitimacy was almost absent from 'public' propaganda organs like the daily press or broadcasts. And when it appeared it was rarely more explicit than for instance when Saddam Husayn in a press conference said:

> If, however, the purpose of the question is to point out that the Socialist Arab Ba'th Party has two different regimes in Iraq and in Syria, then I say that we have a clear and frank opinion regarding everything connected with the party and who represents the party.[119]

Only internal party publications like al-Thawra al-'arabiyya, at least in 1973, seemed to call for the replacement of the Syrian regime with a 'truly Ba'thi one'.[120] That the issue of Ba'thi legitimacy was more openly raised in internal publications is not astonishing, even if the same was not true for internal party publications in Syria. Yet, even in these publications it remained completely secondary.

## Economic and technical relations beyond the pipeline issue

Apart from the rows over the terms and later the termination of Iraqi oil exports via Syria, economic and technical co-operation between the two regimes continued and even expanded. Indeed, neither these two disputes nor the two more latent conflicts, resulting from the needs of regime consolidation and from regional ambitions, had lasting negative effects on domains in which co-operation was beneficial to both sides.

Apart from oil affairs the period from 1972 to 1975 was certainly the most fruitful one for general economic and technical co-operation. So the two sides, despite emerging disagreement in the royalty issue, on 16 July 1972 concluded an agreement providing for the exportation of Iraqi sulphur via the Syrian port of Tartus.[121] On the same day also a protocol was signed according to which bilateral trade was to increase from the previous level of ID4.5 million to ID6 million in 1972.[122] In August two minor commercial contracts followed[123] before the first pipeline row degenerated and temporarily precluded new agreements.

In 1974 a number of further deals and agreements were negoti-ated.[124] Finally, a bilateral protocol of 26 October 1974 renewed the decision to build a railway line linking the two countries, provided for the integration of their electric power networks, and conceded to Iraq a free zone on the Syrian coast; moreover, Syria was to supply Iraq with cotton over the subsequent five years.[125] However, the electricity networks were never integrated, the free zone never established, and the rail link never completed.

On the thorny question of the partition of the Euphrates waters efforts were also made to reach a solution. After an initial attempt by Syria to make Iraq break off the talks[126] a rather promising interim agreement was reached, presumably thanks to Soviet mediation, and preliminary agreements were reached in July 1972 and in November 1973.[127]

*Diplomatic relations*

For the same reasons that economic co-operation continued, diplomatic relations remained 'normal' almost throughout this period. However, towards its close in February 1975 and indeed foreshadowing its end, Iraq recalled its ambassador to Syria in protest at alleged Syrian aid for Kurdish opposition forces in Iraq. Till late 1977 diplomatic relations then only continued at the level of *chargés d'affaires*.

*Official visits and military co-operation*

The relatively high degree of co-operation in various domains also manifested itself in frequent official visits, partly involving high-ranking representatives of the regimes. In some instances members of the ruling groups transmitted personal messages from Asad to Bakr and Husayn and vice versa. Certainly once, but more likely twice, 'summit meetings' were held. The first time this happened was when Saddam Husayn met with Asad in Damascus in March 1972 to submit the proposal for a unity scheme encompassing Syria, Egypt and Iraq, and to prepare the ground for the nationalization of the Iraq Petroleum Company. A second summit involving Asad and Bakr, perhaps also Saddam Husayn, probably took place in the Iraqi desert some months after the October War in early January 1974.[128]

*Protection and subversion*

At the party level the relative *détente* initiated in late 1971 when 'Aflaq was pardoned by Asad – *in absentia*, as he had previously been condemned – continued at least until autumn 1972. At a time when the dispute over the pipeline royalties was brooding and even deepening, Asad in late September 1972 also pardoned

Amin al-Hafiz,[129] who had been condemned in the same trial as 'Aflaq and also *in absentia*. Yet, party relations remained virtually nonexistent and, at least in Syria, party members suspected of sympathizing with the 'other side', continued to be persecuted. On 22 June 1973, for example, 58 officers were arrested and accused of having been involved in a coup attempt.[130] Some of those arrested were pro-Iraqi Ba'this, but it is difficult to assess how far their sympathies were actively exploited by Baghdad. It also appears that the pro-Iraqi Ba'th organization in Syria, due to purges and arrests in the early seventies and the effects of the *infitah*, had become smaller and less efficient.

No pro-Syrian coup attempt is known in Iraq for the period here under review. The only known but finally unsuccessful one was masterminded and staged on 30 June 1973 by the then head of Internal security Nadhim Kzar;[131] there is no evidence suggesting any Syrian involvement, nor did Iraq accuse Syria of such involvement. On several occasions Ba'this and officers were arrested; but there is no evidence that these arrests were carried out on the assumption that they had worked for Syria.[132] Nevertheless, the insignificant Syrian Ba'th in Iraq received fresh impetus in 1974. In that year Ahmad al-'Azzawi, a close confidant of Saddam Husayn, fled to Syria where he was soon entrusted with the reorganization of the pro-Syrian Ba'th in Iraq. Apparently a strong personality, 'Azzawi was said to have been absolutely devoted to his cause and to have personally taken part in many of the commando actions which he organized against Iraqi oil installations or secret police (*mukhabarat*) facilities. However, this increased activity on behalf of the pro-Syrian Ba'th in Iraq came to an end after 'Azzawi, in two attempts on his life in 1975 and 1976, was first badly mutilated and then killed (see p. 114.)[133]

Syria also continued to lend support to non-Ba'thi oppositional forces in Iraq. Not only according to Iraqi propaganda, but also according to independent sources Syria granted support to Iraqi Kurds.[134] As had happened the previous year, in 1972 an official Syrian delegation again went to the Iraqi mountains to see Barzani, the head of the Kurdish Democratic Party (KDP) and then still the uncontested leader of the Kurds, to persuade him to strengthen ties with Damascus. However, Barzani was careful not to let himself be used and only responded more positively after the rift had deepened between the Kurds and Baghdad. Thus in 1974 Barzani received arms via Syria, and towards the end of the year training camps for Kurdish fighters were opened on Syrian territory.[135] However, even then Barzani did not participate in the Damascus-sponsored Iraqi National Gathering (al-Tajammu' al-watani al-'Iraqi) founded in late 1972 by the pro-Syrian Ba'th of Iraq, the Iraqi Communist Party Central Command, and some Nasirist groups.[136]

Unlike the early period of the conflict Iraq now had more limited opportunities to subvert Syria. Apart from the pro-Iraqi Ba'th, which was rather weak at that time, and possibly some supporters of Akram Hawrani,[137] no political actor of any consequence could be relied on. This does not mean that Iraq did not exploit its limited possibilities as much as it could. As in the case of Syria the goal pursued was mainly to weaken the competitor, not to overthrow him. This at least should have been the aim of either side if it realistically assessed its capabilities and strength in this period. It should be noted that conflict during this period never spilled over into military or terrorist action.

# 3

# Escalation and Exacerbation of Regional Competition, 1975–1978

## An overview and chronology

With the agreement of 6 March 1975 between Iraq and Iran, known as the Algiers agreement, the stage was definitely set for an open competition for regional influence and resources between the regimes ruling Iraq[1] and Syria.[2] Since then – and indeed till today – their bilateral relations have been dominated by this competition, even though for a few months in 1978 and 1979 it seemed to have given way to a rather far-reaching *rapprochement*. However, inverting Clausewitz's famous phrase, this was only the continuation of war by other means, and under changing conditions bilateral relations as early as summer 1979 deteriorated again and then reverted to open conflict. The period dominated by regional competition thus can be divided into three parts, corresponding to this and the following two chapters.

The Algiers agreement, at least for a time, ended the long-standing conflict between Baghdad and Tehran that had been exacerbated after the Ba'thi take-over in Iraq in 1968. Under the terms of the accord the two sides would proceed to a precise delineation of their common border in accordance with the Constantinople Protocol of 1913, fix the border in the Shatt al-'arab along the *thalweg*, that is where the river is deepest, and strictly control movements across the border in order to end or prevent all subversive actions in the respective neighbouring country.[3] While the second provision satisfied Iranian wishes, the third one mainly served Iraq as it meant an end to all Iranian support for the Kurdish resistance.

Ironically, by recognizing Iran's dominant position in the Gulf, this agreement enabled the Iraqi regime to strengthen its own internal and regional position economically as well as politically and finally to challenge Iran again. In the long term Iraq, by giving a little, gained more. At the regional level the agreement with conservative and pro-American Iran greatly contributed to making Iraq – so far considered as a 'radical' and a trouble-maker – more acceptable as an ally to the conservative Arab states in the Gulf and thus enhanced its opportunities to vie for Arab support. It became much easier for these states to side with Iraq to counterbalance Iranian power in the Gulf and after 1980 to support Iraq in its war against Iran. Without the moderation symbolized by this agreement the Arab Gulf states, though frightened by the Islamic Revolution in Iran, might not have extended their support to Iraq.

In 1975 the prospect of Iraqi prosperity, consolidation and strength worried the regime in Damascus, which sought to enhance its regional position and to mobilize Arab resources. But although Syria aimed at enhancing its regional position, it did so perhaps less than Iraq in order to become the main interlocutor of the great powers in the Middle East;[4] possibly its ambitions, especially from 1979 onwards, were more limited and remained within the 'red lines' set by Israel.

Due to their regional competition relations between Syria and Iraq greatly deteriorated till the process in the aftermath of the Camp David accords seemed to be reversed in an almost spectacular volte-face. However, this temporary rapprochement articulated in the *Charter of Joint National Action* of October 1978 and the protracted unity negotiations were nothing more than the pursuit of the same competition by different means, corresponding to the needs and opportunities of the hour.

The period from 1975 to 1978 can be divided into three phases, each distinct from the others, though not always by the same criteria:

1   From March till early autumn 1975 bilateral relations were dominated by the argument over the Algiers agreement, reflecting the regional competition, and by the row over the partition of the Euphrates waters which was essentially a narrow conflict of interest, that is a conflict over the allocation of clearly defined resources. Open hostility somewhat decreased in the autumn but Algiers and the Euphrates continued to dominate bilateral relations till December 1975.

2   From then till mid-September 1976 Syria's policy and intervention in Lebanon became the main issue, again reflecting the competition for regional influence. For some time this competition too was paralleled by a narrow conflict of interest, this time due to Iraq's decision to discontinue its oil exports via Syria.

3  Starting with Syria's most serious attempts to control Lebanon, in late September 1976 till October 1978 relations continued to be dominated by regional competition, but this was expressed far more violently than in the earlier phases.

## Regional ambitions

### Syria

Syria's regional policy was pursued in three different ways which can be defined as rallying other actors, as attempting to weaken or subdue them, and as exploiting them; Iraq stuck to the same methods but in addition tried to buy over other actors.

Iraq but particularly Syria tried to rally other actors, either by initiating regional alliances that pretended to serve the Arab cause, or by quickly responding to similar initiatives made by other actors and trying to influence them in their own interest.

In this spirit Syria, for example, in March 1975 put a proposal to the Palestine Liberation Organization (PLO) jointly to set up a 'Unified Political Command', which however never materialized. Syria's intention to control the PLO became even more obvious when shortly afterwards Damascus suggested the Palestinian issue be resolved by creating, not an independent Palestinian state, but a semi-autonomous entity closely linked to Jordan and Syria.

When Syria in 1975 and 1976 became increasingly involved in Lebanon, its policy there apart from military means again relied on alliances, though changing ones, with various Lebanese actors. An author of otherwise dubious views described this as a policy of 'interchangeable allies' in which Asad, as soon as he finds an ally, looks for a potential replacement, never pushes a victory over his adversaries too far, and when helping a friend never enables him to become completely independent.[5]

This kind of policy is also illustrated by the active part Syria played in setting up, in September 1976, a 'Unified Political Command' to 'coordinate political action' and prepare for 'union' with Egypt. In Asad's own words this new *rapprochement* had to be seen in the context of Egypt's growing weakness.[6] In reality, the opposite seems to have been the case as Syria was desperately trying to stop Egypt from concluding a more substantial agreement with Israel than Sinai II which it had bitterly, but unsuccessfully, opposed. As the unified command did not prevent Sadat from visiting Jerusalem in November 1977, Syria redoubled its efforts to mobilize support elsewhere in the Arab world. In November and December 1977 it played an important role in preparing the Tripoli Conference that was intended to organize Arab opposition to Sadat's policy. Although Syria greatly contributed to the organization of the conference, it was convened by the Libyan leader Qadhdhafi, who had his own regional ambitions and was a more acceptable host to the Iraqis than the Syrians would have been. At the conference, which met from 1 to 5 December 1977, the Syrians clashed with the Iraqis but succeeded in winning over the other participants, Algeria, Libya, South Yemen and the PLO. Together with these Syria then formed the Front of Steadfastness and Confrontation (Jabhat al-sumud wa al-tasaddi) which, however, remained frail and failed to meet Syrian expectations.

More recent efforts by Syria to promote its regional interests through the establishment of alliances include the agreement on a 'unitary state' with Libya in 1980, and the project of an 'avant-garde' front discussed in Damascus in 1985 with representatives of Libya, Algeria and South Yemen.

The second way in which Syria attempted to enhance its influence and control over resources was to control and subjugate other actors. These attempts appear most strikingly in its policy in Lebanon, and they are not contradicted by the support it granted to other Lebanese actors, since this support, though increasing their range of possibilities in the short term, finally made them dependent on Syria.

In Lebanon tension between, on the one hand mainly Christian forces trying to maintain the internal status quo in the allocation of wealth and power and, on the other, forces opposed to this distribution pattern, which mainly represented the different Muslim communities and the Palestinians living in the country, gradually built up after the Arab defeat in the 1967 war. Then, and again in 1970 and 1971, after the Black September in Jordan, the Palestinians in Lebanon grew significantly in numbers and enhanced their military strength so that they and their allies, the Lebanese anti-status quo forces, felt strong enough to challenge the Christian, mainly Maronite, defenders of the established order. Heavy fighting broke out in 1975 and as early as January 1976 Syria for the first time intervened militarily by dispatching units of its Palestine Liberation Army (PLA) to Lebanon and to Beirut in particular. This intervention tipped the balance in favour of the anti-status quo forces and thwarted the emergence of a more independent political power in the Christian-controlled area. Such a power would not only have reduced Syria's chances of establishing tighter control over the country, but could also have entailed the creation of another state, in the south of Lebanon, dominated by the anti-status quo forces and, as will be seen, presenting a serious threat to the security and Arab legitimacy of the Syrian regime.

In early March the anti-status quo forces managed to turn the tables on their adversaries and on the fifteenth of that month advanced on the Presidential Palace at Ba'abda. Damascus ordered the Syrian-controlled al-Sa'iqa and Palestine Liberation Army – that is troops under Syrian command pretending not to be troops under Syrian command – to stop this advance, thus opposing its former allies and supporting its previous adversaries.

As Evron put it,[7] Syria was afraid of 'catalytic behaviour of the PLO and related groups' that might drag it, at a moment not chosen by itself, into a military confrontation with Israel. But at the same time the emergence of an independent Palestinian power would have put an end to Syria's role of self-proclaimed spokesman for the Palestinians and consequently diminished its Arab legitimacy.

Finally on 1 June regular Syrian troops entered Lebanon, first to ease the pressure on the Christian forces in the town of Zahla in the Biqa' Valley, and after that to put an end to the anti-status quo resistance in the rest of the country. Syria has ever since pretended that its troops intervened at the explicit request of the Lebanese president but, publicly at least, no such request was made. Nonetheless, Syria's intervention was quickly endorsed by the Arab League countries except Iraq. The League sanctioned the Syrian initiative by deciding to send to Lebanon an Arab Peace Force, to consist of some 22,000 Syrian troops, many of whom at the time of the decision had already entered the country, and some 5,000 token troops from other countries. Not surprisingly, a later Iraqi offer to join the scheme by sending troops of its own was declined. During this offensive Hafiz al-Asad on 20 July made his famous speech on Lebanon in which he explained the Syrian intervention, and also made it clear that the Syrian troops for the foreseeable future were bound to stay in Lebanon. A formal cease-fire with the PLO was signed on 29 July, though it was not actually observed. Soon after Damascus began to circulate a plan to formalize its grip on the country through a Syro-Lebanese federation, which would also be open on a loose basis to Jordan and the PLO.[8]

Syrian military restraint over the summer came to an end on 22 September, when the Palestinian forces were given five days to withdraw from the Lebanese mountains. As the Palestinians and their allies refused the Syrian troops on 28 September launched a second offensive which within two days resulted in their adversaries' defeat in Mount Lebanon. Nonetheless Syria, instead of pushing for the complete capitulation of its adversaries, preferred to use this success as a trumpcard at the Riyadh and Cairo summits in October 1976 where its presence in Lebanon was further confirmed and the Arab Peace Force rebaptized as the Arab Deterrent Force

(ADF). Most important for Syria, the ADF was to be financed by the Arab League countries. Iraq did not endorse the decision, and called instead for Syria's withdrawal from Lebanon.

After the two summits, the Syrian forces on 15 November 1976 finally occupied Beirut. In December they occupied the offices of several newspapers considered not friendly enough to the Asad regime and other measures followed to ensure and further entrench Syrian domination. Although subsequently this position was not always immune to erosion, Syria continued to maintain its military presence in the country, especially in the Biqa' Valley and around Tripoli. Moreover, its intention to maintain control of Lebanon was clearly visible in the role it played at the Lebanese reconciliation conferences in Geneva and Lausanne in late 1983 and early 1984.[9] It made a more far-reaching attempt in December 1985 when it brought about an ephemeral agreement between the militias of the Maronite-dominated Lebanese forces, the Shi'i Amal and the Druze Progressive Socialist Party (PSP) providing not only for constitutional changes but also for close 'co-ordination' with Syria in defence, foreign policy, internal security, information, economic and even educational matters.

As had already become clear in March 1976, one of Syria's chief interests in Lebanon was to control the Palestinians. This aspect came to the fore once more after the Israeli invasion of 1982: first in the tireless attempts from May 1983 onwards to strengthen Arafat's opponents within the PLO, and to establish a parallel organization subservient to Syria;[10] then when Syrian troops in autumn 1983 expelled Arafat and his troops from Tripoli; and finally in the 'War of the Camps' after May 1985 in which Syria's most reliable ally in Lebanon, the Shi'i Amal movement, attempted to crush, though unsuccessfully, the remaining Palestinians in the country.

The intervention in Lebanon was continually justified in Syrian declarations, which often presented Damascus as the legitimate ruler of a territory larger than that of the actual state of Syria, grosso modo coinciding with the area of geographical or Greater Syria.[11] Thus Asad in his major speech delivered on 20 July 1976 not only presented Syria as the defender of the Arab cause by asserting that the intervention in Lebanon served to thwart an imperialist plot staged to cover up the Sinai II agreement between Egypt and Israel, but also specifically as the defender of the Palestinians and of Lebanon. Threatened by partition, Lebanon had to be defended and maintained as a secular state to prove, to Israel and its supporters, the viability of multi-religious states in the Middle East, but also because the Lebanese and the Syrians shared common interests and were bound by specific historic ties. 'Through history,' said Asad, 'Syria and Lebanon have been one country and one people . . . Genuine joint interests ensued . . . A genuine joint security also ensued.'[12]

Lebanon in fact was considered to be the natural extension of Syria, just like Palestine and Jordan. Ever since the struggle against France during the second world war Syria had been 'the guarantor and protector of Lebanon's independence and Arabism'.[13] Indeed, Syrian policy towards the PLO in the 1980s should show that Palestine was considered an extension of the motherland just like Lebanon.

On some occasions Syrian leaders went further and expressed yet more ambitious intentions. Asad, according to Patrick Seale, said in March 1977 that the Syrian aim was to forge an Arab bloc strong enough to become a regional power able to stand up to pressure from either of the superpowers.[14]

Apart from rallying and subjugating, Syria moreover aimed at exploiting other actors for its own purposes. This third policy was pursued not only at an Arab or regional but at a global level.

Before 1975, this was often done through a policy of combining pressure and gestures of friendship or co-operation. To impress and influence the United States the sticks of harsh and violent propaganda and of co-operation with the Soviet Union were combined with the carrots of *infitah* and of action in Lebanon. The latter in many respects satisfied American demands, especially when directed against the PLO.

Support and assistance from Saudi Arabia and the Gulf States, the other countries whose resources Syria tried to tap, was to some extent granted merely because Syria was a confrontation state that had to be kept alive and whose defeat would have shaken the legitimacy of the donor monarchies as well. But Syria also retained a certain nuisance power as it could always threaten to subvert its paymasters.[15] Not surprisingly under Asad the part of Arab financial aid in the government's total budgetary revenues increased from 4 per cent in 1968–72 to 31 per cent in 1973–6 and in 1982–3 still amounted to some 20 per cent. Because of its position as a confrontation state, Syria, at the Baghdad summit of 1978, was promised some US $1.8 billion to $1.85 billion per annum.[16] According to some sources the amount was generous because Asad had earlier gone to Moscow, where the oil states did not want him to seek assistance at all.[17] In addition, oil money covered the lion's share of the costs of the Arab Deterrent Force in Lebanon, not only because the financiers' interests converged with those of Syria, but also because this was the price of obtaining some residual autonomy for the PLO.

Syria's strength again appeared in early 1981 when Saudi Arabia and Kuwait, disgruntled with Syrian policy in Lebanon, held back their part of the monthly instalment for the ADF. Precisely at that moment Syria, though in reply to a previous incident, moved anti-aircraft missiles beyond the Israeli imposed red lines in Lebanon. Saudi and US diplomacy diffused the crisis, probably however not without Saudi money. As the Syrian writer Yasin al-Hafiz once put it, Syria had become a *balad nafti bidun naft*: an oil country without oil.

## Iraq

Attempts by Iraq to gain control over additional resources in the region, and thus enhance its power overtly, appear in numerous official declarations oozing with the self-assurance of oil-wealth. Saddam Husayn in his speech before the congress of the non-aligned countries in Havana in early September 1979 frankly admitted: 'In brief, we want Iraq to play a leading role in the area and especially in the Arab homeland. We want Iraq to play a leading role in the consolidation of anti-imperialist policies at the international level.'[18] Soon, megalomania crept in, as for example in Husayn's later statement to the Iraqi magazine *Alif-Ba'*: 'We aim at rendering our country its actual importance, estimating that Iraq is as great as China, as great as the Soviet Union and as great as the United States.'[19] Iraq, too, tried to rally, weaken and exploit other actors in order to obtain additional resources, including political support and to enhance its regional position, though it pursued each of these aims somewhat differently from Syria. For example, Iraq tried to gain additional support by granting resources, mainly financial aid, to poorer countries of the region as well as beyond.

First of all, however, and in contrast to Syria, Iraq tried to extract political support from other actors, mainly the wealthy oil countries of the Gulf. By obtaining such support, Iraq surreptitiously trapped the supporters in its own designs, which it then could pursue by resorting not only to its own resources, but also to those of its new dependants. To get its way Iraq, very much like Syria, illustrated its usefulness as well as its disruptive capacities or nuisance power, the former often through the latter, and the latter mainly by highlighting its different stances in Arab–Israeli affairs.

Nonetheless Iraq, parallel to its propaganda and overt displays of disagreement, such as the denunciation of Sadat's visit to Jerusalem before it had even taken place, maintained and even improved its relations with Egypt and Saudi Arabia after 1977.[20] Considered in the context of a policy that alternatively blew hot and cold this was entirely consistent with Iraq's participation at the Tripoli Conference. There, Iraq again tried to outdo its partners and called for a complete boycott of Egypt; for the liberation of all Arab territories, not only of the Golan; and for Syria to disavow UN Security Council resolutions 242 and 338, to withdraw from Lebanon and henceforth support the anti-status quo forces – otherwise it would not participate in the anti-Sadat front to be set up by the conference. As neither Syria nor the other participants could be persuaded to adopt this hard line, Iraq refused to sign the final document and walked out of the conference. As a result of the subsequent failure to convene the anti-Sadat forces in Baghdad, the Iraqi regime did not attend the follow-up meeting held in Algiers in early February 1978.

The pressure on the 'moderate' Arab countries was at the same time pressure on the West, especially the United States. Yet, it would be wrong to overrate these pressures and view Iraqi policy towards the West as a policy of confrontation. Rokach correctly pointed out that the Iraqi regime during the 1970s repeatedly acted in the interests of the West,[21] although this may rather have been a convergence of interests than a deliberate policy to please the West as the same author assumes. After the American hostage crisis in Iran in 1979 Iraq again seems to have perceived a convergence of interests with the West, and this perception may have encouraged it to unleash the war against Iran.

Apart from the unsuccessful attempts to push other regimes into rejectionist alliances led by itself, Iraq in its pressure-cum-co-operation policy also sought more positive alliances – among them, Lebanese actors opposed to Syria. As early as December 1975, when Saddam Husayn led an official delegation to Lebanon, Iraq openly supported the Lebanese anti-status quo forces and the Palestinians; in 1989 it granted substantial assistance to the 'Christian government' of General 'Awn.

In the late 1970s Iraq finally began to make serious attempts to become recognized as a respectable Arab power and to rally around itself the more moderate mainstream of Arab politics. The new intention of playing a leading role through consent rather than, as previously, through extremism, appeared most clearly in the regime's *revirement* to moderate positions in the Arab–Israeli conflict after it had failed to muster the support of those opposing Sadat's 'peace policy'. When the ecological niche of rejectionism was firmly occupied by the Tripoli bloc there was indeed no choice for Iraq but to become the link between them and the more hesitant conservatives. On 2 February 1978 it even resumed consular, cultural and commercial relations with Egypt itself, followed by the resumption of diplomatic relations in March, though not at ambassadorial level.

By dropping its demand for the rejection of UN resolutions 242 and 338 and the complete liberation of all Arab territory, Iraq, in

autumn 1978, succeeded in persuading the conservatives as well as
the rejectionists, some of whom like Syria depended on funds made
available by the conservatives, to attend the first Arab summit on
Iraqi soil.

The war with Iran helped to mobilize considerable Arab support,
although the Gulf countries were anxious not to antagonize Iran to
the point that they would be drawn into conflict. The resolutions
of the summits of Amman in 1980, Fez in 1982 and, more
recently, Amman in 1987, despite some reservations show how
far Iraq succeeded in transforming its conflict with Iran into
an Arab–Iranian conflict, into 'Saddam's Qadisiyya' as Iraqi
propaganda describes it. So far as material support is concerned,
Kuwait and Saudi Arabia also sold large quantities of crude oil from
their own production on the account of Iraq[22] to help it finance its
war effort. This war, which started with an Iraqi offensive on 22
September 1980, was in part a reaction to Iranian provocations.
Mainly, however, it was launched to weaken Iran at a moment
when it seemed least capable of resisting an attack, and to secure
for Iraq the dominant position in the Gulf. Thus Iraq like Syria,
though on a much larger scale, also attempted to subjugate other
actors in its quest for resources and influence.

Finally, Iraq also tried to extend its influence by distributing
part of its oil wealth to poorer actors of the region (and beyond).
Jordan and the PLO were repeatedly mentioned as being on the
payroll. According to one source, for instance, Jordan on 5 October
1978 received US $30 million to make it attend the Baghdad
summit.[23]

### March–December 1975: Algiers-upon-Euphrates

*Regional competition and incompatible claims to water resources*

Immediately after the Algiers agreement in 1975 Iran withdrew its
heavy arms and other equipment from the Kurdish areas of Iraq and
put an end to all other support. By early April the Kurdish resistance
had ceased to exist, with the *pashmergas* either surrendering to the
Iraqi army or fleeing across the border as defenceless refugees.
Baghdad was now able to reallocate considerable resources,
military as well as financial, to more profitable ends. Syria clearly
understood the boost which the Algiers agreement implied for
Iraq's future role in the region and the implications for Syria's
own designs and ambitions. Damascus now raged against the
forfeit of Arab rights allegedly inherent in the recognition of the
existing Iraqi-Iranian border, which left to Iran the area known to
the Iranians as Khuzistan and to the Arabs as Arabistan.

Almost simultaneously Damascus started to use the Algiers agreement to divert attention from its less than generous policy over the sharing of the Euphrates waters. Syria at that time was flooding the Asad lake at the newly completed Euphrates High Dam at Tabqa, thus reducing the amount of water flowing into Iraq.

Iraq, for its part, was not ready to give away the new regional advantages it had gained through its accord with Iran by leaving the major claim to Arab legitimacy to the Syrians. Nor was it prepared to accept Syria's privileged use of the Euphrates waters. Together, the conflicts over the allocation of water resources and over regional influence provoked an intensive propaganda war and other hostile acts that continued unabated from early March till mid-July. As the circumstances seemed favourable, Iraq then attempted to win over Syria to its positions in the Arab–Israeli conflict and at the same time to reduce its independence. For some time Iraqi hostility seemed reduced, and they had offered to Syria the carrot of a common northern front. However, by the end of August Iraq abandoned all its limited restraint when Syria showed no sign of accepting the Iraqi proposals, and at about the same time remaining Iraqi hopes of a definite solution to the Euphrates issue vanished.

### The sharing of the Euphrates waters

In early 1975, about one and a half years after the official opening of the Tabqa High Dam in July 1973, Syria and Iraq clashed over the sharing of the Euphrates waters.[24] According to some sources this coincided with the Syrians raising the lake's level to its full capacity,[25] but it is not clear whether the Syrians at that time significantly stepped up the process of filling the lake. It is nonetheless certain that the flooding of lake Tabqa, or lake Asad as it was called in Syria, temporarily deprived Iraq of part of the water it previously received. Apart from this Iraq also saw its share of water reduced in the long term as Syria planned to use the lake to irrigate vast areas of new agricultural land.

Unfortunately, both the short- and long-term losses of Iraq are difficult to assess as information is extremely scarce or, if based on Syrian and Iraqi sources, blatantly contradictory. The different sources do not even agree on the 'natural' amount of water carried by the river at the Syro-Iraqi border, that is the amount of water that would pass into Iraq if there were no diversions or other artificial losses upstream. For the same years in the 1960s the 'natural' amount ranges from 26,200 million cubic metres (cu.m) according to Syrian sources[26] to 31,800 million cu.m according to Iraqi sources;[27] an independent source dealing with the 1980s even puts the figure at 33,730 million cu.m per year.[28] The only factor

actually known is the storage capacity of lake Tabqa. Maximum
output for the generation of electricity and agricultural irrigation
is reached at a water-level of 300 meters above sea level, that is 8
metres beneath the crest of the dam. This corresponds to a storage
capacity of 11,900 million of cu.m water.[29]

The effects of the filling of lake Tabqa on Iraq are difficult to
evaluate precisely, because there is no reliable information about
the beginning, end and speed of this process;[30] nonetheless, Syrian
and Iraqi figures on the amount of water carried by the river, though
contradictory, indicate that Iraq was probably short of water in
spring 1975. While there is no doubt that a large part of the water
of lake Tabqa was stored from early 1975 on,[31] by 1 May 1974 the
lake already contained 4,500 million cu.m. This is the minimum
generating level for hydroelectric production which started on that
date.[32] But it is difficult to know over what span of time the storage
of the remaining 7,400 million cu.m was stretched.[33] As the average
flow of the Euphrates into Iraq prior to the construction of the
Tabqa Dam amounted to some 29,000[34] to 32,000[35] million cu.m,
the storage of 7,400 million cu.m still corresponds to the entire
average amount of water carried by the river into Iraq in two or
three months. The question, however, seems further complicated
by the fact that in 1975 the snows in the Turkish mountains seem to
have melted very slowly and in consequence the Euphrates carried
less water than usual.[36]

In any case, according to Baghdad, the Euphrates in 1975 only
carried some 9,400 million cu.m into Iraq. However, it is important
to note that according to the same sources Iraq had received even
less water in 1974 (9,000 million cu.m) and comparatively little in
1973 (15,300 million cu.m).[37] That Iraq was short of water in these
days is confirmed by an eyewitness who spent most of spring 1975
in Raqqa (Syria) below Tabqa on the Euphrates and asserted that
sometimes the river could be crossed by foot.[38]

Denying Iraqi figures Syria's Minister of the Euphrates maintained that in 1975 Iraq would receive some 12,800 million cu.m,
roughly the same amount as in 1974 when it had not complained.[39]
Nonetheless, even this figure implicitly conceded that Iraq received
just about the amount of water it normally consumed as potable
water and for industrial purposes, including irrigation on the short
section of the river between Hit and Hindiyya. But presumably part
of this amount now could no longer be taken there because of the
river's lower water level.

In the long term also Syria's vast new irrigation projects would
necessarily diquiet Baghdad. Although Syria intended to proceed
slowly and reclaim and develop not more than 20,000 ha per year
of the projected total of 640,000 ha of new arable land,[40] Iraq could

easily anticipate the progressive dwindling of its share of water, which one day would adversely affect its own projects. Apart from irrigation, evaporation from the lake's surface, estimated at 1,570 million cu.m, and the water supply for Aleppo, another annual 80 million cu.m, reduced the amount of water flowing into Iraq.[41] Moreover, the quality of water downstream was degraded by more saline drainage water flowing back into the river from irrigated areas.

According to one authoritative source based on a potential or 'natural' flow of 33,730 million cu.m annually at the Syro-Iraqi border, Syria's share would increase from 2,133.2 million cu.m in the years 1986–90 to 3,493.7 million cu.m in 1990–5, to 12,079.0 million cu.m after 1995. As Turkey also relies increasingly on Euphrates waters the Iraqi share would drop from 29,614 million cu.m annually in 1986–90 to 20,471 million cu.m in 1990–5, 6,369 million cu.m in 1995–2000 and to only 4,960 million cu.m after the year 2000.[42] These figures have to be seen against an estimate that puts the average annual need of water at 12,700 million cu.m between Hit and Hindiyya alone,[43] which is a rather small section of the lower Euphrates. Even should the total Iraqi need for surface waters by 1995 amount to only 12,066 million cu.m,[44] the decrease in the flow of the Euphrates will have effects beyond drying up arable land alongside the river. Certainly, land reclamation in the Syrian Euphrates valley was much delayed so that in 1982 less than 50,000 ha were under cultivation,[45] but Iraq could not base its hopes and policies on such inefficiency.[46]

Both sides justified their claims with 'rational' arguments. Syria mainly argued that it had only extremely limited water resources compared to Iraq and Turkey, the other riparians of the Euphrates.[47] According to one Syrian official, excluding water from the Euphrates, Turkey had annual water resources amounting to some 100,000 million cu.m and Iraq 35,500 million cu.m, while Syria had no more than 3,500 million cu.m a year. Thus Syria should be allowed to develop its use of the Euphrates waters, especially since it was not yet using the share that according to international law appertained to it. In case of need Iraq could always use water from the Tigris.[48]

Iraq, on the other hand, insisted on its 'established rights', also calling upon international law. Accordingly, a distinction should be made between areas already cultivated through irrigation and the development of new areas that needed to be irrigated in the future. In the division of water supplies priority was to be given to the areas already under cultivation[49].

Syria did not actually deny these 'established rights', but contested the figures advanced by Iraq.[50] Iraq claimed these figures were drawn from a report made by the World Bank (IBRD) in 1965 which specified the extent of agricultural land irrigated by the Euphrates in each of its three riparian countries and estimated the respective possibilities for further land reclamation.[51] According to Iraq this report, assuming a total natural flow of 35,000 million cu.m per year, put the needs of Turkey at at 11,900 million cu.m of Syria to 7,000 million cu.m and of Iraq to 16,100 million cu.m.[52] Syria, in contrast, seemed to maintain an older claim of 13,000 million cu.m a year.[53] Iraq moreover claimed to adhere to a Soviet proposal of 1972 which it said was also based on an IBRD report of 1969.

The Soviet proposal, according to Iraq, suggested that for a period of twenty years arable land in the Euphrates Basin, including the Tabqa and Keban schemes in Syria and Turkey, should be extended without encroaching on Iraq's 'established rights'. After these twenty years Iraq would reduce its share of the Euphrates water.[54]

On 7 April Iraq asked for the Arab League Council to discuss the matter. Syria, according to the Iraqi complaint, stored even more water in the lake than was actually necessary for irrigation and the generation of electricity.[55] Iraq thus clearly expressed that contrary to Syria's claim, it considered the dispute 'political' and not simply economic.

Iraq now deployed intensive diplomatic activities to convince other Arab regimes of the rightness of its own position while the Arab League set up a mediation committee.[56] In May Saudi Arabia started its own mediation,[57] and in early June even the Soviet Union was involved in the search for a solution.[58] After a series of visits and meetings[59] and much procrastination Syria, apparently thanks to Saudi intervention, announced on 3 June that it would release 'water of its own share, regardless of the Iraqi regime's attitude'.[60] Iraq acknowledged that more water had been released by Syria, but added that it came too late for the Iraqi summer crops, and that some 70 per cent of the country's winter crops had been lost due to the shortage of water.[61] On 12 August Syria announced that it had accepted a Saudi proposal under which the Euphrates water was to be distributed between Syria and Iraq on a 'proportional basis', according to the amount of water reaching Syria from Turkey.[62] However, no agreement was signed, and the Euphrates issue remained unresolved.

Despite the many uncertainties that surround the flooding of lake Tabqa there seems to be little doubt that with respect to the river's flow in 1975 Syria raised the water level of the lake too rapidly for Iraq to operate its own irrigation and other hydraulic systems. Provided it did not store more water than it needed, Syria's decision to raise the water level may have been taken on a purely economic basis. Although there was still hardly any land ready for irrigation, the power station attached to the dam could reach maximum capacity only if the lake's surface was raised to 300 metres above sea-level. On the other hand if, as claimed by Damascus and confirmed by Baghdad, the Euphrates in 1974 already carried far less water than usual, Iraq should indeed have protested earlier.

In contrast to these speculations about short-term political motives, the long-term aim that Syria pursued with the Tabqa project can easily be identified as the quest for additional material resources. Iraq's opposition to this quest was equally motivated by considerations of material advantage as it sought to defend its access to the very same resources.

### Verbal warfare

#### Syrian propaganda

Syria's propaganda campaign against the Algiers agreement, intended not only to tarnish Iraq's regional position but also to cover up Syria's high-handed treatment of the Euphrates issue, like similar previous campaigns, was started by the media. But with the intensification of the conflict, representatives of the regime became directly involved.[63]

The war of words continued to be fought mainly in terms of Arab legitimacy, even though some explicit references to Ba'thi legitimacy did occur. Once for instance it was claimed that: ' The fascist right-wing in Iraq has forfeited its claim to call itself Ba'th after having conspired against the interests of the party and of the Arab masses.'[64] The alleged Iraqi attempt to overthrow the Syrian government doubtlessly refers to the uncovering of pro-Iraqi activities within the Syrian party in March. This was followed by massive arrests including senior party members which, however, were not officially admitted. Indeed, when these events became known[65] and could no longer be denied outright, the Syrian authorities nonetheless played them down and only admitted to the arrest of some ten party members for having infringed party discipline.[66]

The final statement of the Sixth Regional Congress of the Syrian Ba'th Party (held in Damascus from 5 to 15 April 1975) concentrated on the Iraqi regime's lack of Arab legitimacy, making no references to Ba'thi legitimacy.

Within this framework, the congress considered the Iraqi-Iranian agreement, which was signed by the suspect rightist regime in Iraq, as an unjustified and illegitimate act giving up part of the Arab territory . . . The suspicious policy pursued by the fascist rightist regime in Iraq – whether by forsaking the Arab national rights or . . . fabricating peripheral battles and attempting to draw the Syrian Arab region into these battles to . . . weaken its capability against the enemy – can only serve and assist imperialist Zionist plans.

In the light of all these factors, the congress passed the following resolutions:
1. To condemn the suspicious rightist regime in Iraq for colluding with Iran and signing the Iraqi-Iranian March agreement, which confirms its complete link with imperialism and colonialism, [and for] its persistence in liquidating the revolution in Arabistan and its betrayal of the Arab nation's questions.
2. To condemn [Iraq] for signing the Turkish–Iraqi agreement on the installation of oil pipelines to Iskenderun harbour.
3. To condemn [Iraq's] unnational stand . . . regarding . . . the Palestine question.
4. To condemn [Iraq's] methods of suppression and terror against our Arab people in Iraq.[67]

According to Damascus Iraq's propensity for 'peripheral battles' was moreover clearly linked to its – alleged – refusal to participate in the preparation of the October War that now was unearthed as a topic again. The longer the Euphrates dispute dragged on, the more severe and violent propaganda became. Syria now increasingly pointed to harsh internal repression within Iraq where just about the only fate 'progressives and nationalists' could meet was execution.[68]

At the end of May 1975 and in early June again the alleged 'tribal' and thus atavistic character of the Iraqi regime was insisted on in order to undermine its Arab legitimacy. Far more frequently than in 1973 it was now referred to as the 'Takriti regime'[69] or the 'tribal Takriti regime'.[70]

During the Euphrates crisis the frequency and violence of accusations reached the same pitch as they had in the late sixties. Syria again accused Iraq of having attempted to assassinate persons working for Damascus. According to Syrian sources Iraqi agents had planted the booby-trap that blew up the car of Ahmad al-'Azzawi, a former confidant of Saddam Husayn who in 1974 had fled to Syria and then efficiently reorganized the pro-Syrian Ba'th in Iraq.[71] However, other sources have linked this first attempt to kill 'Azzawi, as well as the subsequent successful operation, to his growing disillusionment with Asad's policies which he repeatedly considered to be opposed to the goals of Arab nationalism and of Ba'thism, especially after Syria supported the pro-status quo forces in the Lebanese civil war.[72]

In the light of Syria's regional ambitions its insistence on Arab legitimacy cannot be seen as anything else but a technique to realize these ambitions. This seems to be confirmed by the unprecedented internal consolidation of the Syrian regime in this period. The substantial economic growth and improvement of the early 1970s[73] obviously had enhanced the regime's internal position, though probably also its appetite for regional influence. However, the economic situation was to deteriorate significantly in 1976, especially towards the end of that year,[74] and the internal legitimacy of the regime correspondingly suffered.

## Iraqi propaganda

Iraqi propaganda, too, dwelt heavily on the theme of Arab legitimacy although, as in the years before, it also continued to blame Syria for unjustly impairing interests that were specifically Iraqi ones, now especially in the case of the Euphrates waters. This issue occupied an important place in Iraqi propaganda throughout the spring and summer of 1975. But very much as before, in the conflicts over the trans-Syrian pipeline, the bulk of Iraqi remarks were again 'descriptive', 'explanatory' and not insulting. Yet, the Iraqi side made it clear on several occasions that, in contrast to Syria, it did not regard the problem as 'technical' but as 'political', stemming from the two sides' controversy over the defence of Arab rights and interests.

Two quotes from Iraqi statements of spring 1975 may illustrate the double concern to the regime in Baghdad to present itself as a defender of specifically Iraqi as well as of wider Arab interests. According to Radio Baghdad Taha Yasin Ramadan al-Jazrawi, a member of the Revolutionary Command Council (RCC), in a speech in late March 'referred to the Syrian regime's hostile attitude to Iraq, an attitude which is manifested in its cutting off of the Euphrates river water, an action which is jeopardizing the livelihood of the Iraqi peasants who rely on this water'.[75]

In contrast Na'im Haddad, a member of the Iraqi Ba'th's Regional Command (RC), in a later speech stressed Arab legitimacy:

> Today US imperialism is pushing certain regimes, particularly the Syrian regime, to cut off water from our masses . . . But

we will be victorious as we have been before. The masses of
our Arab people in Syria will discover this criminal design,
which is neither new to us nor unexpected. The same Syrian
regime adopted a negative policy when the revolution in Iraq
nationalized the monopolist oil companies and even requested
an increase in revenue from the oil flow.[76]

This quotation illustrates the participation of formally high-ranking
– though not really powerful – regime figures in the propaganda
campaign against Syria once it had gained momentum.

When Iraq proclaimed its own Arab legitimacy this served the
same purpose as when Syria did so. Due to the collapse of Kurdish
resistance, the increasing efficiency of internal repression, not least
against the communists, and rapidly increasing revenue from oil,
the Iraqi regime no longer faced serious threats from inside the
country. Certainly, the unequal distribution of wealth created new
or reinforced older cleavages within the Iraqi population,[77] and to
contain discontent Arab legitimacy continued to be the necessary
complement of repression. However, such internal legitimacy
appears to have been sought increasingly by presenting the
regime as the defender of especially Iraqi interests. Like in
Syria, Arab legitimacy in Iraq seems mainly to have served
to enhance the position of the regime not internally but as a
regional power. This was particularly so since the rapid growth
and the formidable dimensions of Iraqi wealth incited the country's
rulers to transform this new economic power into political power at
the regional level.

References to the issue of Ba'thi legitimacy remained rare in Iraqi
statements but did not altogether disappear.[78] Possibly Baghdad
hoped to rekindle intra-party opposition in Syria, exploiting the
egotism of the Syrian regime on the Euphrates question.

## The limited détente of summer and autumn

Attacks on Syria's attitude towards the Arab cause abated somewhat, though far from completely, with Bakr's speech on the
anniversary of the July revolutions on 17 July 1975 and thereafter.
Most importantly, however, they were now partly balanced by
the offer to send Iraqi troops to the Golan, despite 'the known
differences' with Syria. Such co-operation, however, remained
conditional: Syria had to reject UN Security Council resolutions
242 and 338 as well as the idea of the Geneva Peace Conference.
Moreover it had to commit itself to the liberation of 'all the usurped
Arab territories'.[79]

The more conciliatory approach towards Syria was to be pursued
for some time in August 1975, even though Iraqi peasants continued

to suffer from a shortage of water. Combined with heavier accusations, the offer of military co-operation was maintained till the end of November 1975.

Iraq had made its offer against the background of Kissinger's effort in March to make Israel and Egypt agree on a more far-reaching disengagement accord than the first one concluded in 1974. Though these efforts had failed, the Soviet Union's subsequent call for the reconvening of the Geneva Conference made further such attempts easy to anticipate. The prospect of a second accord on the Sinai would certainly disquiet the Syrians, and thus there was a slight chance they might prefer an alliance with Iraq. By entering into such an alliance and granting support to Syria, Iraq could surreptitiously extend its domination over its neighbour and the competition over regional legitimacy could then be pursued by 'co-operation' rather than confrontation. The situation indeed anticipated the one after the Camp David accords, except that in 1975 Syria had not felt as threatened as it did in 1978, and so had then been less ready to enter into an alliance with Iraq.

Despite an exchange of notes between the two countries[80] Syrian public statements continued to be as vitriolic as before 17 July[81]. It is in these days also that Syria rolled out again the old accusation that Iraq initially had declined to participate in the 1973 war against Israel.[82]

By the end of August, Iraq in a tactical move returned to a more vitriolic line. It became less conciliatory towards Syria after the Egyptian–Israeli negotiations over the Sinai II agreement had started, thus bluntly confronting Syria with the alternative of participating in the 'peace process' or of rejecting it.

The combination of aggressiveness and readiness to co-operate militarily with Syria was to illustrate how dangerously alone and friendless Syria could be after Sinai II, if it refused to envisage an alliance with Iraq. Time and again, Iraq reiterated its offer of military co-operation. These reminders were not casual, but well timed – for example an offer was made on 3 September,[83] the eve of the signing of the Sinai II agreement. However, on the following day, when Sinai II was effectively agreed on in Cairo, the Iraqi side again abandoned all moderation and attacked Syria even more virulently than Egypt, who had initialled the agreement. Syria, it was claimed, 'used the Egyptian regime as a mine detector in front of it on the road, letting it receive the explosions, so that when the road is secured, the Syrian regime can march on with few losses.'[84]

The Iraqi stick and carrot policy seemed to pay off. In the second half of October Syria started to move somewhat closer to Iraq. This was noticeable in the rescinding of a certain number of sanctions that had been imposed in spring.[85] Moreover Syria now, though maintaining charges against its neighbour, refrained from violent or insulting statements. There were even rumours that in November the two sides held secret talks 'at the highest level'.[86] However, the transitory *détente* came to an end when Syria in late 1975 renewed the mandate of the UN Disengagement Observer Force (UNDOF) for the Golan,[87] thus ignoring a last Iraqi call, made on 26 November, to establish a 'unified fighting front' and abandon the pursuit of a political settlement.[88]

### Economic and technical relations beyond the Euphrates issue

For the first time now hostility resulting from the dominant conflicts brought about such a deterioration of relationships that technical and economic co-operation in general, even in fields unrelated to the Euphrates issue, was adversely affected.

Not only were no new agreements negotiated, but existing co-operation was halted. First, Syria on 10 May 1975 closed the offices of Iraqi Airways in Damascus and of its own airline in Baghdad; then, on 13 May, it closed its airspace to all Iraqi aircraft and its commercial centre in Baghdad as well as that of Iraq in Damascus.[89]

Only in late August, apparently thanks to a temporary *détente*, were goods from and to Iraq again allowed to pass in transit through Syria.[90] On 3 September, two days after the initialling of the Sinai II agreement – probably as a non-committal sign of goodwill – Syria ratified the 1974 agreement with Iraq to link the two countries' railway networks via Dayr al-Zur.[91] About six weeks later Syria also reopened its airspace to Iraqi civilian planes,[92] perhaps to ensure the participation of an Iraqi delegation at the meeting of the Secretariat General of the Arab Front for the Support of the Palestine Revolution in Damascus on 22 and 23 October.[93] That Iraq actually participated indicated that bilateral relations had improved. In mid-November Syrian Airlines reopened its Baghdad office, and regular flights were resumed between the two capitals.[94]

### Beyond accusations

#### Harsher means: troop concentrations, terrorism and subversion

The deterioration of bilateral relations in spring 1975 did not only affect general economic and technical co-operation. Both sides began more generally to resort to harsher means when dealing with one another or to accuse the other of doing so. However, as it is often impossible to determine to what extent these accusations were justified if at all, the deterioration of bilateral relations need not be reflected necessarily in acts of physical violence but instead in accusations pertaining to such acts.

For the first time now, both sides sent a significant number of troops to their common border. But sources are contradictory as to which side took the initiative. According to one, Iraq sent troops first, which remained at the border at least through March and April 1975.[95] Another puts the responsibility on Syria which at about the same time had dispatched its troops under the pretext that the Iraqis intended to occupy the Euphrates High Dam at Tabqa.[96] By the end of May, Syria was again reported to have sent troops to the border, this time further north to protect the oilfields of Karajuk, close to Turkey.[97]

Syrian troops remained at the border till mid-November, when Damascus briefly moved slightly closer to Iraq. Iraq repeatedly charged Syria with violating its border and airspace[98] while Syria twice accused Iraq of assassination attempts against some of its officials. However, in one of the latter cases there is some reason to doubt the Syrian version.

Already in spring 1975 Syria started to support more openly internal oppositon to the Iraqi regime. On 1 June 1975[99] the Patriotic Union of Kurdistan (PUK) was founded in Europe and almost immediately afterwards opened a permanent office in Damascus. It was presided over by Jalal Talabani who in March 1975 once more broke with the Kurdish Democratic Party (KDP) of Barzani, whose representative in Damascus he had been since 1972. Talabani seems to have resided almost continuously in Syria since 1972.[100] The actual impact of this support should, however, not be overrated, and presumably the Syrian regime intended to taunt its Iraqi neighbour rather than actually combat it by proxy. By that time, the main Kurdish force was still the KDP which, after the honeymoon of 1973–5, again distanced itself from Damascus. Of greater importance was that the situation in Kurdistan proper was sufficiently controlled by the Baghdad regime so that, even with Syrian support, major actions by the Kurdish rebels were impossible.[101]

Unfortunately for Damascus its Ba'th organization in Iraq was in disarray. After Ahmad al-'Azzawi, its leader since 1974, had become increasingly critical of the Syrian regime, an attempt was made to undermine his position, culminating in an attempt on his life on 27 June. Interestingly Iraq, which in the late sixties had entertained close relations with Syrian actors opposed to the Jadid regime, now only had rather limited connections with opposition groups in its neighbouring country. Iraq's appeal possibly continued to suffer from Syria's improving economic performance under the *infitah*. Obviously Iraq's increasing wealth was not propitious for Syria to be able to find support there, but a small group of devoted activists could be formed even under such 'unfavourable' conditions.

### Concern over party contacts

The large-scale arrests of Ba'this, many of them sympathetic to the Iraqi party, carried out by Syrian secret police in March 1975, do not necessarily prove that the pro-Iraqi Ba'th organization was particularly active at that time. They may also indicate continued Syrian concern about such pro-Iraqi sympathies even if they remained constricted when compared to the late 1960s and early 1970s. Different sources agree that some 100–200 Ba'this, many of them officers and senior party members, among them Marwan Hamawi, till then the director-general of the Syrian Arab News Agency (SANA), were arrested and accused of collaborating with and spying for Iraq.[102] Although many of those arrested were actually pro-Iraqi, this is not true of all of them, and the clamp-down must also be seen as a more general preparatory measure or prelude to the Sixth Extraordinary Regional Congress that was to be held in April.

### Diplomatic relations

The increasing tension in spring 1975 also affected diplomatic relations. On 25 May 1975 the Iraqi News Agency (INA) reported that Syria had ordered the closure of the Iraqi Consulate General in Aleppo.[103] Not long afterwards, on 8 July 1975, Syria closed the office of the Iraqi military attaché in Damascus and expelled the attaché and his personnel. This move also put an end to the last though rather symbolical remnant of military co-operation between the two countries.[104]

### Military non-co-operation

It is not surprising that in this growing atmosphere of hostility, party and military co-operation materialized no more than in previous periods of equal or less tension. Yet, the Iraqi offer to send troops to the Golan was not necessarily insincere. Iraq certainly had no great confidence that Syria would accept its conditions, but nor was a positive response entirely excluded at that time.

Had Syria accepted the Iraqi proposal, Iraq would have been in a position of relative strength. This would have been so not only because Iraqi troops would have been stationed in Syria and not the other way round, but also because after rejecting resolutions

242 and 338 Syria would have become extremely dependent on the continuous presence of Iraqi troops on its territory. At least in the beginning this kind of co-operation would not have endangered the stability of the Iraqi regime, although Iraq would have run all the risks of a front-line confrontation state. But perhaps this risk appeared acceptable to the regime in Baghdad after the rather good performance of its troops in the 1973 war.

### December 1975–September 1976: the struggle for Lebanon and the PLO

As Syria with the renewal of the UN Disengagement Observer Force (UNDOF) mandate implicitly rejected the conditions on which Iraq offered to send troops to the Golan, Baghdad had to abandon its strategy of trying to subjugate its regional opponent smoothly, by way of 'co-operation'. Confrontation was again to dominate the search for regional influence and supremacy.

This struggle was unleashed even more violently as Syria's growing involvement in Lebanon began to pose an ever-increasing threat to Iraq's own role in the region. The danger became acute with Syria's later military intervention, which, as by then had become clear, would hardly have been possible without the previous prorogation of the UNDOF mandate. Iraq now had to fear that Syria might establish control over the country and the PLO. The intervention and Iraqi criticism of it far more than Sinai II was a repetition – with the actors inversed – of the situation previously created by the Algiers agreement: a regional initiative was taken by one of the actors with the intention of enhancing its position (then by Iraq, now by Syria) and the other side had to try its best to thwart it. However, the Syrian intervention 'unbalanced' the Syro-Iraqi equilibrium more – and more immediately – than the Algiers agreement. Thus, with Syria's growing involvement, regional influence and competition quickly developed from an issue to be tackled in the long term into an acute problem completely preoccupying both sides and relegating to the background all other affairs. Though harshly criticizing Syria's policy in Lebanon, Iraq nevertheless, at a time when Syrian action ran into great difficulties, again offered its co-operation by participating in a rejectionist alliance against Israel. Essentially this was but a repetition of the earlier attempt made in summer 1975 to reduce Syrian's independence at a moment when its regime needed outside assistance.

As in the previous phase, growing regional competition by pure coincidence was soon paralleled by a narrower conflict of interest quite similar to the earlier one over the Euphrates waters. To make the analogy almost perfect, this conflict of interest again resulted from the conduct of that party, which under the new circumstances was left at a disadvantage in the regional competition, but found itself in a stronger position as to the disputed resources. With the completion of the 'strategic' pipeline linking Kirkuk to the Gulf, Iraq could deprive Syria of oil and royalties, exactly as Syria had deprived Iraq of water.

## Verbal warfare

### Iraqi accusations

Iraqi propaganda, which as early as fall 1975 expressed disagreement over Syria's policy in Lebanon, after the crisis that shook that country in December 1975 and January 1976, developed mainly, though not always, as a function of Syrian action there. Although Iraqi media now permanently charged Syria with supporting the Christian 'isolationists' and thus of working in favour of Western imperialist designs, accusations became fiercer for instance after Asad publicly asserted that Syria was ready to intervene with its own troops.[105]

However, it soon became clear that Syria had manoeuvred itself into a dilemma in Lebanon. So far Damascus had sent into Lebanon only a limited number of troops that could still operate under the guise of Palestinian forces, such as the Sa'iqa and the Palestine Liberation Army. But this limited intervention of March 1976 had failed to produce the expected results and to balance the intra-Lebanese rapport de forces between those in favour and those in opposition to the status quo. The Syrians now found themselves confronted with the difficult choice of whether to acknowledge their failure or intervene more extensively and thus more openly against the anti status-quo forces, especially the Palestinians, with all the concomitant pernicious consequences for their own Arab legitimacy.

Trying to take advantage of Syria's difficulties, Baghdad consequently again offered its co-operation and assistance to Syria, provided it changed its policy in Lebanon and did not align itself with Egypt's ever more accommodating position towards Israel. Like the previous attempt of autumn 1975 this offer again was conceived as an indebting rescue operation for the stranded Syrians: in exchange for its aid Baghdad would have been able to impose its terms, make Syria dependent, and prevent it from enhancing its regional influence. The only difference was that now the offer came in the form of a 'united front' together with Algeria and Libya.[106] Shelved when Damascus launched its June offensive against the anti-status quo forces, the project time and again was referred to later in order to embarrass Syria.

With Syrian troops advancing into Lebanon, Iraq re-intensified its propaganda campaign. Bomb explosions in Damascus were now frequently reported and presented as signs of popular resistance.[107] And when Saddam Husayn in mid-April 1976 cut short a tour of Gulf countries this was explained by the discovery of a Syrian-engineered plot to kill him on this trip.[108] The explanation was later confirmed by a paper not normally hostile to Syria referring to 'informed diplomatic sources'.[109] Syria and Iraq accused each other of planning, supporting or carrying out physical aggression on several other occasions, where, however, the accusations are more easily substantiated with facts (see pp. 114ff.)

### Syrian accusations

From the propagandistic point of view Syria at the beginning of this phase was in the weaker position as it had to justify its intervention in Lebanon. It tried when possible to ignore Iraqi criticisms and accusations[110] or, when this was not possible, to ward them off with the usual replies and counter-attacks.[111] In April 1976, however, the Iraqi decision to cease using the trans-Syrian pipeline provided Syria with a new opportunity to attack Iraq's Arab legitimacy. Now Syria could argue that Iraq treated it unjustly by depriving it of transit royalties. Iraq replied to these accusations, referring to Syria's high-handed increase of royalties in 1972; but basically it continued to concentrate its propaganda on Syria's intervention in Lebanon. Although Syria soon stopped using the pipeline row in its verbal warfare, the later propagandistic defence of its position in Lebanon cannot be dissociated from the economic harm it estimated Iraq had done to it. Syrian propaganda was largely the mirror image of Iraqi propaganda, justifying opposite positions in the same terms of Arab legitimacy. Apart from the arguments over Lebanon and the oil pipelines only a few new features appeared in Syrian propaganda, for instance a stronger insistence on infighting within the Iraqi regime,[112] and on widespread arrests there.[113]

An alleged Iraqi defector held that the Iraqi army actually intended to attack Syria. In late August Damascus claimed that it had broken up a terrorist group and arrested its members who had links with Iraq.[114] However, there is no reliable evidence confirming that Iraq had anything to do with the bombs that in the first two weeks of August exploded in public places, or in front of government buildings, in Syria.[115] Even less is known about the blasts reported by the Iraqi media in June. Unrest and discontent were running high in Syria after the regime had decided in favour of a full-scale invasion of Lebanon to quell Palestinian resistance and independence, and thus bombs may well have been planted by Palestinians, or by Syrians sympathetic to their cause, and not necessarily by Iraqi agents or even with Iraqi participation.[116]

It seems almost natural that both sides in this phase of the conflict again concentrated on the theme of Arab legitimacy. Syria had to prove to the Arab world and, of course, to the Lebanese in particular that its intervention in Lebanon was well-founded, while Iraq for the same reason of regional competition had to uncover Syria's selfish motives behind its ostensibly altruistic peace-keeping mission. But the Syrian regime also had to defend itself against strong criticism of its intervention from within its own country and even from within its own party. This criticism was expressed in demonstrations,[117] but also in more serious forms of resistance, including a coup attempt in late March[118] after the regime had changed sides and begun to support the pro-status quo forces. Possibly another coup attempt was made in June. And at the end of August President Asad was reported to have narrowly escaped death when a bomb exploded in Ladhiqiyya.[119]

### The pipeline row of spring 1976

In late April 1976 conflict re-erupted over the use of the trans-Syrian pipeline. Despite the agreement of 18 January 1973, the issue had started to come to the surface again in late December 1975 when the financial provisions of the 1973 agreement[120] had to be renewed. Now, however, Iraq was in a position of relative strength. The 'strategic' pipeline linking the Kirkuk oilfields to the Gulf port of Faw, itself a child of the previous pipeline row, was about to reach completion when, from 12 to 19 December, the first talks were held to renegotiate the financial terms of 1973. Moreover, the project of the trans-Turkish pipeline went ahead and, in December 1975, the two countries exchanged the instruments of ratification.[121]

The negotiations with Syria duly failed and had to be adjourned till after the inauguration of the 'strategic' pipeline on 27 December.

Once the 'strategic' pipeline was completed, it would have been uneconomic not to use it, not only because Kirkuk crude shipped via the Gulf was slightly cheaper than via the Mediterranean,[122] but also because maintenance created expenses, whether the pipeline was in service or not. So quite naturally Iraq, as soon as possible, diverted as much Kirkuk crude as possible to the Gulf. Certainly in March 1976, but perhaps earlier, Iraq channelled some 500 thousand barrels a day through this new pipeline to Faw, which amounted to about one-half of its total exports from the northern oilfields.[123] For Syria this meant already now the loss of half of its revenue from royalties, roughly US $63 million.[124] From 12 to 15 February[125] and then in early April 1976[126] two more rounds of talks were held.

As again no agreement could be reached, on 12 April 1976 Iraq completely stopped its oil exports via Syria and ceased to supply the Homs refinery with crude at a preferential price.[127] By that time the 'strategic pipeline' was expected to reach a capacity of about 800 to 850 thousand barrels a day.[128] However, as was to be known later, technical difficulties persisted beyond its opening and until at least June Iraq was not able to pump more than 500 thousand barrels a day through it.[129] While these technical difficulties were an unexpected mishap, the reduction of oil exports from Kirkuk and the smaller oilfields around it from an average of about 915,343 barrels a day in 1975[130] to some 800–850 thousand barrels a day was deliberate and shows that the Iraqi regime was ready to incur financial losses in its dealing with Syria. Indeed, much of the demand for Kirkuk oil in spring 1976 could not be satisfied due to limited export capacities.[131] Of course, Syria could have refused to maintain the pipeline if Iraq did not maintain the throughput at the minimum level it had guaranteed in the 1973 agreement, but confronted with the alternatives of receiving some royalties or none, Syria probably thought it better to keep the line open.

While Iraq's losses still seem relatively modest if calculated on average exports, in 1975 they were potentially much higher calculated on the maximum capactiy of the trans-Syrian pipeline, which was 1.4 million barrels a day.[132] It should still be pointed out that the difference could by no means be absorbed by the Kirkuk refinery, whose capacity as late as 1977 did not exceed 20 thousand barrels a day.[133] The old export capacity was only reached again when the Iraqi-Turkish pipeline was put into service.

Iraq officially justified the discontinuation of oil exports via Syria by pointing to Syria's intervention on the side of the pro-status quo forces in Lebanon. However, more disquieting for Iraq was the fact that Syria intervened there at all and thus attempted to enhance its regional position. Apart from revenge for 1972–3, depriving Syria of transit royalties – even if it was only for the remaining 150–200 thousand barrels a day – was one way of reducing its potency in Lebanon. Nonetheless, the construction of the 'strategic' pipeline was primarily motivated by economic considerations and in order to ensure Iraq's independence.

Syria estimated its loss at about US $272 million for the current year, including the losses from the discontinued supply with Iraqi oil at preferential prices.[134] In terms of the budget the Syrian government had planned for 1976, which was to total the equivalent of US $4,507 million, this meant a loss of some 6.03 per cent.[135]

Only in early 1981 did Iraq reverse its decision and, on 25 February, start again to pump oil to the Mediterranean. Not long afterwards, however, the pipeline was closed again, this time by Syria, which thus intended to support its new ally Iran against Iraq in the so-called Gulf War.

Returning to 1976, the mutual accusations to which the closure of the pipeline gave rise show that each side, despite being motivated by mainly economic reasons, used the matter to increase its own Arab legitimacy, primarily in their competition for regional influence. While Iraq presented its decision as a protest against Syrian action in Lebanon,[136] Syria though admitting its interest in the royalties, claimed that Iraq by disusing the trans-Syrian pipeline deprived Syria of the funds it needed to fight against Israel.[137]

As in the quarrel over the sharing of the Euphrates waters, the outcome of the narrow conflict of interests[138] seemed to reinforce the loser's determination to fight out the struggle over regional hegemony. Thus it was not regional competition that caused the conflict of interests, but the conflict of interests that became an additional cause of the conflict over regional influence. However, the termination of Iraqi oil exports via Syria in April 1976 is the last genuine narrow conflict of interests in Syro-Iraqi relations to date; all subsequent rows over resources have been manifestations of the overriding competition for regional influence.

*Hostilities and their limits*

*Subversion*

While there was little or no proof that Syria or Iraq were involved in terrorists activities, both granted some support to oppositional forces in the neighbouring country. Syria continued to support the PUK created in 1975,[139] while it continued to be at odds with the KDP. At the same time the pro-Syrian Iraqi Ba'th, already weakened in the preceding phase, now received a further blow when the second attempt on the life of its principal figure, Ahmad al-'Azzawi, succeeded on 10 July 1976. Though blamed on the Iraqis, the assassination according to other sources was perpetrated by the Syrian regime itself. In contrast, the pro-Iraqi Ba'this in Syria apparently expanded, though modestly, due to the support of Ba'this opposed to Asad's policy in Lebanon.[140] Massive arrests of civilian and military party members critical of the intervention in Lebanon occurred in March[141] or in April 1976,[142] but it is not known how many of those arrested were actually sympathetic towards the regime in Iraq.

*Troop concentrations*

Soon after Syria launched its June offensive in Lebanon, Iraq started to move troops to the border with Syria.[143] On 8 June the Iraqi Foreign Ministry, according to its own version, informed Syria that Iraq would dispatch troops to the Syro-Iraqi border. At the same time it expressed its hope that Syria would allow these troops to pass through its territory and proceed to the front line in order to liberate the Golan and eventually Palestine.[144] Baghdad claimed that Syria had agreed to the entry of Iraqi troops, and was to renounce the UN Security Council resolutions 242 and 338 and thus meet the Iraqi requirements for establishing a common Arab front together with Libya, Algeria and the PLO (on this front, see p. 110).[145]

On 17 June Iraq announced that yet another army unit was on its way to the border, and again it alleged that an agreement had been reached with Damascus under the terms of which a common northern front would be established and Syria would reject the UN Security Council resolutions 242 and 338.[146] Five days later, on 22 June, Syria presented two alleged Iraqi defectors, who claimed that Iraq had stationed three divisions in the Uwaynat area[147] not far from the Karatshuk oilfields in the very north of Syria and that they planned to attack Syria.[148]

The Iraqi troops camped near the border till November 1976[149] when Syrian troops entered Beirut. When this happened Iraq could no longer reasonably hope that its pressure on Syria would prevent the latter from pursuing its 'pacification' of Lebanon. Consequently Iraq withdrew its troops from the Syrian border. Syria then withdrew its own troops[150] which it had sent to the border as soon as it had become aware of the Iraqi troop movements.[151] According to one well-informed Syrian source, however, Iraq had sent its troops to the border in June in a tacit understanding with Asad to thwart a coup attempt in Syria. This coup was allegedly planned by officers hostile to Asad's decision to send the regular army into Lebanon and in part to be carried out by the very units then sent to the Iraqi border.[152] This is not implausible as Baghdad's Arab legitimacy would have suffered from a Syrian regime that sided with the Palestinians and the Lebanese anti-status quo forces.

*Diplomatic relations, military and party contacts*

Despite the return of tension in December 1975 and the continuous degradation of bilateral relations thereafter, diplomatic relations did not deteriorate in this phase. To some extent there was also such continuity in general contacts between the inhabitants of the two countries as well as in the domains of technical and economic co-operation where some of the improvements brought about during the thaw of October and November 1975 seemed to survive. There were no rumours about official contacts at military and party levels, with the possible exception of tacit Iraqi support for Asad in his thwarting of a *coup d'état* in early June 1976.

This second phase of the post-Algiers period in Syro-Iraqi relations came to an end with Syria's second offensive against the anti-status quo forces in Lebanon, starting in late September 1976. The Iraqi side correctly interpreted this offensive as the final stage in imposing Syrian overlordship on that country and accordingly stepped up verbal as well as non-verbal action to make Syria pay the highest possible price for this new regional acquisition, and if possible to make it lose or abandon it.

### September 1976–autumn 1978: the fierce fight from Syria's victory in Lebanon to its defeat at Camp David

Things came to a breaking point on 22 September when Damascus made it publicly known that it was determined to crush the opponents of the still fragile *pax siriana*. This threat to the anti-status quo forces in Lebanon, quickly followed by their defeat, was also a threat and a defeat for Iraq as it enhanced Syrian influence in Lebanon and ultimately on the PLO. In terms of regional influence, any such gain for Syria was a loss for Iraq. And indeed, Iraq's reaction was strong and violent.

Tension came to a head again in February 1977 when Iraq blamed Syria for the serious riots that had broken out in the holy cities of Karbala' and Najaf during the 'Ashura celebrations. Open conflict, however, continued throughout this phase and was interrupted by a transitory and limited thaw only in late November 1977 after Sadat had travelled to Jerusalem. The circumstances under which this modest *détente* materialized were similar to those prevailing in summer and autumn 1975, as well as in late spring 1976, with the noteworthy difference, however, that this time it was Syria that sought the *rapprochement* and not Iraq. But since Iraq, like Syria in the earlier attempts, refused to accept the soliciting party's terms, the reconciliation failed once again, and after two months of mutual restraint bilateral relations deteriorated. Tension further heightened during summer 1978 when intensive contacts between the United States, Egypt and Israel showed that an Egyptian–Israeli agreement was in the air. The conflict developed into a war of succession with both sides attempting to assume Egypt's leading role in Arab politics. However, Syria's position was far weaker than Iraq's since an Egyptian agreement with Israel, though theoretically enabling Syria to assume this role, at the same time made it extremely vulnerable in regard to Israel. This 'imbalance of strength' increased with the Camp David accords which left Syria more vulnerable than ever, and consequently led to the most far-reaching, though purely tactical, *rapprochement* between the two sides yet.

With the exception of the brief *détente* in late 1977 and early 1978 relations were more violent than in any other period before. In addition to the propaganda campaigns, merciless terrorist attacks now marked the conflict. Although it seems that both sides instigated or sponsored such action, Iraq seems to have done so far more efficiently than Syria.

## *Verbal attacks and worse*

### *Iraqi propaganda, subversion and terrorist involvement*

Iraqi propaganda had intensified with the growing tension in Lebanon before Syria's ultimatum to the Palestinians. Yet, it basically repeated old accusations: Syria was held to be guilty of 'capitulationism' and 'defeatism', of betraying the Arab or Palestine cause, and of collaboration with imperialism – a charge not always levelled in previous times and hence indicating the acidity of the conflict.

Shortly after Syria had made its ultimatum to the Palestinians on 22 September, Iraqi-supported terrorists launched their first major action inside Syria. On 26 September four *fida'iyun* of the 'Black June' organization which had its headquarters in Iraq occupied the Semiramis Hotel in central Damascus and took a number of hostages. They demanded the release of several fellow *fida'iyun* imprisoned in Syria and a radical change in Syria's policy in Lebanon.[153] Not long after the Semiramis action, 'Black June' on 11 October 1976 staged almost simultaneous attacks on the Syrian embassies in Rome and Islamabad, and on 1 December the organization claimed responsibility for an unsuccessful attempt on the life of the Syrian Foreign Minister Khaddam.

Soon and for almost a year assassination attempts and other terrorist acts became a frequent and increasingly disquieting feature of Syrian political life.[154] After a second attempt on the

life of Khaddam on 25 October 1977, while he was on a visit
to Abu Dhabi, there was a pause in terrorism till the end of
January 1978 while secret mediation and negotiations between
the two countries went on (see pp. 131ff.) But when these failed,
assassinations and bomb attacks quickly resurged. As earlier,
explosions mainly occurred in or in front of government and
party buildings, and the victims of assassination attempts were
all persons closely associated with the regime or representing it,
and they were almost exclusively 'Alawis.[155] Most of these acts
after autumn 1976 were perpetrated by Syria's Islamic opposition,
often incorrectly lumped together as Muslim Brothers (al-Ikhwan
al-muslimun) who at that time emerged as the chief internal
challenge to the regime. Expressing the economic grievances of
parts of the population as well as wider discontent and problems
of political participation, the Islamic opposition received weapons
and financial assistance from the Iraqi regime. But only the
recrudescence and extreme intensification of terrorism in spring
and summer 1978 seemed to be directly the work of the Iraqi
regime, which wanted to pressurize Syria into an alliance when
it became very clear that Egypt intended to reach an agreement
with Israel.

When Syria put its ultimatum to the Palestinians Iraq also stepped
up its propaganda campaign, which quite naturally reached its first
apex during Syria's second offensive in Lebanon. Propaganda
warfare also intensified in February 1978, during the incidents
in Karbala'[156] and Najaf, and again in the summer of the same
year. As previously, the seriousness of the conflict was thrown into
relief by the interventions of high-ranking regime representatives,
among them President Bakr,[157] and by the raising of the issue on
anniversaries celebrated by the regime.[158]

Also a radio station was set up that broadcast in the name of the
Syrian opposition, or part of it. This station, the Voice of Arab Syria
(Sawt Suria al-'arabiyya), began transmissions on 26 October 1976,
the very day the Cairo summit legalizing Syrian military presence
in Lebanon was concluded,[159] and thus about a month later the
Syrian regime had started a programme for the Iraqi opposition.
The station repeatedly broadcast calls to the Syrian people to
overthrow their present regime, and to the Lebanese people to
rise against the Syrian invaders.[160]

However, each time terrorist acts were reported from Syria,
Baghdad persistently denied being involved, though it gave wide
publicity to them and even justified them.[161]

Instead of admitting its own involvement in the violent resistance
within Syria, Iraq presented itself as a victim of terrorism organized
by the regime in Damascus.

An intelligence agent of the Damascus regime on television here last night made known important information about the role of Syrian Intelligence in carrying out sabotage operations and assassinations in Iraq with the help of the Syrian Embassy in Baghdad. A Syrian intelligence agent, Captain 'Izz ad-Din Wahdan, disclosed the role of Syrian intelligence in creating the Lebanese crisis and in kidnapping and assassinating Lebanese and Syrian politicians exiled in Lebanon. He also disclosed the role of the branch of Syrian Intelligence in Kuwait, where there is a sizeable Palestinian presence, in collecting information about the Palestine rejection front, spreading lies about events so as to serve the liquidation plot and masterminding sabotage operations against Iraq.

The agent admitted that he entered Iraq to carry out sabotage operations against Government establishments and utilities and to assassinate a number of Syrian political refugees in Iraq . . . He said that acting against the revolution in Iraq is one of the main objectives of the Damascus regime . . . The agent also said that the Syrian regime had assassinated the former Syrian Interior Minister, Major General Muhammad 'Umran.[162]

Iraq later continued to present itself as one of the prime targets of Syrian terrorism and subversion, and generally explained this Syrian choice by referring to itself as the incarnation of Arab legitimacy. So when on 14 December 1976 a bomb exploded at Baghdad airport killing at least three persons and injuring many others, the incident was blamed on Syria.[163] And after the 'hired gangs' of imperialism had been held responsible for the unrest in the holy cities of Karbala' and Najaf on 5 and 6 February 1977,[164] during the Shi'i 'Ashura celebrations the authorities, according to their own version, on 7 February arrested a Syrian soldier named 'Ali al-Na'na', allegedly in the act of planting a bag with ten kilos of explosive in the courtyard of the Husayniyya in Karbala'. Except for the short period of December 1977 and January 1978 similar incidents were reported with breath-taking frequency throughout these two years,[165] including, on several occasions, alleged Syrian support for a 'defunct agent pocket',[166] as Kurdish resistant groups were called.

Generally Iraq presented these subversive and terrorist activities as illustrations of Syria's acts against the 'Arab people'[167] or plots against the 'Arab national cause'.[168] Only on rare occasions did Iraq still claim that Syria sought to damage specifically Iraqi interests. When Syria was accused of sabotage against economic installations in Iraq, it was accused of doing this in order to prevent Iraq from effectively defending the Arab cause. Thus Iraqi propaganda in this respect began to resemble Syrian propaganda.

However, although Iraq boasted of being a target, or the prime target, of Syrian terrorist activities, it did not pretend to be its only victim. Thus according to Baghdad Syrian terrorism abroad was complemented by large-scale arrests, torture and the execution of political prisoners at home. 'The regime of Hafiz al-Asad', it was claimed for instance 'sends its agents and intelligence men to persecute Arab strugglers. These agents have orders to assassinate or abduct such strugglers, who are added to the thousands of persons detained without trial and who are suffering the worst kind of psychological and physical torture.'[169] Syrian terror and repression in Lebanon were worse than in Syria itself. In Lebanon, Syrian forces or agents were reported to have launched 'vile attacks' on Palestinians,[170] and of having assassinated Kamal Junblatt,[171] the Druze leader, and others.

Thus Syria, in Iraq's description controlled a highly developed terrorist apparatus that was spreading its tentacles over the whole Middle East, and which received its orders from the highest echelons of the regime. Its final aim was to implement the 'liquidation plot against the Palestinian revolution', in connivance with Zionism and US imperialism, whose spies it protected. As Bakr once succinctly put it,

> The operation of slaying the nationalist forces and the Palestinian resistance in Lebanon is only one major link in the chain of the imperialist-Zionist liquidation scheme being implemented by the renegade Syrian regime, which has transformed itself into a handy tool in the hands of its masters in order to achieve their evil intentions of dismembering fraternal Lebanon and plotting against its Arabism.[172]

Similar comments identifying Syria with Zionism and US imperialism accompanied the visits to Syria by the US Secretary of State Cyrus Vance in February and August 1977, the assassination of Kamal Junblatt in March 1977, and Asad's meeting with President Carter in Geneva in May 1977. These somewhat abstract accusations were paralleled by more concrete statements about the nature of the ties cementing Syro-American friendship. In March and again in September 1977 it was revealed and reasserted:

> that Rifa'at al-Asad was the one who received the bribe offered by the CIA and handed [it] over to his brother, the president of the Syrian regime. The bribe amounted to [US $12] million. It is worth mentioning that the CIA made it clear that it is offering these bribes for services rendered by its

agents in the interest of what is called the security of the United States.[173]

Terrorism, repression, the renewal of the UNDOF mandate, (in November 1976 and again in May 1977), contacts with the United States, and bribery from the CIA according to Iraqi propaganda illustrated that the Syrian regime was a servant of imperialism and served the chief aim of imperialism in the Middle East: namely, the 'peaceful settlement' of the Arab–Israeli conflict.[174] The charge of Syria's readiness to 'settle' the conflict with Israel became more prominent after Sadat's visit to Jerusalem in November 1977.[175] Responsibility for this visit, it was even claimed, lay with Damascus as 'the Arab reactionaries guided by the renegade regime in Damascus . . . have used him [i.e. Sadat] as a minesweeper on the road to treason.'[176]

In a detailed 'analysis' of Syro-Iraqi relations following the collapse of the winter *rapprochement* in 1977–8, the Iraqi *al-Thawra* presented Syria's 'policy of settlement' as the main cause of the conflict between the two regimes; the second most important was the 'party aspect' which, however, was not elaborated on. The author of this analysis denied that Iraq attempted to outbid Syria as Syria claimed. Iraq, he wrote, merely took a 'principled stand' in the defence of the Arab cause. This stand it had not adopted to obtain benefits for itself. Rather it was a policy of sacrifice that entailed a whole bunch of disadvantages such as the Euphrates issue, the pipeline dispute of 1972–3, and the temporary interruption of Iraqi imports and exports through Syria.[177] Syria's search for an accommodation with Israel, Baghdad stressed, precluded moreover the dispatch of Iraqi troops to the Golan that Damascus had presumably asked for during the contacts in December and January.[178]

Minor themes in Iraqi propaganda against Syria were economic mismanagement,[179] widespread corruption,[180] and, more significantly, infighting among members of the regime itself.[181] But while in Syrian propaganda against Iraq the subject of infighting served primarily to show what a base and quarrelsome lot the rulers of the neighbouring country were, in Iraqi propaganda this aspect only played a secondary role. The main aim of pointing to such internal wrangling was to make the rival regime appear fissured, shaky and weak and, by showing its action was contested from inside, to further strip it of legitimacy. Similar delegitimizing intentions were behind the charges of corruption and economic incompetence.

Towards the end of this third phase of the post-Algiers period the Iraqi side paid back in kind Syrian talk of the 'Takriti tribal regime' by pointing to the power of the Asad family in Syria,[182]

which was soon referred to as the 'Asad family regime'.[183] Iraqi
reports for instance deplored the low standard of the Syrian armed
forces, imputing that their main *raison d'être* was to keep the 'Asad
family' in power. For this reason, the reports also said, two more
or less private parallel 'armies' had been set up. Foremost among
them were the Defence Brigades Saraya al-Difa of Rif'at al-Asad.
And yet another, third parallel army was being created.[184] Defining
the Syrian regime as a 'family regime' insinuated, of course, that it
could not possibly represent wider Arab interests.

### Syrian propaganda, subversion and terrorist involvement

Syrian propaganda markedly intensified during September 1976,
and also reflected the developments in Lebanon and their corollaries. After the relevance of this issue had somewhat subsided
by the end of the year, anti-Iraqi campaigns reached new heights
during February and March 1977. Their intensity subsequently
returned to a 'normal' but nonetheless elevated level. There it
remained more or less, except for a few articles published in June
in which the Syrian press called for an improvement in relations
with Iraq. These articles followed the election victory of the Likud
bloc in Israel, which Syria no doubt saw as a new threat. However,
Iraq at that time did not seem to react to the message.

The more tangible attempt to iron out differences with Iraq,
made in November 1977 and December 1978 (see pp. 131 ff.),
then led also to a marked improvement. Though it failed and
propaganda returned to its previous level, Asad as late as in
May 1978 apparently had not abandoned all hope of anti-Israeli
co-operation with Iraq.[185] Till this hope at least transiently
materialized after Camp David, however, yet another wave of
vitriolic verbal warfare, starting in summer 1978, had to run its
course.

In the struggle over Lebanon that opened this new phase of the
conflict, Syria occupied the stronger position and unlike Iraq did
not have to try to oppose a military intervention with the sheer
force of words. But from late September 1976 terrorist attacks
began to shake the country. These were in most cases blamed on
Iraq, who was said to carry them out directly or in collaboration
with other forces hostile to the Syrian regime. Syrian wrath against
Baghdad was unleashed after each of the four attacks carried out
in autumn 1976 by the Black June organization. In early January
1977 the Supreme State Security Court in Damascus sentenced
to death a group of 'Iraqi criminals' found guilty of having
planted explosive charges in a number of 'populated areas' in
Damascus and Aleppo.[186] Iraq was also held responsible for

most of the subsequent and increasingly frequent bomb blasts and assassinations;[187] for instance for the murder in February 1977 of Muhammad al-Fadil, a prominent 'Alawi Ba'thi and the president of Damascus University.[188] As in the case of Ahmad al-'Azzawi, however, there were indications that Fadil was assassinated by forces loyal to his 'Alawi rival Rif'at al-Asad.[189] In March 1977 Saddam Husayn was even reported to be heading a special office in charge of the organization of terrorist activities in Syria.[190]

In July a number of explosions in public building, in their environs or in the proximity of the homes of prominent officials or members of the ruling group again were blamed on Iraq. In the same vein 'Abd al-Halim Khaddam, after escaping another attempt on his life while on an official visit to Abu Dhabi, accused Iraq of having 'teleguided' the action 'which only serves Israel'.[191] Such charges continued till the end of November 1977[192] when terrorist activities in Syria came to a temporary halt. Both were resumed after January 1978 when the secret bilateral contacts did not lead to any tangible results, thus strongly indicating Iraqi involvement.

Terrorism then escalated sharply.[193] Though perhaps it was chiefly due to internal causes, it seems that this escalation was not unconnected to the regional developments that were then leading to the Camp David accords. The last Iraqi terrorist plot of the 1976–8 season Syria claimed to have discovered on 17 September 1978, the very day on which the Camp David negotiations were concluded.[194]

Though Syrian accusations varied somewhat according to circumstances, they may be hypostasized by a broadcast comment on the explosion in front of the Amiriyya, the air force headquarters close to the offices of the Regional Command, on 4 July 1977:

> The criminal plan of the rulers in Baghdad was nothing but a cowardly attempt which can only be described as an ugly criminal operation . . . The crimes can be explained as attempts to quench the thirst of the rulers of Baghdad for more Arab blood. The Takriti rulers have revealed their true identity . . . If by these criminal acts the revengeful Takriti clique hopes to disrupt the national and progressive regime in Syria by diverting attention from the main battle with the Zionist enemy and its allies in the interest of insignificant or secondary disputes . . . then our steadfast country is determined to head off every revengeful enemy who places itself in the service of the Zionist and imperialist plots.[195]

Like Iraq, Syria denied any involvement in terrorist activities that were carried out in the neighbouring country. Nothing definite can be asserted about the veracity of these denials, any more than about Iraqi denials. But apart from the bomb blast at Baghdad airport on 14 December 1976 there is indeed little evidence of Syrian involvement.

Easier to verify is Syrian support for part of the Iraqi opposition. Partly confirming Iraqi accusations, independent sources hold that Syria provided the Patriotic Union of Kurdistan (PUK) with money as well as with weapons, and that members of the PUK repeatedly, though not very frequently, infiltrated Iraq from Syria. However, such actions from Syrian territory were extremely complicated because not only did Iraq heavily guard its border but also the PUK bases in Kurdistan could only be reached after crossing territory controlled by the Kurdish Democratic Party (KDP). The KDP was far from friendly towards the PUK and in the period from 1975 till 1979 did not co-operate with the Syrian regime. Apart from the PUK, the Syrian regime also supported the rather tiny Democratic Union of Kurdistan founded in 1976 by 'Ali al-Sinjaghi.[196] Any aid, however, was apparently suspended during December 1977 and January 1978.[197]

Syria did not only denounce the Iraqi regime's lack of Arab legitimacy in statements relating to terrorist events. Rather, Arab legitimacy – as in Iraqi propaganda – was the underlying theme of most of the charges levelled against the neighbouring regime. Almost the mirror image of Iraqi propaganda, the Syrian side proclaimed that all Iraqi evils sprang from the regime's collaboration with 'imperialism'. Except for late 1977 and early 1978, hardly a day passed without news and comments on 'the chartered role of the treacherous Iraqi stand', trying 'to undermine Syria's steadfastness';[198] Iraqi participation in imperialist 'plots';[199] or the 'evasion of national responsibility', by which Iraq 'placed itself in one trench with the forces hostile to the Arab struggles'.[200]

Several issues were currently referred to in order to illustrate more concretely Iraq's 'treacherous' stands. Iraq's role in Lebanon was one of them. This role, it was claimed, at the same time revealed Iraq's attitude towards the Palestinians:

> It is a known fact that this deviationist bloody regime is still squandering funds to foment sedition . . . for the continuation of the massacre in Lebanon in order to disunite the Arab ranks and to drive the Palestinian Resistance towards pitfalls which will keep it away from its goals and ultimately lead to its downfall and liquidation.[201]

Allegedly also the outlets Baghdad chose for its oil exports revealed its basic hostility towards Arab interests. Syrian statements on oil affairs sometimes even went so far as to praise the nationalization of the Iraq Petroleum Company as a Syrian rather than as an Iraqi success:

> The plot against Syria and its steadfast revolution, which is confronting the attempts to liquidate the Arab cause and the Palestine question, is still going on . . . The fascist Tikriti tribal regime in Iraq has laid the Kirkuk–Mediterranean pipeline across Turkey in order to deprive Syria of its annual revenues . . . It goes without saying that this will diminish our chances to prepare ourselves well for the confrontation battle with the Zionist enemy and his allies . . . If we ask ourselves about the reasons for the blind Tikriti spite against Syria . . . we find that the cause is the successful experiment by Syria, in its capacity as one of the Third World countries in making oil a national industry . . . It suffices to say that the nationalization experiment of the Iraqi oil company would not have succeeded had not Syria given its complete support.[202]

More than ever these unpatriotic and 'treacherous' policies pursued by the Iraqi regime now were related to the non-representative and undemocratic nature of the 'Takriti clique'.[203] Also the reference to its 'tribal' character, already fashionable in 1973 and in May and June 1975, and in some way the match of Iraqi talk about the Syrian 'family regime', now made an extremely successful come-back and remained one of the watchwords of Syrian anti-Iraqi propaganda till its temporary end in October 1978.[204] These tribal features of the Iraqi regime were often compared to the Arab character of 'steadfast'[205] Syria, the 'strong homeland of the Arabs'.[206]

Tribalism stood for backwardness, internecine fights, and quarrels that had so often opposed Arabs to Arabs. It could in no way be reconciled with claims to be nationalist or even 'progressive'. *A fortiori* tribalism contradicted the declared aims of the Ba'th Party as expressed in the constitution of 1947:

> National ties are the only ties within the Arab state. They guarantee harmony between its citizens, their unity in the crucible of a single nation, and protection against ideological (*madhhabi*), religious (*ta'ifi*), tribal (*qabali*), racial and regional solidarities (*'asabiyyat*).[207]

In Damascus it was more important to demolish the Arab legitimacy of Baghdad than its Ba'thi credentials, and so divert attention from the monopolization of power in Syria by 'Alawis that from 1976 on had led to growing resentment. To further discredit the regime in Baghdad, 'bloody infights' were

reported between its different factions, especially those led by
Saddam Husayn and Ahmad Hasan al-Bakr.[208]

The non-representative character and nature of the Iraqi regime
together with its anti-nationalist policies, presented as not unrelated to its very nature, were described as the causes of unrest
among the people and military, and of merciless repression, carried
out by the regime in response to or in anticipation of such unrest.
Thus the incidents in Karbala' and Najaf, in February 1977,
according to Syrian sources were caused not by a Syrian agent but
by political executions in Baghdad.[209] Presumably in an attempt to
divert attention from the claims of the increasingly active *Ikhwan*
in Syria the Iraqi authorities were then accused of 'preventing Iraqi
citizens from performing their religious rites in those holy places
last week and in closing the mosques in An-Najaf and Karbala' as
a result of the surge in the popular current against the terrorist rule
of the Tikritis and their unjustified repression of the people.'[210]

Syrian propaganda did not spare the details on torture practices
either. In one instance 'the clique of the Takriti regime' was
reported to have

> perpetrated a terrible mass massacre . . . in Nazi style . . .
> by decomposing [the victims] with acid after they were
> murdered in torture dungeons in which the henchmen of
> the tribal regime practise their savage liquidation acts against
> honourable Iraqi citizens who oppose their regime and stand
> against their domination and treacherous policies.[211]

But opposition was growing and 'The Iraqi National Group (*Al-
tajammu' al-watani al-'iraqi*) . . . urged the Iraqi masses to act to
topple the family regime in Baghdad.'[212] The mere reporting of
opposition calls to overthrow the regime was then quickly followed
by genuine Syrian calls on the Iraqi people to rally around the
Tajammu' and thus 'free Iraq'.[213]

From mid-1978 on, when the propaganda war intensified even
more, Syrian media repeatedly predicted – and welcomed in
advance - outbursts of popular wrath: 'The recent escalation of
terror is the sign of an imminent popular uprising which we expect
to usher in a new era in fraternal Iraq.'[214] In addition to the
previous charges such as the dismissal or arrest of officers,[215] Syrian
propaganda now almost continuously reported on 'campaigns of
terror', 'missing persons' and 'mysterious murders' in Iraq.[216]
Rather originally it once stated that 'If one counts the number
of people held in the Iraqi prisons in the Takriti era, one finds
that it exceeds even the number of people detained in the days
of Nuri al-Sa'id and the Regent 'Abd al-Ilah.'[217] In line with the
charges that Iraqi policy was directed against the interests of the

Palestinians, the regime in Baghdad was also accused of 'campaigns to liquidate PLO representatives'[218]

Like high-ranking Iraqi regime representatives, their Syrian counterparts did not hesitate to participate in person in the war of words. On the anniversary of the 23 February movement in 1977 for instance the National Command member Bakr Yasin levelled serious accusations against the Iraqi regime. But high-ranking officials participated in the debate on other occasions too, for instance the Defence Minister, Mustafa Tlas, in his speech on 28 July 1977.

## The motives behind the propagandistic choices

Syrian and Iraqi propaganda concerning Arab legitimacy first of all articulated the bilateral competition over regional influence, since it increased either when the one or the other side attempted to enhance its regional position – as Syria did in Lebanon; or at moments that appeared propitious for such attempts, such as with the developments in the Egyptian–Israeli 'peace process' which Iraq, due to persisting Syro-Egyptian bonds, could exploit to compromise Syria. As far as the argument served this regional competition, it was addressed on the one hand to a non-Syrian and non-Iraqi audience, to groups liable to exert pressure on other Arab regimes or directly to these regimes, either to tout for their support or to intimidate them; on the other hand it was designed to appeal to the people in the respective neighbouring country, to encourage them to increase their opposition to their regime and thus weaken it, not only internally but also in the competition for regional influence. However, weakening the competitor regime was not intended to lead to direct domination over that country, as both sides seem to have been aware that this enterprise would almost certainly fail.

The claim to sole Arab legitimacy, as in previous periods, also served to enhance the internal legitimacy of the claimant. The need to justify policy choices was extremely acute in Syria. The intervention in Lebanon was controversial in the party and in the country at large, particularly from the moment the regime shifted its support to the pro-status quo forces. Even party dignitaries and army officers criticized the intervention. The extent of internal opposition may moreover be guaged from Asad's speech on 20 July 1976,[219] which attempted to explain and justify the action and in this was unprecedented. Thus the intensification of propaganda against Iraq, at the time of the two offensives in Lebanon in June–July and in September 1976, was to a great extent intended for home consumption.

In the second half of 1976 and especially towards its close the Syrian economy slowed down significantly, and the results of the slump were felt by an increasing section of the population.[220] The balance of payments by the end of the year showed a heavy deficit,[221] and in 1977 economic growth even declined, by some 2 per cent overall and in the commodities section by 9 per cent.[222] From that time on the Syrian economy never really recovered, and in the 1980s the situation further deteriorated. Among those most concerned were the conservative and mainly Sunni *petite bourgeoisie* – also referred to as the bazaar bourgeoisie – which already in the past had been a fertile ground for the Muslim Brothers or other Islamic fundamentalist groups.[223] The economic decline probably contributed more to the rapid increase in terrorist activities during the second half of 1976 than other factors, such as the intervention in Lebanon or the actual resentment of 'Alawi domination, in terms of which opposition was generally couched;[224] Iraqi involvement, though undeniable, largely depended on these primarily Syrian factors. The intervention in Lebanon, however, in turn reinforced the economic crisis. While the purely military costs of the intervention were estimated at some US $80 million per month,[225] the Arab subsidy for the so-called Arab Deterrent Force in Lebanon, that had been decided at the Cairo summit, only amounted to US $180 million annually.[226]

In comparison to Syria, the internal and economic situation in Iraq was excellent. Oil revenue continued to grow, and large sections of the population, though to very different degrees, drew benefit from this development.[227] Nonetheless, the rapid economic growth also led to the redistribution of wealth and prestige and to social dislocation.[228] The solace provided by ideology under these circumstances served to becalm the less fortunate. Finally, reference to Arab legitimacy as in Syria, also sometimes served to embellish egotistic state or regime interests.

The theme of Ba'thi legitimacy continued to play a minor role in the propaganda of both sides.[229] Iraqi treatment of this matter was mainly limited to dispersed and irregular references to the 'renegades of Ba'thism'.[230] There were also a few statements, such as the previously mentioned analysis in *al-Thawra*, which affirmed that there was a 'party aspect' to Syro-Iraqi relations.[231] However, the issue was never enlarged upon. Even President Bakr's interview on the occasion of the party's anniversary in 1977 did not contain a single remark about the matter.[232]

In Syrian propaganda as well, it seemed that the issue no longer retained much importance. Remarks were mostly veiled and hardly more explicit than the assertion by the NC member

Bakr Yasin that: 'The right-wing mentality in the Party conspired with the Right and the enemies outside the Party. The 8th February Revolution in Iraq was the victim of that plotting, which contributed to the success of the ill-omened apostate coup on 18th November 1963.' The 18 November 1963 coup, Yasin added, was then 'perpetuated' by the 17 July 1968 'coup', thus implicity denying the Iraqi version of the July Revolution of 1968.[233]

## The negative effects on economic and technical relations

Relations in this phase deteriorated so far that even mutually beneficial co-operation in technical and economic matters was abandoned. Both sides now pursued a policy of causing maximum damage to the other – even at the price of disadvantages to themselves. In place of co-operation sanctions were imposed, and there was a reduction in economic interdependence. No agreement on economic or technical co-operation was made between the two sides, not even to continue existing schemes.

First of all Iraq in this phase could bolster its independence vis-à-vis Syria regarding oil exports. With the completion of the trans-Turkish pipeline export capacity from the northern oilfields was restored to its level prior to the closure of the trans-Syrian pipeline in April 1976, even if this happened more slowly than expected. Indeed, the trans-Turkish pipeline was officially opened on 3 January 1977, but for a variety of reasons lifting at Dörtyol was delayed till May or June.[234] According to figures released in January the capacity was to reach 25 million tons a year in 1978 and 1979 and then be raised to 30 million in 1980 and to 35 million in 1983.[235] This meant that in 1977 exports from the northern oilfields could not reach their potential maximum level of April 1976, even if the capacity of the 'strategic' pipeline had by then already been increased to the 1 million barrels a day that had been projected.

Another unfavourable aspect for Iraq was that in 1976 ten of the 15 million tons of throughput and in subsequent years some 40 per cent had to be sold to Turkey below the market price.[236] And though royalties received by Turkey were only US $0.39 per barrel in 1977,[237] and thus still lower than those obtained by Syria in 1973, Kirkuk oil lifted at Dörtyol was nonetheless 66 per cent more expensive than the same oil from Faw on the Gulf.[238]

But already on 9 July 1977 it was decided to increase the capacity of the trans-Turkish pipeline. Moreover, the two sides agreed on linking their countries through a new railway line, also bypassing Syria, providing additional transit facilities for Iraq, and expanding the port of Iskanderun, which was in open defiance of Syrian claims on this part of Turkey.

Syria, for its part, had already on 2 December 1976 closed all its ports and frontiers to the transit of goods to or from Iraq;[239] only the Turkish–Iraqi railway line which passed a short distance through Syrian territory was still exempted from this measure, manifestly taken in response to the attempted assassination of Khaddam the day before. Again in reply to alleged Iraqi involvement in terrorist activities, this time within Syria, Damascus about a year later, on 10 November 1977, closed its border with Iraq.[240] This measure, however, was aimed at disrupting contacts between the two countries in general, not only to curb terrorist activities within Syria, but also the spread of subversive news. About a week later the Turkish–Iraqi railway line was closed first for goods on 16 November, and then for passengers on 19 November 1977.[241] The closure came on the very day on which Sadat arrived in Jerusalem. Rather curiously, however, a day later, on 20 November, Asad sent a message to Bakr attempting to end or ease the conflict between their two regimes. Apparently the railway line was temporarily reopened during the bilateral contacts in late 1977 and early 1978.[242] When referred to by the media of either side, these sanctions and other measures to reduce economic co-operation were more often than not linked to the overriding argument over Arab legitimacy.

### Relations and contacts at the military and party levels

The exacerbation of the conflict quite naturally continued to prevent the two sides from co-operating in military and party matters. However, there was one remarkable exception to that rule. During Israel's invasion of South Lebanon Damascus according to its own reports, and apparently confirmed by other sources, at Baghdad's request allowed a unit of Iraqi volunteers to cross Syrian territory on its way to Lebanon. Why it did so remains a mystery, but presumably it was part of the deal struck at the Riyadh and Cairo summits in autumn 1976 where Syria had to accept some conditions in exchange for Arab endorsement of its presence in Lebanon.

More typical of the situation after summer 1976 was the use of military strength to thwart, embarrass or weaken the other side. It must be stressed, however, that no fighting took place at the border, except perhaps for a minor incident mentioned by Iraq.[243] Iraq was reported to have granted military support to Syria's adversaries in Lebanon and, at an unspecified date in 1976, to have assisted them with a smaller troop contingent, dispatched by air or sea.[244] In December 1976, after Syrian troops had entered Beirut, they occupied a number of newspaper offices in the Lebanese capital, among them obviously the pro-Iraqi ones, but also others.[245] During the second half of 1976 or first half of 1977 at least one open clash occurred in Lebanon between the pro-Iraqi Arab Liberation Front and the Syrian al-Sa'iqa.[246]

At the party level the policy of no-contact was continued as previously, except of course for the secret messages and talks of December 1977 and January 1978 which, however, were restricted to the party leaders. Ba'this who sympathized with the 'other side' continued to be arrested – a policy that Syria could now extend to Lebanon, as in December 1976.[247]

### Diplomatic relations

Again the deterioration also affected diplomatic relations. On 3 November 1976 Iraq recalled its chargé d'affaires from Damascus in protest against Syria's policy in Lebanon.[248] On 8 September 1977 a first secretary of the Syrian embassy in Baghdad was declared *persona non grata*, thus being the first official of such rank expelled from one of the two countries since 1968. But on 22 October Iraq filled the post of ambassador to Syria, vacant since February 1975. Not even the attempt on Khaddam's life three days later, blamed on the Iraqis, prevented the incumbent from arriving in Damascus on 30 October.[249] But cold water again followed hot, and on 22 August 1978 Iraq expelled the Syrian counsellor for alleged terrorist involvement.

### The transitory rapprochement from November 1977 to January 1978 and its collapse

A transitory respite came about in late November 1977 and ended in late January 1978. Apparently it was initiated by a letter that Asad wrote to Bakr on 20 November,[250] the day on which Sadat concluded his controversial visit to Jerusalem – even though as late as 19 November Syria had imposed economic sanctions against Iraq. The letter, in which Asad reportedly asked Bakr to forget the past and open a new page in Syro-Iraqi relations, was taken to Baghdad by the Libyan Prime Minister Jallud[251] who during the following two months continued to offer his good offices to mediate between the two capitals.[252] According to Iraqi sources, on 29 November 1977 Bakr addressed a letter to Syria, Algeria, Libya, South Yemen and the PLO who, like Iraq itself, had all responded positively to a Libyan summit call and were to convene for the Tripoli Conference from 2 to 5 December 1977. As published by the Iraqi media in early February 1978, Bakr's letter began with an analysis of the Arab situation after Sadat's trip to Jerusalem in which he held the Syrian regime co-responsible for Egypt's 'treason':

> To be fraternally frank . . . we believe that the brothers in the Syrian Government shoulder a basic responsibility for the deterioration of the Arab situation to this extent. After the October war they followed the same line as that followed by Sadat, although sometimes differed with him on details and methods of implementation and expression.[253]

To confront such settlement solutions Bakr proposed the establishment of an 'Arab front' comprising Iraq, Libya, Algeria, South Yemen and the PLO, but not Syria, even though its president also received a copy of the letter.

Syria was considered eligible to join the front only after it had withdrawn from Lebanon and rejected the UN Security Council resolutions 242 and 338. To formally set up the front the addressees of the letter were invited to convene in Baghdad on 5 December 1977, and Libya was asked kindly to postpone the Tripoli Conference. The invitation to other Arab heads of state to convene in Baghdad had already been made public in November.[254]

However, Qadhdhafi maintained his invitation to the Tripoli Conference and, as all other parties decided to attend, Iraq had little choice but to go as well. It now took its proposal to Tripoli where it was presented under the title of Front of Steadfastness and Liberation. But Iraq found little support for its insistence that Syria should reject resolutions 242 and 338.[255] The other participants all sided with Syria, some presumably from an understanding that an alliance without a country bordering on Israel would be a rather odd construction. The Iraqi delegation in the end walked out of the conference and Iraq did not sign the final statement which decided on the creation of the Front of Steadfastness and Confrontation (Jabhat al-sumud wa al-tasaddi).

Again according to Iraqi sources published in early February 1978, Bakr at an unspecified date invited the participants of the Tripoli Conference to a follow-up conference in Baghdad from 15 to 20 January 1978. There Iraq apparently intended to resubmit its own more far-reaching proposals.[256] Together with this invitation the Iraqi media published the draft charter for the Front of Steadfastness and Liberation as well as a secret appendix to it.

Apart from securing for Iraq the leading role in Arab politics, Baghdad's initiative also and more specifically aimed at establishing Iraqi supremacy over Syria. This appeared from two provisions of the draft charter: firstly the commitment to the liberation of 'all the occupied Arab territories', and secondly the formation of a 'Supreme Political Command' of the Front, which was to 'adopt the principal decisions in all domains'. According to the secret appendix this body would designate a 'Supreme Military Command' which alone would decide on waging war and concluding cease-fires. Equally unpleasant for Syria, the appendix moreover stipulated the explicit rejection of UN resolutions 242 and 338, the establishment of a joint northern command, and the support in Lebanon of the Palestinians and of the Lebanese Nationalist Movement. This last stipulation was not made more acceptable to Damascus by the severe tutelage the document elsewhere tried to impose on the PLO.[257]

Bakr's messages of 29 November and after the Tripoli Conference, together with the charter and its appendix, reflected two concerns. First, to make Iraq appear the driving force for Arab steadfastness after Sadat's visit to Jerusalem, and thus to rally the 'rejectionist' regimes around Baghdad instead of losing this advantage to Damascus or, perhaps, Tripoli or Algiers. This first aim involved some sort of *rapprochement* with Syria, to control 'access' to the other 'rejectionists'. Secondly, by moving closer to the 'rejectionist' the Iraqi initiative tried to enhance Iraq's relative position *vis-à-vis* Syria itself.

Despite disagreement over how to confront Egypt's policy towards Israel, Syria and Iraq continued to receive the mediators dispatched by Libya, Algeria, South Yemen, certain quarters of the PLO[258] and, according to some sources, even the Soviet Union.[259] Algerian efforts seemed to be more successful than others, and a tripartite meeting of Syria, Iraq and Algeria was scheduled for the end of January.

While these contacts took place behind the scenes, the propaganda warfare was greatly reduced, and terrorism in Syria came to a temporary halt. Syria, for its part, was reported to have suspended its aid for the faction of Jalal al-Talabani,[260] who had become their Kurdish *enfant chéri* in early summer 1975. In January, as a sign of goodwill, Syria even allowed Salah al-Din Bitar, the co-founder with 'Aflaq of the Ba'th Party, to visit Syria from his exile in Paris.[261] Though not actually pro-Iraqi, Bitar had sometimes defended Iraqi policies, but he was first of all a symbol of the party's old 'nationalist' wing, many of whose members had, like 'Aflaq, found shelter in Iraq after 1968. Finally, the railway line from Iraq to Turkey, which passes through Syrian territory, was temporarily reopened.

However, the tripartite meeting on 29 January to which Algeria had invited Syria and Iraq did not take place.[262] The Iraqis at the last minute refused to attend, apparently because the talks were to include a follow-up meeting to the Tripoli Conference[263] from which they had walked out. Yet the final decision to end the *rapprochement* seems to have been taken in Damascus. This could be confirmed by the visit the Iraqi RC member Na'im Haddad paid to Syria on 9 February 1978: he probably represented the only high-ranking visit between the two countries during this phase in a last attempt to prevent the failure of the *rapprochement*.

# 4

# The *Rapprochement* in 1978–1979 or the Continuation of War by Other Means

### *The causes and aims of rapprochement*

A little more than a month after Camp David, Syro-Iraqi relations seemed to have undergone a complete change. The Egyptian–Israeli agreement had apparently induced a swift transition from deep hostility to close co-operation, manifesting itself in the Charter of Joint National Action of 26 October 1978, and in far-reaching projects towards uniting the two countries.

But this volte-face belonged to the realm of appearances. What looked like co-operation in all fields, even in military matters, was just a subtler continuation of the old competition for regional supremacy; it was, to invert Clausewitz, the continuation of war by political means, as had already been attempted several times in the past. The *rapprochement* of October 1978 was basically the repetition of similar attempts in the summer of 1975, the summer of 1976, and December 1978, the only difference being that this time Syrian vulnerability was critical enough and Iraqi flexibility sufficiently strong to bring about the temporary *mariage contre nature*. That the *rapprochement* ensued from an entirely external event was evidence enough to doubt the protagonists' real intentions.

The sudden frenzy of co-operation and unification was a direct sequel to the Camp David accords, and would otherwise never have occurred. After Egypt and Israel had concluded these accords, Syria found itself in an extremely delicate position. It could no longer count on Egyptian help in the event of Israeli aggression, and Israel no longer needed to fear Egypt siding with Syria. Certainly, by the time of Sinai II at the latest, Egypt had largely ceased to be a force Syria could rely on and Syrian statements repeatedly expressed this concern. Nevertheless, the possibility of Egyptian intervention had not yet been formally excluded. But now Syria badly needed support from other sides to compensate the new strategic imbalance, and Iraq was the only country capable of replacing part of that loss by at least providing Syria with what both countries then designated as 'strategic depth'. An accommodation with Iraq thus was indispensable for the Syrian regime. This does not mean that Damascus at any time thought of sacrificing its long-term ambition in the region for short-term assistance from Iraq. Rather, Iraqi aid was to be used against Iraqi interests, not only to give the regime in Damascus some temporary respite, but also to realize these ambitions under more propitious circumstances in the future.

The Iraqi side, for its part, tried to take advantage of Syria's new vulnerability and offered its assistance in the hope of reducing Syrian sovereignty and independence. To enhance its chances of success, Iraq this time was careful to adopt a more flexible attitude than in its previous two attempts, by omitting an explicit demand for Syria to reject UN resolutions 242 and 338.

Iraq's new advances to Syria also served the long-cherished project of holding an Arab summit in Baghdad, and by late 1978 different factors, among them the Camp David accords, brought it closer to realization. A boycott by Syria might have entailed the absence of the other signatories of the Tripoli declaration. Even if this consequence could be avoided, the absence of the strongest confrontation state would have reduced the summit's importance and moreover foiled the Iraqi plan to get its new leading role recognized also by its main competitor.

### Setting the process in motion

The *rapprochement* in October was presumably initiated by Iraq although it held that both sides simultaneously contacted their counterparts[1] and President Bakr on the evening of 19 September reportedly still declined an appeal made on the telephone by the Libyan leader Qadhdhafi to reconcile differences with Syria.[2] As Syria needed Iraqi assistance and knew that Iraq would not grant it unconditionally, it would have been unwise for the Syrians to appear as the instigators, thereby forfeiting part of their bargaining power – especially as Iraq appeared anxious to hold its first Arab summit ever.

Indeed, on 1 October the Iraqi Revolutionary Command Council (RCC) released a statement calling for a summit conference to be held in Baghdad in order to concert Arab action after Camp David. The wording of the RCC statement was chosen to be acceptable

to the Syrians, and to indicate that further contacts could ensue
where the issue of closer ties between the two countries could be
examined. The statement by the RCC was without any reference to
UN resolutions 242 and 338 and yet proposed the dispatch of Iraqi
troops to the Golan. Under these conditions the Syrian side could
respond positively without losing face. If Iraqi sources are correct,
Asad did so as early as 2 October in a personal message to Bakr.[3]

Later Syrian officials on different occasions presented the
*rapprochement* as initiated by the Syrian President Asad.[4] This
was, of course, after the event, when Iraq had already made
known its basic conditions. Taking credit for the initiative at that
time would serve Syria's reputation as the driving force in bringing
about Arab unity.

The initial exchange of messages was immediately followed by
more concrete events. As early as 3 October an Iraqi trade
union delegation led by Mu'ayyid 'Abdallah, then chairman
of the General Federation of Iraqi Trade Unions, left Baghdad
for Damascus.[5] The symbolic importance of this visit can only
be measured if seen against the background of the complete
interruption of similar visits during the preceding years. On 7
October, for the first time in eight months, a high-ranking official
from one country visited the other. On that day Tariq 'Aziz, a close
confident of Saddam Husayn and a member of the Iraqi RCC,
travelled to Damascus, carrying a written message from Bakr to
Asad;[6] it was presumably the invitation to visit Baghdad.[7]

When he received 'Aziz, Asad had just returned from Moscow
where, apart from seeking increased Soviet aid he probably also
explained Syria's new policy towards Iraq. According to one
interpretation he also intended to threaten the rich Arab countries
with a Soviet–Syrian *rapprochement* and thus pressurize them
into granting more support to Syria. Indeed, before the Baghdad
summit Syria had obtained assurances of significant Arab financial
support.[8]

Nevertheless, contacts and visits between the two sides had been
resumed and were soon to continue and expand. Tension was
further eased when by mid-October mutual propaganda campaigns
were significantly scaled down. Even the Iraqi radio broadcast,
the Voice of Arab Syria changed its terminology; it ceased, for
instance, to speak of the 'Asad clan' and returned to the neutral
term 'Syrian government'.[9] Some sources also reported that the
Syro-Iraqi border was reopened as early as 22 October,[10] while
others put it at only 29 October,[11] three days after the conclusion
of Asad's meeting with Bakr and Saddam Husayn. In any case,
however, police on both sides seem to have strictly controlled
movements across the border as soon as it was reopened.[12]

*Between unification and co-operation: the Charter of Joint
National Action*

After this prelude and in view of the ongoing preparations for the
first Arab summit conference in Iraq, Asad's visit to Baghdad from
24 to 26 October – the first bilateral summit after almost five years
– did not come as a real surprise.

His meeting with Bakr and Husayn led to the Charter of Joint
National Action (*Mithaq al-'amal al-qawmi al-mushtaraq*), signed
amid much pomp and circumstance on 26 October.[13] In their
speeches at the signing ceremony, Bakr and Asad admitted, in
veiled terms, that Camp David had paved the way for their new co-
operation, although subsequent statements sometimes presented
it as entirely unconnected to the accords between Egypt and
Israel. Asad, moreover, gave the impression that this co-operation
scheme, which also envisaged an as yet undefined form of unity,
was better prepared than previous Arab units schemes, and he
acknowledged that it would take time and effort to materialize.[14]

The Charter itself (for the complete text, see the appendix)
remained extremely vague and contained no details of the co-
operation or unity that was now to characterize Syro-Iraqi
relations. After an extensive preamble evoking the motives of
the contracting parties, in which the Egyptian–Israeli accords
again were only hinted at and presented as just one of several
reasons, it spoke only of 'joint action between the two countries
in the various political, military, economic, cultural, information
and other fields including a determination to seek arduously . . .
to bring about the closest form of unity ties between Syria and
Iraq.' The issue of unity was thus reduced to 'unity ties', whose
realization was only to be sought. Even the determination to seek
their realization was just one of apparently many aspects of the
'joint action' that was agreed but again not enlarged upon. The
Charter then mentioned the participants in the talks and finally
came to concrete decisions that had been agreed on. These were
almost completely limited to setting up different committees and
sub-committees whose composition was given in enough detail as
to make up a substantial part – about half – of the text, but whose
tasks were only briefly referred to and only in general terms, such
as to 'supervise co-ordination, integration and co-operation' or the
'strengthening and developing' of relations in the 'various . . .
fields'.

The main body created by the Charter was the Joint Higher
Political Committee (usually referred to as such, although in
Arabic designated as al-Hay'a al-siyasiyya al-'ulya), made up

of the two presidents and their closest aides. Reporting to this committee or body were four specialized committees (*lijan*; sing. *lajna*). The first of these was concerned with 'political, information and cultural affairs'; the second with 'education and science'; the third with 'economic affairs and technical co-operation'; and the fourth with 'military co-operation'. Only this last committee was entrusted with a more concrete task and to 'undertake the formulation of a joint defence pact providing the groundwork for complete military union'.[15] Despite this promising precision, military co-operation would remain as bad as ever, and the committee for military affairs would meet only once, on 16 January 1979.[16] The defence pact also never materialized and 'complete military union' was a non-starter.

The Charter lacked especially any exact information such as a time schedule or the structure and functioning of the union to be created. In its vague and non-committal form it definitely reflected the Syrian intention to temporize and to get as much support as possible for as little loss of sovereignty.

## Promoting and preventing unification

The different aims pursued by the two sides through the Charter and the *rapprochement* in general were manifest in their positions over the two sensitive issues of party and military co-operation or unification. A third controversial issue was the shape of a common constitutional framework, but this depended largely on decisions in matters of party co-operation or merger.

For Syria, military support, including the financing of arms purchases, was the most important motive for improving relations with Iraq. But this support had to be organized in such a way as to guarantee the continued independence of the Syrian regime. Accordingly, Damascus sought clear and definitive assurances on the part of Iraq on sending its troops and granting other military assistance should Syria require this, but to safeguard its independence opposed the Iraqi proposal that had already been made in the RCC statement of 1 October 1978 to station troops immediately on Syrian soil.[17]

However, although Iraq wanted to send troops and sought the 'closest form of unity ties' with Syria, it was in no hurry to merge its armed forces with those of its neighbour. It made this dependent on the unification of the two Ba'th parties. Only after merging the two parties into one, which the Iraqi party due to its more efficient organizational structures would have inevitably dominated, could the rulers in Baghdad hope to impose themselves on their Syrian counterparts. Ideological hegemony and a monopoly of legitimacy were indispensable, as it would have been impossible to prevail upon the Syrian officers by military means alone. This is not to suggest that the Syrian officers, especially those close to Asad, would have easily obeyed the directives of a party leadership which was not under their own control. Such a leadership, however, would have helped to tip the balance against Asad and his faction, who at that time were not uncontested in the army – and this was not only because of the intervention in Lebanon. Insiders of the time say that till the clamp-down on all opposition – suspected or real – in March 1980, a great many officers in the Syrian armed forces quite freely expressed their reservations about the regime.[18]

Syria in accordance with its own aims tried to avoid not only an early but also a later merger of the two armies. Statements like the one made by the then Information Minister Ahmad Iskandar Ahmad, according to whom it was 'logical and natural to have one army for both countries',[19] should not be taken at face value. Unifying the armies would have exposed the members of the Syrian armed forces to dangerous Iraqi ideas, or made it easier for the Iraqi side to distribute financial favours and thus corrupt officers still loyal to the less well-off Syrian leadership. Furthermore, the basic pay of the Syrian military personnel, like that of civil servants and party officials, would have had to be adapted to the higher Iraqi standards and, in view of the notorious difficulties of the Syrian treasury, be financed with Iraqi funds. Informed sources attested that in order to safeguard its independence, Syria moreover refused to disband the Defence Brigades (*Saraya al-Difa'*) or integrate them into a unified army.[20]

The Syrian leadership also worked against any significant increase in exchanges, contacts and co-operation between the two party organizations and their members, even though it paid lip-service to such changes. Certainly, party unification was extensively discussed within the Syrian party and honestly advocated by many of its members, but never seriously envisaged by the ruling group around Asad. Some important representatives of the regime, most prominent among them Rif'at al-Asad, even overtly opposed the unity scheme, fearing for the continued independence of their parallel armies such as the *Saraya al-Difa'*. Presumably it was also Rif'at who was behind the Guardians of the Homeland (Hiras al-watan), who in leaflets distributed within the armed forces strongly criticized the unity scheme. Reports according to which the transfer to the diplomatic service of 'Ali al-Madani, till January 1979 a high-ranking official in the country's 'security' apparatus and Tawfiq al-Jihni, the commander of the first division, was prompted by their opposition to party unification[21] seem to be unfounded.[22] The same applies to the assertion that 'Abdallah al-Ahmar, the assistant secretary general of the party, and Muhammad Haydar, a former Syrian minister and one of the architects of the *infitah*, were in favour of the scheme.[23]

Expressing the point of view of the inner core of the regime, the then Minister of Information Ahmad Iskandar Ahmad, had already said in early November 1978 that before the question of party unification could be taken up positive developments had to be achieved in other fields.[24]

Another indication of Syrian hostility to any changes at the party level were the travel restrictions imposed on the Ba'thi exiles of 1966, who had settled in Iraq and now wanted to take advantage of the thaw and revisit Syria. These restrictions remained in force throughout the period of *détente*.[25]

In contrast to Damascus, Baghdad sought and advocated the complete unification of the two party organizations, as well as the constitutional unity of the states. So Bakr on 6 November, in a joint press conference with Asad, said: 'We will work in Baghdad and Damascus as one party and one state.'[26] And on 26 November, Saddam Husayn expressed much the same when declaring: 'Our relationship with Syria should be a unionist relationship. It is not a relationship of a neighbourly policy, because Syria is not a foreign country to us.'[27]

Nonetheless at that early stage Iraq did not make party and state unification an explicit precondition for all progress in other fields. It increased its pressure only, but significantly, when in late January the process of *rapprochement* had been put into motion and the Syrian side would be less able to jump off.

The unbalanced *rapport de forces* between the two regimes was also reflected in their positions on the form of unity to be achieved. Again, and consistent with its attitude towards party unification as well as with its overall strength, Iraq advocated a complete merger that would have led to a unitary state with only one centre of decision making.[28]

Aware of its relative weakness, the Syrian side on the contrary tried to reduce the 'closest form of unity ties' to a federation between the two states,[29] even though there was no Syrian statement unequivocally rejecting a complete merger.[30]

As the overall aims pursued by the two sides differed completely from one another, so did their chronological priorities in organizing the new *modus vivendi*. While the Iraqis attempted to push ahead the unification of the parties and apparatuses under their own pre-eminence, the Syrians tried to start with rather anodyne technical agreements that would assure them some practical benefit without losing their independence. Initially the Syrian point of view prevailed and only from January onwards Iraq insisted on modifying the timetable in favour of its own priorities.

## An overview of events

After the meeting of Asad, Bakr and their respective delegations from 24 to 26 October 1978 had crystallized in the Charter of Joint National Action, visits and other contacts, joint declarations or unilateral ones on the progress of common projects and the intimate friendship of the two sides succeeded each other in a daily rhythm. The most salient events, apart from the Baghdad summit between 2 and 5 November 1978 and the preparatory meeting of the foreign ministers on its eve, were the two meetings of the Joint Higher Political Committee, first in Baghdad from 5 to 7 November 1978, and then in Damascus from 28 to 30 January 1979. However, not long after the second meeting of this body, the intense bilateral exchanges sagged markedly, and the third meeting of the Joint Higher Political Committee, held from 16 to 19 June 1979, was nothing else but the funeral party for the entire project. But the intense early activities could already be seen to be mainly pure activism devoid of any substance. Sensitive issues were eschewed anyway as the Syrian side had got its way and forced Iraq to agree to initiating the process with lesser topics. Co-operation started to fade at the point when the Iraqi side realised that settling these minor affairs with their Syrian counterparts was in no way a prelude to moving on to the more 'serious' matters of party and state unification.

## October 1978–January 1979: the activism of small steps

Already two days after the Charter a trade agreement was signed which provided for the doubling in volume of bilateral trade and for the establishment of Syrian and Iraqi trade centres in the respective capitals of the neighbouring country.[31] In fact, however, the Iraqi side used the increase in bilateral trade to destabilize the Syrian regime. During the *rapprochement* Baghdad bought goods worth just £S17 million from the Syrian public sector. From the private sector it bought goods worth £S183 million, the aim being to weaken the regime by strengthing the local bourgeoisie.[32] A few days later Syria reported that henceforth identity cards instead of passports would suffice for travel from one country to the other,[33] possibly coinciding with the reopening of the border.

From 5 to 7 November, 1978, Asad in Baghdad co-chaired with Bakr the first meeting of the Joint Higher Political Committee, but, apart from the generalities reported by the official media, nothing of substance emerged from these talks.[34] Meeting at the same time the Committee for Political, Information, and Cultural Affairs on 6 November announced measures to co-ordinate diplomatic and information services.[35] On 11 November air traffic was resumed,[36] and two days later it was announced that restrictions on the sale of newspapers to the other country had been lifted.[37] However, if such a decision was actually made it was certainly never implemented, at least by Syria, where throughout the period of *rapprochement* no Iraqi newspapers could be found.[38]

Talks, visits and declarations continued at the same rate till late January. As these mostly failed to produce tangible results and even agreements and protocols remained just paper and ink, only the more important events will be mentioned.

If 'unity ties' were to be established it was evident that Syria would partake, in one way or another, in Iraq's oil wealth. After rather vague talks about 'joint oil projects', the resumption of Iraqi oil exports through the trans-Syrian pipeline which had halted in April 1976, was discussed on 25 November 1978.

An agreement between the Damascus Chamber of Commerce and the Union of Iraqi Industrialists of 16 December showed that to some extent non-governmental, though not completely independent institutions took part in the co-operation effort – and presumably did so more seriously. Calling for 'cooperation in industry and industrial development, and to facilitate the transfer of labour and expertise between the two countries',[39] their agreement was one of the most precisely worded ones made during the *rapprochement*.

It strongly contrasted with the decisions made earlier in the month by the Committee for Education, Higher Education and Research to form two further subcommittees, charged with supervising another eight committees or sub-subcommittees, that were to bring about the 'harmonization' of laws, regulations and different kinds of activities in the domains of education and research. The committee moreover agreed on a working paper, whose clearest commitment was to 'unify efforts and educational activities'.[40]

Towards the end of December it seems a joint decision was taken to expel a certain number of political refugees, who had once fled from Syria to Iraq and vice versa; Iraq was reported to have expelled the former Syrian president Amin al-Hafiz and several others, while Syria was said to have deported at least 25 Iraqi opponents.[41]

Early in the new year the Committee for Economic Affairs and Technical Co-operation convened in Damascus.[42] Its meeting ended on 8 January and according to an official Syrian report 'a number of agreements and minutes was signed . . . These included the basic points of bilateral co-operation and integration in most economic fields, including industry, agriculture, planning, oil and others.' The precision of this statement spoke for itself, although a few slightly more concrete details were added.

Eventually, on 16 January the first meeting of the Committee for Military Co-operation took place. For this purpose the Iraqi Defence Minister Khayrallah al-Tulfah and a delegation, comprising among others Foreign Minister Hammadi and Chief of Staff 'Abd al-Jabbur al-Shanshal, left for Damascus on 15 January. On the Syrian side the Defence Minister Tlas, Foreign Minister Khaddam and Chief of Staff Hikmat al-Shihabi took part in the talks. As usual, information about illustrious participants was a substitute for news about scarce results.[43]

Talks on 23 January led to a decision to increase co-operation in postal matters. What this meant exactly was again not stated very clearly. Apart from the joint issue of a stamp bearing the insignia of the Ba'th Party to commemorate the first anniversary of the Charter of Joint National Action, and the usual litany about harmonization of laws, regulations and procedures, it could only be learnt that 'Iraq and Syria have agreed to regard the postal service between the two countries as a single domestic service.'[44] The stamp met the same fate as the projected joint tourist board, since at the Charter's first anniversary relations had already turned sour.

Altogether the tangible results of the many talks and contacts preceding the second meeting of the Joint Higher Political Committee were few. Most significantly, no progress had been made on the key issues of the resumption of Iraqi oil exports via Syria, and the partition of the Euphrates waters. The same applies to military co-operation, even though Iraqi sources claimed that Baghdad had guaranteed Syrian army purchases in the Soviet Union, including MIG-27 aircraft.[45]

### January–February 1979: unification now or never

Some time before the Joint Higher Political Committee convened for the second time, the Iraqi side must have come to the conclusion that the more serious questions should now be raised. Pressure on the Syrians at the meeting itself was preceded by an increased insistence on the subject in official and semi-official statements. An editorial in the Iraqi al-Thawra, for instance, claimed that the Iraqi-based and Iraqi-dominated National Command, with Michel 'Aflaq at its head was to be recognized as the supreme organ of the reunited Ba'th Party.[46] The purpose of the claim was, of course, to enhance not the position of 'Aflaq and his remaining followers, but of the Iraqi rulers who pulled the strings of the puppets in the NC.

No more doubt was left as to Iraq's aims at the second meeting of the Joint Higher Political Committee. At Baghdad airport, shortly before flying to Damascus, Husayn – who led the Iraqi delegation due to Bakr's alleged illness – unequivocally stated that 'complete unity' had to be reached; the Damascus meeting was to 'accomplish the tasks stipulated in the Charter of Joint National Action', and to fix the date for another meeting, in which the two sides would 'discuss the constitutional and political formulas for . . . Iraqi-Syrian unity'.[47]

The reasons for Iraqi insistence on party unification and Syrian resistance to it are quite clear. The Iraqi party since 1968 had become a highly efficient instrument in the exercise of power that also kept a close watch on the armed forces whose military command structure was doubled by a network of political commissars. In comparison, the Syrian party was far less streamlined and efficient. Its main weakness with respect to its Iraqi counterpart was certainly the latter's function as an internal intelligence service, a task that in Syrian was exercised by services not subservient to the party.

Why the Iraqi regime waited so long to press for its demands can only be conjectured, but the undeclared policy seems to have been to draw Syria slowly closer to Iraq and increasingly to entangle and finally trap it. Accordingly the few and relatively minor agreements passed between 26 October and 28 January were intended to prove Iraqi goodwill and the advantages that co-operation could bring. Although not particularly attractive to Syria in their conditions, these agreements certainly were attractive for the Iraqi contribution to the fund the Baghdad summit had set up in favour of Syria, Jordan, Lebanon, the PLO, and the occupied territories. Of the approximate sum of US $3.66 to be annually allocated to these recipients, US $1.80–1.85 million was to be paid to Syria. Iraq alone was to pay US $520 million annually into the fund.[48]

Repeatedly, the increasing difficulties characterizing Syro-Iraqi co-operation from early spring 1979 were linked to the personal attitude of Husayn towards the *rapprochement* and unity scheme. Bakr, in this interpretation, was seen as a traditional Ba'thi imbued with the pan-Arab dream, while Husayn was depicted as the 'regionalist' (in Ba'thi parlance), whose efforts were concentrated on the development and strengthening of Iraq. This view of Husayn's political goals is certainly correct,[49] with the proviso that the strengthening of the country is understood as a means of strengthening his own personal power, and to some extent, that of his close associates. However, the pan-Arab or Arab nationalist stands ascribed to Bakr were less real than supposed.[50] Bakr had greatly influenced Iraqi politics after 1968[51] and, despite all Arab nationalist propaganda, in none of the regime's domestic or foreign policy decisions since then had considerations of Arab unity prevailed over specifically Iraqi interests.[52] The difference between the two persons was rather a difference of appearances, with Bakr looking more modest and partly effacing, while Husayn was more pretentious and boastful.[53] Moreover Bakr, together with Husayn, built up Takriti dominance within the Iraqi apparatus,[54] thus pursuing a policy of 'elite co-operation' that was hardly compatible with unity schemes involving the sharing of power. If Bakr had been more in favour of the union than Husayn, it would also be difficult to explain why Iraqi pressure for party and state unity increased about the time Husayn led the negotiations on the Iraqi side.

In the final communiqué after the second meeting of the Joint Higher Political Committee, it became clearer than ever that the Iraqi side now wanted to pass on to the more substantial issues of the project; it was asserted that 'the Committee studied formulae of action during the forthcoming stage to set up constitutional unity between the two countries as well as the unity of the party.[55] The explicit reference to 'party unity' and 'constitutional unity' was indeed much more concrete than the earlier and vaguer formulations of 'unity ties'.

No agreement was reached on the further steps and the communiqué only stated that the sides had agreed 'to hold a meeting soon in Baghdad to approve the constitutional formula for the two countries' unity and the accomplishment of party unity'. So far the January meeting had not been a failure, as even Saddam Husayn, in his statement of 28 January, had assigned this task to a later meeting; the unsuccessful turn of the talks could, however, be inferred from the absence of a broader outline of the unity project and from the failure to fix a date for the next and decisive meeting.

In his press conference immediately after the meeting Husayn expressed his disappointment at the outcome of the talks. Before reiterating the need for party unification he admitted that the two sides did not share much more than a certain goodwill to resolve problems: 'There exists a readiness by the two sides to resolve all the problems facing them with equal concern and interest. As long as this is so, things are good.'[56]

Iraq now made what seems to be a last attempt to obtain the desired concessions from Syria by even more clearly illustrating the benefits the union could bring for Syria. The lure was to be the resumption of Iraqi oil exports via Syria and the significant relief that this would mean for the Syrian treasury. On 9 February, a formal agreement was signed in Baghdad that provided for the passage of Iraqi oil through Syria and the supply of crude oil for Syria's own consumption. At what time oil was again pumped through the pipeline, however, remains unclear. According to some reports, the flow of Iraqi crude oil started again on 24 February 1979;[57] while from a statement made on 28 May by the Iraqi Oil Minister it could be inferred that the pipeline was still disused.[58]

### February–June 1979: estrangement and erosion

After that, the frequency of contacts declined markedly. Despite Iraqi concessions, no signals seemed to arrive from Damascus to prepare the ground for the next top-level meeting at which Iraq hoped to approve concrete measures on the unification of the parties and states. According to the Charter of 26 October 1978, such top-level meetings of the Joint Higher Political Committee were to be held at least every three months (see text in appendix), but when these three months had passed at the end of April 1979, no new meeting was in sight. Rather a long period of non-events indicated that the unification process had started to flounder. Around 12 April minutes were still being signed in Baghdad concerning the supply of Iraqi fuel oil to Syria,[59] and on 7 May others concerning the even more hypothetical common five-year plan.[60] This meeting was to be followed only by the third meeting of the Joint Higher Political Committee in June, which consecrated the failure of the unity scheme.

While the Iraqi side increasingly pressed for the unification of the parties and states from late January onwards, the Syrians correspondingly tried to curb contacts and efforts liable to facilitate these Iraqi aims. Reportedly Muhammad Haydar, a former prime minister,[61] in an 'internal party publication', had demanded that in the future Syro-Iraqi entity two separate party organizations had to coexist.[62] A similar statement was made in June by the assistant secretary general of the Syrian Ba'th Party, 'Abdallah al-Ahmar.[63] Despite discussion within the party, the ruling group at no time seriously countenanced party unification.[64] Also the Party Security Law of April 1979 seemed to indicate the hostility of the rulers towards such a merger. Among other things this law provided for prison terms of up to ten years for Ba'th members concealing knowledge about anti-party activities, obstructing the party's functioning, joining other political organizations (*munazzamat*) and even 'working' for other organizations or 'sides'.[65] Interestingly, this law was passed at a time when terrorist activities by Islamic opposition groups were insignificant, after autumn 1978 and before April 1979. Thus it seems likely that the law was intended to prevent subversion by Iraqi Ba'this, or spontaneous pro-Iraqi activities by Syrian Ba'this, even though it did not expressly exclude a merger of the two parties. The Syrian attitude also clearly appears in the fact that between October 1978 and the definite end of the thaw in July 1979 only one single pro-Iraqi Ba'thi was released from gaol in Syria.[66]

The third meeting of the Joint Higher Political Committee, in due alternation, was convened in Baghdad where it started on 16 June 1979. Either because participating did not involve any travelling, or because in the meantime he had recovered, Bakr again took part in the deliberations, alongside Husayn; the Syrian delegation was of course, headed by Asad. As in the previous meetings, nothing substantial transpired while the talks were being held. But their failure was manifest in the 'political declaration' published by the two sides at the end of their talks on 19 June.[67]

According to this declaration the two delegations approved 'the principles and the bases for the realization of constitutional unity' which they were, however, careful not to enlarge upon. Far from keeping their promise made at the previous top-level meeting to approve the details of the new constitution, they set up a 'constitutional committee' to draft a 'unified state constitution' and the legal structure of a 'unified military leadership'. Another committee was entrusted with the task to 'prepare the basis . . . for party unity'. This was doubtful progress, if compared to the previous meeting of the Joint Higher Political Committee which, according to its final statement, had already studied formulas concerning constitutional and party unity.

Until the realization of such unity the Joint High Political Committee was to be replaced by a Unified Political Leadership (*Qiyada siyasiyya muwahhada*) whose responsibilities, however, did not seem to be much different from those of its predecessor. Finally also a 'military commission' was to be formed, but its distinction from the Committee on Military Co-operation set up under the Charter of 26 October remained equally unclear.

Manifestly disappointed, President Bakr following the signing ceremony stated: 'We all hoped that our unionist steps would be greater than the ones achieved.'[68] Asad agreed that there was wide disagreement when he said, 'We are not where we should be.[69] He seemed, however, more disquieted by Iraqi exasperation than by the lack of progress itself. Though completely hostile to the far-reaching unity projects of the Iraqi side, the Syrian regime certainly did not seek a rapid end to the *rapprochement*, at least not as long as the strategic imbalance following Camp David could not be redressed by other means.

A month after this last top-level meeting between Syria and Iraq Bakr more or less willingly resigned from his post as President of Iraq and chairman of the RCC.[70] Immediately after his resignation speech on 16 July coinciding with the ceremony commemorating the July 'revolutions' of 1958 and 1968, Husayn was sworn in as his successor. The Syrian Foreign Minister Khaddam, as early as 17 July, went to Baghdad to congratulate Husayn on his 'election'. According to some sources Husayn then confronted Khaddam with information about an important Syrian-engineered plot against the Iraqi regime and Khaddam acknowledged some Syrian involvement prior to the *rapprochement* of 1978–9; another version suggests that the plot Husayn referred to was Asad's and Bakr's alleged wishes to unite the two countries but this seems doubtful, even though it would give an explanation of sorts for Bakr's sudden retirement.[71]

Eleven days later, on 28 July, Iraqi authorities publicly disclosed that such a plot had been discovered against the 'party and revolution', and five members of the RCC, the country's highest political body, were accused of having conspired over several years with an unnamed foreign power.[72] Most likely, however, and despite a number of 'confessions',[73] the alleged plotters were Saddam Husayn's inner-party opponents,[74] who may have organized themselves.[75] Striking at these opponents could be conveniently linked to the divorce with Syria. The opponents would be more disqualified in the eyes of the public if accused of conspiring against the 'revolution', and at the same time a plausible excuse was found to end the *rapprochemant* with Syria which had not yielded the results the Iraqi rulers had hoped for. Certainly, the existence of a real pro-Syrian or Syrian plot cannot be discounted which, as one version goes, aimed at bringing about Syro-Iraqi unity with Asad as president and 'Abd al-Khaliq al-Samarra'i, an Iraqi Ba'thi then in prison, as vice-president.[76]

Only gradually did the Iraqi regime come out with charges clearly directed against Syria.[77] The first unequivocal but still indirect reference to Syrian involvement came in August from the RCC member Tariq 'Aziz who said the uncovered plot would affect the Syro-Iraqi unity scheme.[78]

Though the Iraqi side viewed the divorce as complete and publicly declared this, Asad displayed confidence that after a period of interruption the process might continue: 'Maybe it is necessary and advisable to let some time pass until our brothers

in Iraq will be ready to embark again on the common way. This
is entirely up to the Iraqi leadership. We will do our part.'[79]
The contents as well as the language chosen to transmit it can
be taken as an indication that Syria would indeed have preferred
some co-operation with Iraq to continue.

The incompatibility of the goals which the two sides had pursued
through the *rapprochement*, and eventually Iraqi exasperation at
Syria's intransigence – from an Iraqi point of view so unbecoming
and malapropos for a weaker partner – was the main but not
the only cause of the rupture. Other factors were significant
too. The Syrian regime in spring 1979 saw itself confronted with
a recrudescence of the activities of Islamic opposition groups,
including terrorist activities,[80] which reached their final apex
with the killing of 83 army cadets in the Military Academy in
Aleppo on 16 June 1979.[81] The massacre coincided with Asad's
arrival in Baghdad where he co-chaired the third meeting of the
Joint Higher Politicial Committee. Presumably, these dangerous
developments seemed impossible to the Syrian regime to tackle
without preserving its full independence in decision making,
unburdened by the complications ensuing from collaborating with
an unfamiliar and untrusted partner, who moreover, perhaps, even
had a hand in these subversive activities.

Baghdad, for its part, after the revolution in Iran bringing
Khomeini to power, had reason to maintain its freedom of action.
The new regime in Tehran could become a threat if it appealed to
Iraq's Shi'i population, but its weakness would also enable Iraq to
take a premier place in the Gulf. In fact, the new situation in the
Gulf promised to open an easier road to regional influence that the
one leading through Damascus.

In this new constellation it could seem more beneficial to Syria
– and actually was – to move closer to Iran. As early as February
1979, Rif'at al-Asad, who seemed extremely hostile to the unity
scheme with Iraq,[82] entered into contacts with close collaborators
of Khomeini, even before the shah's regime finally expired; these
contacts were said to concern Syrian arms supplies to the then
Iranian opposition and a later co-ordination of foreign policies
once they were in power.[83] Undisputed, in any case, is the
visit by the Syrian Foreign Minister and Information Minister to
Tehran in April 1979, which introduced a period of ever closer
co-operation.

The transfer of power in Iraq from Bakr to Husayn may also have
affected the fate of the unity scheme, but as already pointed out it
should not be thought that Husayn was generally less interested
in it than Bakr. From the course taken by the unity negotiations
as described above it rather appears that Husayn pushed more

impetuously for full union and thus made the Syrian side shrink back.

Finally, it must not be forgotten that, at the time and under the circumstances, no foreign power was sympathetic to the unity scheme, including those who wished some improvement in Syro-Iraqi relations. The West, and foremostly the United States, continued to prefer a divided Arab world, preoccupied with internecine conflicts, probably not only to defend Israel but also in a general attempt to maintain its divide-and-rule policy. The Soviet Union, although not opposed to a higher degree of cohesion among its allies in the Arab world, nonetheless objected to any closer form of 'unity ties' between the two countries; as Primakov, the director of the Institute for Middle East Studies of the Soviet Academy of Sciences, warned at the congress of the (pro-regime) Syrian Communist Party in early 1979,[84] this would entail increasing openings to the West. But, and this is what Primakov did not say, a union of the two countries would also have enhanced their bargaining position *vis-à-vis* the Soviet Union.[85]

Among Arab regimes the Syro-Iraqi *rapprochement* was not very popular either. It promised to unbalance the inter-Arab *rapport de forces* by creating an axis, or even a state, whose strength and resources would be immensely greater than those of all others. Saudi Arabia especially seems to have deployed all its efforts to prevent a substantial improvement in Syro-Iraqi relations. Traditionally Saudi Arabia had pursued policies to ensure that Syria would not pass under the control of other Arab states, particularly Egypt and Iraq.[86] This aim, of course, did not contradict Saudi interest in 'normal' good neighbourly relations between Syria and Iraq, and consequently the attempts prior to the Baghdad summit to improve them; improved Syro-Iraqi relations and some access for Syria to Iraqi resources would also keep Damascus away from the Soviet Union – a major concern of Saudi policy. But in view of the possibility that Iran, due to internal developments, was no longer able to check Iraqi expansionism in the Gulf, an independent Syria had to be preserved as a counterweight.

# 5

# The Period After 1979:
# Return to Open Conflict

### Motifs and developments

Following a period of latency that appeared somewhat tense but was still without visible or audible hostilities,[1] Syro-Iraqi relations, after a transitory crisis in March 1980, in June and July 1980 returned to the state of open conflict that had characterized them prior to the 1978–9 *rapprochement*. Though the means resorted to largely resembled the pre-*rapprochement* period, a few differences can be discerned. Foremost among these differences was the establishment of a firm alliance between one of the conflict parties – Syria – and another regime in the region – Iran – that served to combat Iraq as their common adversary, or even enemy. In the aftermath of the *rapprochement*, Iraq initially continued to be the stronger side and accordingly provoked the deterioration in relations in and after spring 1980. Syria, on the contrary, was still weak when the conflict broke open again and would have liked to preserve with Iraq a relationship as co-operative and free from conflict as possible. However, the initial Syro-Iraqi imbalance of strength, first 'rebalanced to the bottom', was temporarily reversed after Iraq, having lost the initiative in its war against Iran, found that from July 1982 onwards it had to defend its own territory, instead of attacking that of its neighbour.

The main factor determining Syro-Iraqi relations after the *rapprochement* was again the competition for influence and perhaps supremacy in the politics of the region. Syria, of course, was at a great disadvantage in comparison with Iraq as it was a direct neighbour of Israel, and as the accords of Camp David had further reduced its freedom of action, Syria indeed had to compete within general limits imposed by Israel. Some observers even hold that it only tried to acquire the regional influence that Israel was ready to grant it – a possibility which, however, would not make it less of a rival to Iraq.[2] To some extent Iraq also had to think about the limits imposed by Israel, as is shown by Israel's bombing of the Tammuz reactor in 1981, but for geographical reasons it was less exposed to Israeli threats. A distinguishing feature of this phase is that the two sides no longer competed for regional influence by fighting – or pretending to fight – the same adversary. But although Iraq now chose the road through Iran instead of the one through Palestine, this change in means did not affect the goal.

The competition over regional influence became even more central to the conflict in the 1980s when Syria supported Iran in the war with Iraq. Nonetheless, then as before, secondary causes continued to contribute to this conflict. As in previous periods, the dispute over Arab legitimacy was not only used by each protagonist to canvass support from all over the Arab world at the expense of its competitor and to undermine its competitor's internal legitimacy, but also to enhance its own internal legitimacy.

The Syrian regime had to assert continuously its Arab legitimacy, and not only because this was the *conditio sine qua non* of the legitimacy of Syrian regimes in general. Increasing inequalities as well as the general economic decline after the short-lived boom of the early seventies[3] led to growing unrest, culminating in the strikes and open calls for reform in early 1980. Though presenting religious demands, especially the application of the *shari'a* (Islamic law) and an end to 'Alawi rule, the Islamic opposition largely took its strength from the floundering economic position of the predominantly Sunni 'bazaar bourgeoisie'.[4] At the same time secular opposition, especially among doctors, chemists, engineers and lawyers, was growing rapidly. The unrest culminated in a strike of shopkeepers, merchants and professionals in Hama and Aleppo on 31 March 1980, but it was severely repressed: the secular opposition was crushed in spring 1980, and the Islamic movement ended in the massacre of Hama in 1982. Repression, however, served the regime better if it was combined with an emphasis on the positive aspects of its policies or justified as a means to such positive ends. The regime's policy in Lebanon, and finally Israel's unchecked invasion of that country in 1982, further diminished Syria's Arab legitimacy.[5]

In Iraq the insistence on Arab legitimacy was no less important as the people had to be continuously mobilized in the war against Iran, and the ensuing heavy burdens on many individuals and different social classes had to be made more acceptable to them.[6]

### The latency period

During the months between the alleged discovery of a plot in

Iraq and the return to hostility in bilateral relations, anti-regime terrorism strongly increased in Syria. Heralded by the Aleppo killings this, between late June and late September 1979 alone, led to the assassination of some seventy 'Alawis close to the regime.[7] On 26 June 1980 an attempt was made on the life of Hafiz al-Asad, though it is not known how closely the authors of this attempt were linked to the Islamic opposition.[8] But although the Islamic groups responsible for these acts received external assistance, this was far from being decisive in their growth in numbers and importance.[9]

That Syria in these months never publicly accused Iraq of being involved in terrorism should, however, not be taken as an indication of Iraqi innocence, for Syria was anxious not to antogonize Iraq. In a statement to the Kuwaiti paper *Al-Ray al-'amm* in May 1980, the Syrian Prime Minister 'Abd al-Ra'uf al-Kasm admitted that the regime in Damascus had decided not to say anything about Iraq and that it had given instructions to the media not to offend any Arab country.[10] This conciliatory attitude was pushed to the extreme by Asad, who at the Seventh Regional Congress of the Syrian Ba'th Party in late 1979 gave expresision to his hope that the 'Iraqi brothers' would return to the 'common path'.[11]

In propaganda matters Iraq returned the silence observed by Syria till in spring 1980 it changed its policy and started again to heavily attack its neighbour. But till then Iraqi officials – like their Syrian counterparts – if at all, tended to describe bilaterial relations as 'normal' or marked by only minor differences.[12]

Despite this mutual restraint in propaganda matters the relationship was evidently far from cordial and the scope and importance of bilateral interaction at most levels tended to contract. Certainly no co-operation took place in military affairs. Though resembling an empty shell diplomatic relations were maintained, while in the fields of economic and technical co-operation and general communications no major deterioration seems to have occurred.

The state of *no-war-no-peace* received its first blow in March 1980 when Iraq came out openly in favour of elements of the Syrian opposition. At the Arab Popular National Conference held in Baghdad in that month Syrian opposition figures were given the opportunity to attack Damascus. Iraq had for that occasion succeeded in securing the participation not only of its long-standing allies like Hawrani but also of more independent opponents such as Salah al-Din Bitar.[13] Bitar's participation there may well have been the last straw that led to his assassination in Paris in July 1980.[14] Though far from being unconditionally pro-Iraqi, he was buried in Baghdad. The killing and the ceremony were exploited by Baghdad to enhance its own Arab and Ba'thi legitimacy at the expense of its counterpart in Damascus.[15]

### June 1980 and after: crisis, escalation and implacability

Bilateral relations lastingly deteriorated in June 1980. Though both sides stepped up their propaganda campaigns, the intiative was first taken by Iraq. The frequency and vehemence of verbal hostilities increased slowly at first till Saddam Husayn in a major speech on 18 June[16] gave the *coup d'envoi* to the resumption of the large-scale propaganda war of the pre-*rapprochement* period. Finally, in early March 1981, the Voice of Arab Syria resumed its anti-Syrian broadcasts, about two months after Syria had put its Voice of Iraq back into service.[17]

### Mutual propaganda and subversion

Iraqi as well as Syrian propaganda again centred on the theme of Arab legitimacy in all its possible variations. With a few exceptions and updated to current events these were the same as prior to the *rapprochement*. Even the vocabulary remained the old one so that official or press statements of the 1980s seemed to be a reprint of those of the late 1970s. And again high-ranking representatives of the two regimes up to the presidents themselves actively participated in the campaigns. Ba'thi legitimacy was hardly ever referred to by either side, but when it was the terms were also identical to those used in the late 1970s.

Nor was the purpose of these propagandistic choices any different from previous periods. Now, as then, the theme of Arab legitimacy served each actor primarily to enhance its regional position and secondarily as a means to gain internal legitimacy. Not unconnected to their regional ambitions, both regimes had to meet or pre-empt internal challenges: the Syrian that of the Muslim opposition; the Iraqis that of potential unrest resulting from the protraction of the war that it had launched against Iran.[18]

As previously, all the adversary's evil, whether in Syrian or Iraqi propaganda, sprang from its betrayal of the Arab cause and its being a handmaiden of imperialism. That it was the handmaiden of imperialism could be seen first of all in its approach to the Palestine issue[19] and, if further illustration is needed, in the corollaries of this policy, ranging from the massacre of opponents, even of entire cities,[20] to the creation of secondary battles.[21]

In the same vein the 'fascist' regime in Damascus, 'foster-son of the CIA',[22] was again accused of subverting the regime in Baghdad for defending Arab rights and interests.[23] One of the proofs

supplied was the large quantities of arms and ammunition that
Iraqi 'security forces' discovered after entering the Syrian embassy
in Baghdad on 18 August 1980.[24]

More credible than the embassy plot were the claims that Syrian
agents placed the bomb at the door of the Iraqi-sponsored daily,
*al-Watan al-'arabi*, in Paris on 19 December 1981 (though it failed
to explode). Syrian together with Iranian agents were also blamed
for other terrorist acts, for instance the explosion that in December
1981 devastated the Iraqi embassy in Beirut. The second attempt
to detonate a bomb at the offices of *al-Watan al-arabi* in Paris on
22 April 1982 was successful. When another bomb exploded at
the pro-Iraqi German–Arab Society in West Berlin on 30 March
1986, police and judicial authorities found evidence of Syrian
involvement.[25] Damascus moreover, seemed to have a hand in
the assassination of Salah al-Din Bitar in Paris in 1980. Syria also
granted support to Iraqi opponents. Possibly as early as 1979 it
offered shelter to Iraqi communists of the wing headed by Amir
'Abdallah.[26] In any case, Idris, son of the Kurdish leader Mulla
Mustafa Barzani, in the second half of 1979 came to Damascus,
where he was Asad's personal guest. The visit resulted in formalized
relations between Syria and the Kurdish Democratic Party in Iraq
(KDP). This did not prevent the Syrian regime from maintaining
and developing its relations with Jalal Talabani's Patriotic Union
of Kurdistan (PUK).[27] Soon afterwards the news spread that the
different Iraqi opposition groups had organized into two 'fronts'
in order to ensure a better co-ordination of their activities.[28]

The Jabha wataniya qawmiyya wa-dimuqratiyya fi al- 'Iraq,
usually translated as the Democratic National Patriotic Front
(DNPF), was founded in Damascus on 12 November 1980 and
comprised the Patriotic Union of Kurdistan (PUK), the pro-
Syrian Iraqi Ba'th Party and several minor groups. According
to one source they numbered six, with among them some Iraqi
communists supporting 'Aziz Muhammad,[29] who seems to have
been in favour with Asad by whom he was received at least
once, on 14 October 1980.[30] Another source put membership
of the DNPF, though for a later date, at altogether 27 groups
and splinter groups, many of them consisting of not more than a
few individuals; this source also counted the – rather unimportant
– Iraqi Ikhwan among the members of the DNPF while denying
any significant communist participation.[31] The Jabha wataniyya wa
dimuqratiyya, or National Democratic Front (NDF), founded in
1980 or 1983/4 either in Damascus or inside Iraq,[32] was comprised
of the Iraqi Communist Party,[33] the Kurdish Democratic Party – or
rather its wing opposed to the regime in Baghdad – and the United
Socialist Party of Kurdistan;[34] later the Shi'i Da'wa Party and,

in summer 1981, General Hasan Mustafa Naqib, calling himself Leader of the Iraqi Revolution (*Qa'id al-thawra al-'iraqiyya*), and his supporters, were also said to have joined this front.[35] Naqib's membership and that of the Islamists seem to have resulted in a change of name to the Front of Revolutionary, Islamic and National Forces.[36] Both fronts seem to have been ineffective, and apparently did not even meet the limited hopes of the Syrian regime. In any case, Damascus was reported to have continued its support for the Iraqi Communist Party and the Patriotic Union of Kurdistan directly, without passing through the fronts in which they participated.[37]

Further reports affirm that by summer 1981 General Naqib had become the rallying force of what they call the Islamic National Front in Iraq,[38] presumably more or less identical to the National Democratic Front but rebaptized to better accommodate its Islamist members. At the same time the Syrians did not stop granting direct support to the Kurdish Democratic Party and the Patriotic Union of Kurdistan.[39] Continued Syrian support for the Iraqi communists around 'Aziz Muhammad was apparent when Muhammad publicly expressed his gratitude to the Syrian government in February 1982;[40] in the same month he was moreover reported to have been received by President Asad.[41]

Talabani momentarily incurred the displeasure of the Syrian regime in late 1983 when it transpired that since 1982 he had been in secret negotiations with Baghdad.[42] However, when the talks failed in 1984, the PUK and the Syrian regime reconciled themselves. The price the PUK had to pay was a marked and lasting improvement in the relations between the Syrian regime and the Kurdish Democratic Party (KDP), its old rival.[43]

Since at least 1984 the two main groupings of Iraqi oppositional forces in Syria have again operated under the names of Jabha wataniyya qawmiyya wa-dimuqratiyya fi al-'Iraq (DNPF) and Jabha wataniyya dimugratiyya (NDF), their composition being the same as they had been initially. The NDF published the daily *al-Rafidayn* which was temporarily suspended in 1986 when after the Iranian occupation of Faw the front issued a communiqué in support of the Iraqi army, though not of the Iraqi regime. Since 1983 yet another Iraqi oppositional grouping operated from Syria. Publishing the monthly *al-Ghad al-dimuqrati*, this extremely small grouping, the Iraqi Democratic Gathering (al-Tajammu al-dimuqrati al-'iraqi), is neither affiliated to the DNPF nor to the NDF.

During the whole of this phase the pro-Syrian Ba'th organization in Iraq was of hardly any importance at all, and for some time was non-existent. There was little spontaneous pro-Syrian sympathy in

Iraqi Ba'thi circles, and the Syrian regime lost most of even this in 1976 when 'Azzawi, the central figure of the pro-Syrian Iraqi Ba'th was assassinated. Some sources say that from 1976 until about 1983 the pro-Syrian Iraqi Ba'th was virtually non-existent. During these years only the family of the former Vice-president Salih Mahdi 'Ammash was said to collaborate with Syria.[44]

It is noteworthy that there are very few indications of Syrian links with Islamic opposition groups in Iraq, apart from unconfirmed membership of the National Democratic Front (later the Iraqi Front of Revolutionary, Islamic and National Forces); as far as the Shi'i Da'wa is concerned all evidence suggests that it co-operated only with Iran.

Except for the KDP which received most of its support from Iran, none of these oppositional fronts and groups had any significant influence within Iraq, not least because they were busy fighting each other. In November 1980 the Patriotic Union of Kurdistan started to operate a radio station in Syria, the Voice of Revolutionary Kurdistan, broadcasting to Iraq;[45] and later in that month, on the eve of the Amman summit, the Voice of Iraq resumed its broadcasts[46] which had been interrupted in late 1978. Communist and Kurdish groups were reported to have made a number of incursions into Iraq and committed some sabotage. However, these actions were far less important and frequent than similar ones undertaken by Kurdish groups operating from Iran or Turkey.[47]

Far more than in 1976–8, the Syrian regime's lack of Arab legitimacy was linked to its being 'sectarian' in character. The country was said to be dominated by 'Hafiz al-Asad and his clique' or 'afflicted by Hafiz al-Asad and his brother Rif'at', and their 'special forces and defense squads'.[48] Their patrimonialist rule was described as violently selfish and corrupt, 'sucking people's blood, profiteering at the expense of national wealth, encouraging bribery . . . and exploitation, starving people, undermining the national economy and liquidating all the socialist gains.'[49]

As the entire people opposed this 'sectarian' and 'treacherous' regime, Saddam Husayn in his speech on 18 June 1980,[50] and other regime sources later, expressed their conviction that it was only a question of time till the people overthrow Asad and his supporters. On other occasions, however, representatives of Iraqi public opinion including the pro-Iraqi Syrian Ba'th Party openly called for action to overthrow the regime in Damascus.[51] In the meantime the Syrian people supported Iraq's valiant position in the defence of the Arab cause. This could be readily seen from messages of support that after the Iraqi attack on Iran in 1980 were allegedly sent to the Iraqi authorities by 'the masses of the struggler city of Aleppo',[52] and others who praised 'Saddam's battle of Qadisiyya',[53] thus drawing a parallel with the battle of 636 AD/15 H. in which the Muslim Arabs defeated the Persian 'infidels'.

When in October 1980, less than three weeks after the outbreak of this war, Baghdad broke off diplomatic relations with Damascus, this was done with reference to Syrian arms deliveries to Iran.[54] Soon afterwards, the Syrian regime was accused of having sent some 2,000 military experts to Iran, in part to maintain and command missile bases there.[55] Accusations of some sort of military involvement were then frequently made.[56]

Typical of the official Iraqi assessment of Syrian policy in the Iran–Iraq war was the statement released on 27 June 1982 by the Regional Congress of the Iraqi Ba'th Party. It stated that 'the alliance between the regimes of Iran, Syria and Libya . . . has stabbed Arab solidarity in the back', and that it had also destroyed the results of the Baghdad summit; Syria and Libya, the statement continued, had committed one of the 'most serious crimes in modern Arab history' by supporting Iran, because they thus prolonged the war and prevented Iraq from fighting Israel. At the end of the statement the congress expressed its confidence that the Syrian and Libyan regimes 'will certainly receive their punishment at the hands of the Arab masses'.[57]

Syrian accusations continued to be almost the mirror image of those of Iraq. So Iraq too was accused of subversion, especially of granting support to terrorism in Syria and even of instigating it. Indeed, Iraqi support for opposition groups in Syria was more than verbal, even though its extent is more difficult to evaluate for the early part of this period than for that commencing in 1982.[58]

In October or November 1980 the clandestine Islamic Front (al-Jabha al-islamiyya) was founded in Damascus, according to its own sources, although other sources claimed it was founded in Aachen, West Germany.[59] This front united all the important Islamic opposition groups active in Syria.[60] It was headed by 'Adnan Sa'd al-Din, who was the leader of the Aleppo-based *mujahidun* ('strugglers'), the 'military wing' of the Party of the Muslim Brothers (Hizb al-ikhwan al-muslimin) led by 'Isam al-'Attar. The front moreover included 'Adnan 'Uqla, the commander of the Struggling Vanguard (al-Tali'a al-muqatila li-hizb al-ikhwan al-muslimin, later al-Tali'a al-muqatila) founded by Marwan Hadid who, in the 1960s, broke away from the Ikhwan. However, there seems to have been no clear-cut distinction between the *mujahidun* and the Tali'a, and militants frequently changed from one to the other,[61] the term *mujahidun* moreover being a substantive adjective applicable to all strugglers. After the assassination of his wife in 1981, ′Attar seemed to reconcile himself with the leaders of the Front whom, like Sa′d al-Din, he had often opposed in the past.[62]

These groups were responsible for numerous explosions and assassinations that all followed the pattern of the period before the *rapprochement*. The targets again were government buildings and representatives of the regime.[63] These actions and the underlying popular unrest culminated in the Hama uprising in early February 1982. After about a fortnight the government forces finally succeeded in putting down the armed resistance in the city; according to reliable sources, at least 10,000 persons had been killed, mostly in indiscriminate shellings and summary executions. The Islamic opposition not only in Hama but in Syria in general was exhausted and, despite a few other bold actions, virtually at its end.[64]

Hafiz al-Asad, in his speech on the occasion of the anniversary of the 'March Revolution' on 7 March 1982, identified Iraq as the outside force responsible for the Hama rising and dwelt at length on Iraq's role in it.

> Sons, our experience has shown that we can be certain that the concern of the United States is to kill us *en masse* whenever possible. We also do not doubt that the concern of the agents of the United States from overseas and on our borders is to kill our citizens, particularly *en masse*. [But] the one who has the biggest share this time is a very generous person. It is the ruler of fraternal Iraq. It is the ruler of fraternal Iraq who honoured us with this big quantity of various weapons. Sons, it is obvious that the hangman of Iraq was not content with how many Iraqis he has killed and is still killing. He was not content to see us in Syria far from the acts of killing and assassination. It is obvious that the hangman of Iraq was not content to only kill tens of thousands of the fraternal Iraqi people. He came to Syria to carry out further of his favourite hobbies: killing, assassination and sabotage.[65]

Not long afterwards, and to underpin the claim, on 3 April 1982 Syrian television presented an alleged Iraqi agent of Syrian origin who was forced to admit that he had been sent from Iraq to carry out sabotage in Syria.[66]

On 11 March 1982, shortly after the Hama rising had been quelled by force, the National Alliance for the Liberation of Syria (al-Tahaluf al-watani li-tahrir Suria) was founded in Damascus, according to its supporters, or Paris, according to independent sources.[67] This alliance comprised all the allies of Iraq in the Syrian opposition, though it also comprised a few others who had more distant ties with the rulers in Baghdad. It set up its permanent secretariat in Baghdad[68] and its charter (*Mithaq*) was broadcast in full over Baghdad Radio on 22 March 1982. The Alliance, renamed in 1990 the National Front for the Salvation of Syria (al-Jabha al-wataniyya li-inqadh Syria), must not be confused with the National Democratic Gathering (al-Tajammu' al-watani al-dimuqrati), founded in 1980 and comprising, among others, the communists loyal to Riyad al-Turk and the Socialist Union led by Jamal al-Atasi; they were all independent of Iraq.[69] The Alliance comprised the *mujahidun* of Sa'd al-Din, the pro-Iraqi Ba'th of Syria, the supporters of the ex-Ba'thi Hamid al-Shufi, also called 'independents' at the time, some Nasirists and the Hawrani wing of the Party of Arab Socialists (Hizb al-ishtirakiyyin al-'arab). Though Hawrani himself did not sign the charter, he continued to be one of Iraq's most reliable allies in Syria.[70]

Interestingly, of the Islamic opposition groups, only the Ikhwan around 'Adnan Sa'd al-Din participated in the Alliance. Adnan 'Uqla and his Tali'a al-muqatila did not join and thus presumably provoked the collapse of the Islamic Front of 1980. 'Uqla, who had previously received aid from Iraq, fell out with the rulers in Baghdad and some time after March 1982, together with his fighters, was expelled from there.[71] The Iraqis thus lost influence over a component of the Islamic opposition in Syria that had been of considerable consequence, not least in the Hama rising.[72]

After March 1982, of the different Islamic groups, only the one led by 'Adnan Sa'd al-Din continued to co-operate with Iraq and soon was granted half an hour of broadcasting time a day on the Voice of Arab Syria.[73]

When Damascus succeeded in bringing 'Uqla's faction into negotiations in 1983 and 1984 and finally in neutralizing it, Sa'd al-Din's group emerged as the only real force of the immensely weakened Islamic opposition in Syria. But at the organization's congress in late May 1986 in Baghdad it split into two factions itself, one still led by Sa'd al-Din, and the other by Munir Ghadban. After the split Baghdad continued to support Sa'd al-Din who, together with Iraqi agents, seems to have been responsible for blowing up several crowded buses in spring 1986. At about that time Iraq is said to have sheltered 484 Islamic activists from Syria, who were mostly followers of Sa'd al-Din.[74]

At times also pro-Iraqi sentiment in the Syrian Ba'th seemed to run high. This was barely reflected at the level of Syrian propaganda, presumably because, unlike in the late 1960s, the regime itself was now cynical about the ideological commitments of its supporters. Scores of Ba'this with pro-Iraqi sympathies were quickly arrested in 1982 and 1983. The first wave of arrests took place around March 1982 and concerned Ba'this all over Syria;[75]

the second wave, carried out in mid-July 1985, was limited to the party branch of Raqqa, which had become almost completely dominated by pro-Iraqis.[76]

Baghdad also seems to have been involved in the plot uncovered in January 1982 and later extensively dealt with in the Iraqi media. At least partly in conjunction with the Islamic opposition, pro-Iraqi officers had planned a coup that was to coincide with the rising in Hama. In this most serious and best prepared conspiracy during the Asad period, an air strike was planned on the building in which the Ba'th Party Central Committee convened, and possibly also on the residences of Hafiz and Rif'at al-Asad. It was foiled at the last minute and a great number of officers, particularly in the air force, were arrested and executed.[77]

From about summer 1980 onwards, as Syria drew increasingly closer to Iran, it began to claim that Iraq lacked Arab legitimacy because of its hostility towards Iran. By attacking the profoundly anti-imperialist regime of Iran, Iraq fought an army and a people that would otherwise have fought alongside the Arabs against Israel. Asad put this in these terms:

> When the revolution in Iran said: We are with you, Arabs, the Iraqi ruler invaded it. He now demands that all the Arabs go and fight with him against the Iranians in their country as a punishment for them because of their support for us in our battle against Zionism and because they say that the cause of Jerusalem is their own cause.[78]

Again repeating previous themes Iraq's lack of Arab legitimacy also had to be shown in relation to the central issue of Arab nationalism, the defence of the Palestinian cause. So Iraq participated in carrying out a most dangerous crime against the Arab nation, its present and future, and its major cause of struggle, the cause of Palestine.[79] And in his Revolution Day address in 1982 Asad said:

> The Iraqi regime was not satisfied with pulling Iraq out of the arena of struggle against Israel. It was not satisfied with this and its role did not stop at this, but exceeded that to fragmenting forces in the region, particularly the forces which can be an effective front in confronting Zionism.[80]

Because of its crimes the Iraqi regime, in Syrian eyes, would not last long. Frequently after the beginning of the Iraq–Iran war Syrian sources either predicted the imminent downfall of the Iraqi regime or openly called on the people 'to topple this treasonous regime to save our people in Iraq and to fortify the Arab confrontation front against the reactionary conspiracy linked with the United States and Israel'.[81]

In 1985, when Iraq was under heavy Iranian pressure, these calls were abandoned in favour of calls to bring about its unification with Syria which alone would be able to end the Iraq–Iran war.[82] Although certainly nobody in Damascus thought the Iraqi regime would accept such a unity scheme, the offer could help Syria repair the breach in its own Arab legitimacy, battered by the obstinate support it granted to Iran even after its occupation of the Iraqi peninsula of Faw.

*Economic and technical relations*

As they had between 1976 and 1978, relations deteriorated to such a degree that contacts and co-operation in all other fields were affected; first they reduced, and then stopped.

After the end of the *rapprochement* in early summer 1979 no new economic agreement was concluded between the two sides. Only in one instance was previously discontinued co-operation – temporarily – resumed. This happened when Iraq on 25 February 1981 reversed its decision of April 1976 to stop its oil exports via Syria. Iraq in 1981 urgently needed the trans-Syrian pipeline, as shipping in the Gulf had become increasingly dangerous. The co-operation, however, did not last much longer than a year as on 10 April 1982 Syria shut down the pipeline.[83] Syria claimed in May 1983 that it had reopened the pipeline on one occasion but that Iraq had not had enough oil to export, allegedly because Iranian shelling and bombardment of the Kirkuk oilfields had greatly reduced production.[84] Until the closure in 1982 about one-half of Iraqi oil exports were routed via Syria,[85] and Iraq reportedly lost potential income of almost US $6 billion, though the actual net less was estimated at far less.[86] Syria's closing of the pipeline, according to well-informed sources, was the last straw that led Iraq to terminate its financial support for Syria agreed at the Baghdad summit in 1978; till then it had apparently been continued first to entice and then to appease Syria.[87] Two days before closing the pipeline Syria had already closed its border with Iraq, accusing it of being involved in terrorism in Syria.[88] At least on one occasion, however, the border seems to have been reopened. This was in late November 1983 when Abu Nidal's followers, though perhaps not Abu Nidal himself, were deported by Iraq to Syria.[89]

The economic 'disentanglement' of Syria and Iraq led both sides to increase their co-operation with third parties. Syria pursued its policy towards Iran (see p. 165) adroitly enough not only to enhance its political weight in the Middle East, but also to obtain economic advantages, especially oil supplies free of charge or at preferential prices (see pp. 167ff.). Iraq, for its part, in October signed an agreement with Turkey to build a second oil pipeline to the Mediterranean with a capacity of 35 million tons a year[90] to be completed by mid-1987.[91] Towards the end of November 1983 the Iraqi Oil Minister announced that an agreement had been reached with Saudi Arabia to link Iraq to an existing Saudi pipeline, the Petroline, to carry oil from an oilfield near the Gulf to Yanbu on the Red Sea.[92] This link, with a capacity of 500 thousand barrels a day was completed in September 1985.[93] A completely new and independent pipeline from Southern Iraq to Yanbu was completed in 1989 and inaugurated in January 1990. This new pipeline has a capacity of 1.65 million barrels a day, thus ending Iraq's use of the older Petroline.[94]

At the beginning of December 1983 Iraq and Turkey set up a committee of experts to study a gas pipeline project – also to the Turkish coast on the Mediterranean. At the same time it was announced that the capacity of the trans-Turkish oil pipeline had been increased to 900 thousand barrels a day and that it was to be expanded to 1 million barrels by April 1984.[95] Moreover, Iraq and Turkey in January 1984 passed a 'security agreement' under which each side is allowed to pursue Kurdish rebels into the territory of its neighbour.

*Party relations, contacts between party members and cross-border communications*

Party relations, difficult even during the *rapprochement*, had quickly returned to complete non-existence at the official level, and thus again were restricted to clandestine contacts, mainly between the Iraqi party and dissatisfied Ba'this in Syria. Neither of the sides authorized uncontrolled contacts between party members in the two countries, so as to forestall any danger of subversion and transfer of loyalty to the other side. Accordingly those involved, or alleged to be involved, in such unauthorized contacts continued to be persecuted; this is shown by the wave of arrests in the whole of Syria around March 1982 and more specifically in Raqqa in mid-July 1985.

But not only were contacts between members of the two parties prevented; the politics of severed communications were generalized, extending to the closure of the common border by Syria on 8 April, and its decision, in force at least since 1986, to prevent its nationals from travelling to Iraq.[96] In contrast, Iraqi passport holders were not in principle denied entry into Syria when they arrived via third countries.[97]

*Recourse to armed force*

The policy of cutting communication applied to the armed forces at least as much as to the Ba'th parties. Instead of co-operating in military matters and of co-ordinating military action, Syria in this last period continued – and Iraq started – to use its armed forces for its own designs of regional hegemony. While Syria still maintained a sizeable troop contingent in Lebanon, Iraq launched its offensive against Iran. But this was not all. Until now the use of military forces had been restricted to intimidation of the adversary by concentrating troops on the common border or combat against its allies, mainly in Lebanon, and if possible by proxy. Now, however, one side – Syria – with military personnel and material engaged in war against its adversary, though this was not fought on their common border but on Iran's. At the same time Syria continued to resort to troop concentrations to express its disagreements and demands; now, however, these concerned Arab supporters of its adversary rather than the adversary itself. Moreover, both sides continued to oppose each other militarily by proxy in Lebanon.

An airlift of weapons and other military material from Syria to Iran was mentioned for the first time on 6 November 1980. This information was later verified and confirmed, not only on this date[98] but also subsequently, even after Iran had occupied Iraqi territory;[99] moreover, Syrian missile experts and other advisers reportedly assisted the Iranian military.[100] Also in November 1980 Syria concentrated troops on its border with Jordan where the Eleventh Arab summit was to be held. This summit conference was to come out in support of Iraq in its war against Iran and was boycotted by Syria. The Syrian troops camped at the border till around 10 December,[101] about a fortnight after the end of the summit meeting. Syria's official justification for the action was the pursuit of 'murderers' – meaning members of the Islamic opposition in Syria, who allegedly sought and found refuge in Jordan. As related by one of the best-informed and most reliable observers of Syrian policy, the troop concentrations had earned Syria some US $500 million of 'protection money' as against £S300 million of expenses.[102] According to unconfirmed reports Syrian forces later, in early May 1982, moved to the Iraqi border,[103] possibly in connection with the closure of the trans-Syrian pipeline in April.

Direct use of military force by the adversary was reported only by Iraq, which repeatedly accused Syria of having violated its airspace[104] and once of having shot and killed five Iraqi border guards.[105] However, clashes by proxy in Lebanon became more frequent and violent, and they increasingly involved – though this was not admitted – Syrian troops which granted substantial, support to and intervened on the side of their Druze and Shi'i allies or their few remaining Palestinian pawns. So in February

1982 fighting was reported from Tripoli in Northern Lebanon
in which Syrian troops were opposed by the militias of the
local Islamic opposition group, the Ittihad, and of the pro-Iraqi
Lebanese Ba'th Party, supported by the Palestinians of al-Fath.[106]
Clashes between Syria and its Lebanese allies on the one hand and
Lebanese Christian troops and militias on the other developed into
an unacknowledged Syro-Iraq war since, in August 1988, Baghdad
concluded its cease-fire with Iran and became free to open a
new front, now against its enemy in the West. The Syro-Iraqi
confrontation in Lebanon escalated in late September 1988 when
the Lebanese presidency fell vacant, resulting in the existence of
two parallel governments, one 'Christian' and anti-Syrian, and one
'Muslim' and pro-Syrian. The 'Christian' government has since
received not only verbal and diplomatic support from Iraq but
also tanks and ammunition, though not missiles as initially thought.
In August 1989 this Syro-Iraqi war on Lebanese soil led to the
heaviest fighting, severest shelling and worst killing since 1975 when
the Lebanese civil war began.

*Diplomatic relations*

The heavy deterioration in Syro-Iraqi relations led to the severing of
diplomatic relations. After surviving the arms search at the Syrian
embassy in Baghdad on 18 August 1980 and the ensuing expulsion,
first, of all Syrian diplomats from Baghdad, and then of all Iraqi
diplomats from Damascus, relations were finally broken off by
Iraq on 10 October 1980, over the issue of Syrian arms supplies
to Iran.[107]
    The participation of both sides in mediation efforts, especially
those undertaken by King Husayn of Jordan in 1986 and 1987, was
first seen as an indication that relations had somewhat improved.
However, both sides had enough tactical reasons to accept King
Husayn's mediation, particularly Syria which sought to alleviate
Arab pressures by appearing to participate. Developments since,
especially in Lebanon, show the vanity of all hopes that had been
attached to these mediation attempts.

*Attempts at mediation*

The first attempt at mediation seems to have been made at the
second Fez summit in early September 1982, only a few months
after Iranian troops had entered Iraqi territory. During this summit
Hafiz al-Asad and Saddam Husayn met in committee with King
Husayn, King Hasan of Morocco, the Amir of Kuwait and King
Fahd of Saudi Arabia. After the meeting Asad was ready to
accept the summit resolution on the Iraq–Iran war and even to

have another meeting with Saddam Husayn and King Fahd in a month or two. Saddam Husayn after the Fez meeting remained sceptical about the prospects of a Syro-Iraqi *rapprochement*,[108] and indeed neither the second meeting with Asad nor any other progress materialized. Other equally unsuccessful attempts were undertaken by Saudi Arabia in January 1983, Kuwait and the United Arab Emirates in September and October of the same year, and at the Arab emergency summit held in Casablanca in August 1985. The latter at least led to several secret meetings between intelligence officials of the two countries at the common border. Though a failure[109] the experience was repeated under Soviet pressure in March 1986, when intelligence officers again met somewhere in the desert. At these talks which were later confirmed by Tariq 'Aziz, the Syrian side reportedly insisted on immediate unity, which according to several Syrian statements was also the only way to put an end to the Iraq–Iran war.[110] According to another well-informed source, 'Ali Dubah, Head of Military Intelligence (*al-Mukhabarat al-'askariyya*), led the Syrian delegation, and the whole meeting consisted of not more than an exchange of insults.[111]

Jordanian efforts in May 1986[112] appeared to be more likely to come off as it became known that the World Bank had just sent a letter to the riparians of the Euphrates saying that further financial support for irrigation and agricultural development schemes was dependent on a definite agreement between them on the partition of the Euphrates waters.[113] In Kuwait on 28 May 1986 the Iraqi Foreign Minister and member of the RCC, Tariq 'Aziz, publicly though with great caution acknowledged the mediation efforts of King Husayn,[114] but on 6 June he said Syria and Iraq would hold talks soon.[115] A few days later King Husayn announced that this meeting would take place on 13 June.[116] However an official Jordanian statement issued on that very day said that the planned meeting of the two Foreign Ministers had been postponed for 'further preparations'.[117]

Syria's initially positive response to King Husayn's mediation was partly a response to the anxieties of its paymasters in the Gulf that rose sharply in February 1986 when Iran occupied the Iraqi peninsula of Faw. More important for Syria's initially co-operative attitude, however, were its difficulties with Iran at that time. To a minor extent the problems stemmed from the growing antagonism between Syria and Iran and its allies in Lebanon. Mainly, however, it consisted of the expiry on 15 May 1986 of the Syro-Iranian agreement of 1981 under the terms of which Syria received 100 thousand barrels a day of crude oil at a preferential price and another 20 thousand a day free of charge.[118] As Syria was US

$1.5 billion behind in payment, Iran ceased to supply it with oil.[119] Indeed it appears that Syria during the five years of the agreement had not paid anything to Iran.[120]

The pressure paid off and indeed, shortly before the scheduled meeting of Asad and Saddam Husayn, an Iranian delegation came to Damascus. The head of the Iranian delegation, Besharati, was received on 12 June by Asad, who the Iranians thought was going to meet Saddam Husayn on 13 June. After the meeting Besharati said Iran had resumed its shipments of oil to Syria,[121] and this was confirmed by independent sources.[122] Moreover, Besharati at the end of his visit promised that Iran would send Syria an extra 500 thousand barrels of crude and give it more time to repay the outstanding debt of US $1.5 billion.[123] A new agreement was then signed in Tehran in early July. Under this accord Syria was to receive 2.5 million tons of Iranian crude oil between October 1986 and March 1987, when this agreement was to expire.[124]

However, King Husayn could not be discouraged so easily. And indeed, combined with Soviet pressure, Jordanian efforts succeeded in bringing together Hafiz al-Asad and Saddam Husayn in late April 1987; according to some sources they met twice within a few days. The meetings were preceded by an encounter, under Soviet supervision, of the two Foreign Ministers 'Aziz and Shara' in Moscow in March 1987.[125] In the eyes of the Soviet Union Asad's Arab policy was quite inapt to pressurize Israel and its Western allies into concessions at a Middle East Peace Conference – a prospect about which Syria was anything but enthusiastic. Although presumably no more in favour of a complete merger between Syria and Iraq than it had been in 1978–9, the Soviet Union particularly disagreed with Asad's policy towards the PLO and Iraq, for it created unnecessary divisions within the Arab world.

The first meeting, in the Jordanian desert near the H4 pumping station of the disused Kirkuk–Haifa pipeline, apparently lasted some six hours. For Asad it was reportedly a stopover on his way to Moscow, where he went on an official visit which lasted from 23 to 25 April. At the meeting Asad is said to have developed, over four hours of discussion, his unification proposal, repeating an old argument according to which Syria and Iraq either had to unite or live in conflict. Unlike in 1978 when Syria had been the weaker side, it now called for an immediate merger, and even offered Saddam Husayn the office of president. Adopting Syria's stance of 1978, Husayn in his reply proposed the creation of commissions to discuss the bones of contention and suggested proceeding step by step.[126] Presumably only as a result of Soviet pressure Asad agreed to meet Husayn a second time; they met again near H4, and Syria agreed to the commissions previously demanded by Iraq. This second meeting, the only one officially confirmed, took place on 27 April.[127]

Apart from Soviet pressure, by April 1987 Syria again needed oil as the previous agreement with Iran had expired in March. The first meeting between Asad and Saddam Husayn indeed seems to have impressed Iran since, as quickly as 25 April when Asad was still in Moscow, the Iranian News Agency IRNA announced that Iran had donated 1 million tons of crude oil to Syria.[128] And, still in April, Syria and Iran renegotiated a new oil agreement to run for ten years, under which Syria was to receive annually 1 million tons of crude free of charge, and 2 million tons of crude at a reduced price.[129]

About a month later the two Foreign Ministers, Tariq 'Aziz and Faruq al-Shara', had a follow-up meeting, again in Jordan, but reportedly separated 'without having exchanged one serious word'. This meeting was followed by yet another one that involved secret service chiefs.[130] However, both remained inconclusive. And although both sides were weakened – Iraq by its eight-year-long war with Iran – and Syria by the worst economic crisis since independence, they were strong enough to confront each other in Lebanon as soon as the cease-fire between Iraq and Iran was concluded.

# Conclusion

The Ba'th regimes of Syria and Iraq have been in conflict since the very beginning of their coexistence in July 1968. Until early March 1972 this conflict chiefly resulted from the desire of the Syrian rulers to monopolize Ba'thi legitimacy to prevent certain categories of their Ba'thi supporters from shifting their political allegiance to the regime in Baghdad. Although the Syrian rulers partly overestimated the danger, such tendencies did exist among certain members of the Syrian apparatus, that is among those who occupied key positions in the army and the party, threatening to erode the regime in Damascus from within. Reviling and attacking the more attractive Ba'thi neighbour seemed to be the most adequate self-defence. With the increasing consolidation of the Syrian regime *vis-à-vis* its apparatus bilateral relations in 1972 entered a calmer period that nonetheless was marked by transient though serious narrow conflicts of interest. But after Syria's 'victory' in the Arab–Israeli October War of 1973 and then definitely after the Algiers agreement passed in March 1975 between Iraq and Iran both regimes felt strong enough to pursue more ambitious regional policies. Ever since, the resulting competition for regional resources and influence has dominated their bilateral relations, even during the short-lived *rapprochement* of 1978–9.

Having described Syro-Iraqi relations since 1968 as developing from a consolidation conflict into a competition for regional influence and resources, this evolution has yet to be analysed in its relevance for the views according to which the contemporary Arab state is a territorial state rather than a nation-state, and inter-Arab relations are characterized by a blurred distinction between internal and external affairs.

Over the twenty years covered by the present analysis it is manifest that Syrian and Iraqi actors increasingly distinguished between internal and external affairs, although the two domains remained blurred to some extent. But generally actors do less and less conceive of the Arab world as of an overarching polity, and the strength of cross-border solidarities at the level of other ties such as between Sunnis of different countries has also decreased.

The increasing distinction between internal and external is most obvious from the dwindling instances since March 1972 of shifts in political allegiance of Syrian Ba'this to the regime in Iraq and corresponding fears by the Syrian rulers, which have ceased to be large-scale phenomena. This is clearly apparent from the greatly reduced reference to Ba'thi legitimacy in the mutual propaganda onslaughts.

This tendency towards greater distinction is not contradicted by the co-operation in the late 1970s and early 1980s between the Iraqi regime and the Islamist opposition in Syria. Co-operation between the two sides was purely pragmatic or utilitarian and by no means based on any kind of Sunni solidarity that might have linked the regime in Iraq to the opposition in Syria. From an Islamic or Sunni point of view the Syrian Islamists, generally referred to by the eponym 'Ikhwan', had no particular reason to consider the Ba'th regime in Baghdad as more acceptable than the Ba'th regime in Damascus for both claimed to be secular in their outlook even though their secularism was and remains speckled with religious references. Conversely, the Iraqi Ba'th could not have too great an interest in promoting Islamic rule in Syria; spill-over effects were not to be excluded even though the Iraqi regime was rather firmly rooted in the Sunni segment of its country's population.

Seeing the Iraq–Ikhwan connection in purely pragmatic terms must of course not be taken as an indication that dichotomization of inside and outside has now become generalized. First of all, both regimes have continued to canvass for wider Arab support as expressed in their continuous insistence on Arab legitimacy when comparing themselves to each other or to third parties. At least in the minds of the rulers in Baghdad and Damascus, the possibility has persisted that political allegiance could be obtained from actors external to their own country. Through the mobilizational strategies that it engendered, belief in this possibility has contributed to the continued blurring of the distinction between inside and outside, and the successes of these strategies have ensured that this blurring has remained a feature of Arab politics. In part, these successes are again based on the expectancy, or rather fear, that inter-Arab politics continue to function like communicating vessels. An example is the Gulf monarchies which over years have readily agreed to finance Syria for fear of being subverted by Damascene agents and propaganda – a fear that implied that Damascus could appear a more legitimate representative of Arab interests, even in the Gulf, than the local dynasties. Yet, these expectations and fears have often been based on actual events and interactions that provide more 'real' indications for the persisting tendency not to distinguish between internal and external affairs. While these examples first of all provide evidence of centrifugal tendencies in third countries there are also indications that shifts in political allegiance and changes in preference have continued to recur between Syria and Iraq, again mainly in favour of Iraq. Sympathy for Baghdad increased in Syria in 1976 after the regime in Damascus intervened on the side of the Maronites in Lebanon, and more strongly during the Iraq–Iran war, especially when it continued to side with Iran after Iranian troops had occupied Iraqi – and therefore Arab – territory.

Syrian policy in Lebanon and towards Iran also affected the loyalty of Syrian Ba'this towards their regime. More generally, the survival of a clandestine pro-Iraqi Ba'th organization in Syria throughout the period after 1972, though of a much reduced and sometimes minimal size, testifies that outside and inside remained partly confused in relations between Iraq and Syria. This is confirmed by the temporary successes of the Syrian Ba'th to mobilize support among Iraqis.

At this stage it should be added that the above examples also show that the fusing of internal and external affairs occurred when actors sought to mobilize or invest resources for their policies. As already mentioned, the attempt to mobilize resources is quite evident in the bilateral competition for Arab legitimacy which amounted to a competition for regional influence and power, necessarily based on the control of symbolic and material assets. The case of mobilizing resources through prior investment of resources, yet more significant for diagnosing a blurred vision of inside and outside, is most clearly illustrated by those Syrian Ba'this who supported the Ba'thi rulers in Baghdad. By doing so they invested their political capital – their loyalty as well as their physical, material and intellectual capacities – in the Iraqi regime and thus attempted to mobilize a force that, hopefully, would advance their own interests in return. Equally significant, though less conspicuous, is the example of those Syrians who supported Baghdad in 1976 or after the Iranian occupation of Iraqi territory. Modest though it was, the transfer of allegiance or sympathy in these two instances also meant a transfer of political capital that was expected to yield some benefit for its investors, even if only in the form of the defence of what they considered their common Arab land.

Such political loyalties that are not contained within the borders of a given state have remained of relatively minor significance since 1972, and may remain a marginal feature of Arab politics. But although inter-state relations in the Arab world have tended to develop into a pattern more similar to those between European nation-states, this need not necessarily become a definite and irreversible state of affairs. The question of whether the distinction between internal and external affairs and with it the overarching Arab polity will now finally expire should not be answered too hastily or categorically. The element of uncertainty resides in the very causes that in the Syria of the early 1970s led actors to mobilize and invest their political resources from and within Syria itself. As shown above, the increase in loyalty to the regime and to the state resulted from the material advantages the regime could provide through the policy of *infitah* and its corruptive corollaries. The allegiance in particular of the apparatus, the key personnel on whom rested the survival of the regime, was secured by offering them generous opportunities for personal enrichment that arose from the need for private business people to have influential patrons. The necessary licences and authorizations could only be obtained through such patrons who, in more ruthless cases, could also use their power for blackmail and simple racketeering. Allegiance thus depends on profit which in turn depends on a flourishing economy whose functioning, however, is in many ways impeded by its subjection to a largely autonomous political power. The regime indeed wants the economy to function, but only to the degree necessary to live parasitically on it, as anything beyond that would threaten its autonomy. As a result of this attitude, but also partly because of factors outside the control of the Syrian regime, the country's economy started to slump in the second half of the 1970s and continues to decline. When the regime is no longer able to provide the material advantages it disburses to its apparatus, their support may falter and allegiance shift to alternative recipients. Then again actors from beyond the country's borders but eligible to be considered as internal may be rediscovered and play a more significant role as political partners or allies. Obviously in Iraq too, where shifts of allegiance to external actors had always posed far less of a problem than in Syria, the regime's ability to grant material benefit has enhanced its internal stability, particularly with the increase in oil prices after 1973.

However, should co-operation and alliances between Syrian and Iraqi actors increase in the future it will be difficult to determine how far this will be due to a renewed blurring of the internal–external distinction between the two states; shifts of allegiance from Syria to Iraq may instead be caused by very material considerations enticing members of the Syrian apparatus to desert. Provided Iraq reaches favourable agreements with its international creditors, despite the debts and damages incurred from its war with Iran, it may be able to attract Syrian actors by means not of legitimacy but of finance.

In the late 1960s and early 1970s such a policy of financial inducement was open to Iraq only to a limited extent, even though its annual gross national product per capita exceeded that of Syria more than 20 per cent.[1] At that time the Iraqi regime had to operate within narrower financial constraints and, unlike today, within an extremely hostile international environment, especially at the time of the nationalization of the Iraq Petroleum Company whose success was not completely certain. Moreover, of course, Iraq's regional ambitions during this early period were generally far more limited. After the increase in oil prices in 1973 Iraq clearly had the means to buy allegiance abroad, and the regional ambitions which required it. But either it did not use its new resources to this end, or the Syrian apparatus was already too much under the spell of the prospering *infitah*.

Since the increase in loyalty to the state, especially in Syria, seems dependent on immediate economic benefits it may well turn out to be fragile and reversible, thus leaving unfulfilled a main condition for making the state a nation-state. The decline after 1972 in the tendency by Syrian actors to extend their interior beyond the country's borders – a tendency indicative of the more territorial type of state – in fact may have created the appearance of a nation-state rather than an actual nation-state. Indeed it remains doubtful whether Syria, as well as several other Arab countries, has become sufficiently consolidated in itself not to fall victim to centrifugal tendencies in times of crisis when the cement of distribution and enrichment networks starts cracking. Spatial and interactional continuities other than those within the state, especially those based on shared cultural and historical references, may then be reactivated and further contribute to the disintegration of the apparent nation-state. Certainly, no nation-state, however solidly established, is immune to the distintegrating effects of protracted economic breakdown and crisis. But many states, such as in Europe, have acquired far more *raison d'être*, independent of immediate material returns, than Syria. Doubts about Syria's nation-state character are reinforced by the absence of political participation that – in the simultaneous absence of total mobilization – is the precondition of internal legitimacy and thus of the inhabitants' loyalty to the state.

This, of course, is not to deny *a priori* that, since about 1970, Syria may have become less of a territorial and more of a nation-state, and that despite all adversities it will turn out to be a political entity accepted by its inhabitants and a polity of its own rather than part of a wider one comprising the Fertile

Crescent, the Mashriq or the Arab world. Such a success largely depends on the efficacy of identity-generating devices, for instance the creation of a Syrian past through the reinterpretation of history in schools and universities, or the creation of a Syrian space through architecture or the imagery on banknotes and stamps. Such a Syrian space will probably collide with the still common equation in Syria of 'Arab' with 'Syrian'. Though useful to mobilize wider Arab support, this equation at the same time enhances centrifugal tendencies within Syria. There also exist the potentially and at least partly homogenizing and outwardly differentiating effects of state-imposed frameworks of interaction such as internal trade and military conscription. However, the increase in the means of communication and interaction, far from homogenizing the 'modernizing' societies of the periphery, often have further exacerbated internal differences and cleavages. In Syria itself the factional and ethnic divisions within its army have, since the 1950s, resulted in the present divisions of the country.

# APPENDIX

# *Charter of Joint National Action*[1]

In response to the historic pan-Arab[2] responsibility shouldered by the two leaderships of the two struggling Arab countries – Iraq and Syria – in harmony with their deep belief in the principles of pan-Arabism and Arab unity; out of realization of the great dangers threatening the Arab nation, particularly in the current stage, from the imperialist – Zionist alliance, which have increased in gravity with the signing of the treacherous agreements between the Egyptian regime and the Zionist enemy; out of a feeling of the need to insure effective struggle requisites to face these dangers threatening the Arab nation's destiny, dignity, sovereignty and future; and out of a determination to achieve a qualitative change in relations between the two fraternal countries, the leaderships of the two countries met in Baghdad from 24 to 26 October 1978 in an atmosphere of deep awareness of the historic responsibility, deep understanding and firm determination to realize the pan-Arab aspirations and hopes which the Arab masses pin on these two leaderships.

The two leaderships agreed upon a charter for joint action between the two countries in the various political, military, economic, cultural, information and other fields, including a determination to seek arduously – within a continuous and scientific plan – to bring about the closest form of unity ties between Iraq and Syria.

The historic meeting of the two leaderships which took place in October 1978 signifies an important qualitative change in relations between the two countries on the road to Arab unity, which is the highest aim of the Arab masses.

The two leaderships particularly stress the profound and comprehensive militant purport of their historic agreement with regard to the just struggle of the Arab nation against the usurping Zionist enemy for the liberation of the occupied land and for the restoration of the legitimate rights of the Arab nation.

The delegations of the two leaderships consisted on the Syrian side of: President Hafiz al-Asad, president of the Syrian Arab Republic; 'Abd al-Halim Khaddam, deputy prime minister and foreign minister; Jamil Shayya, deputy prime minister for economic affairs; Fahmi al-Yusufi, deputy prime minister for services affairs; and Ahmad Iskandar Ahmad, information minister.

On the Iraqi side: President Ahmad Hasan al-Bakr, chairman of the RCC and president of the Iraq Republic; Saddam Husayn, RCC vice chairman; Taha Yasin Ramadan, RCC member and minister of housing and construction; Tariq 'Aziz, RCC member; 'Adnan Husayn, RCC member and planning minister; 'Adnan Khayrallah, RCC member and defense minister; and Dr Sa'dun Hammadi, foreign minister.

The two delegations have decided on the following:

First, to establish a joint higher political committee composed of the leaderships of the two countries to supervise all the affairs of bilateral relations between the two countries in the political, military, economic, cultural, educational, information and other fields and to achieve coordination and integration between them to realize the unity objectives specified by this charter.

Second, the committee will include, on the Iraqi side:

1 President Ahmad Hasan al-Bakr, RCC chairman and president of the republic.
2 Saddam Husayn, RCC vice chairman.
3 'Izzat Ibrahim, RCC member and interior minister.
4 Taha Yasin Ramadan, RCC member and minister of housing and construction.
5 Tariq 'Aziz, RCC member.
6 'Adnan Husayn, RCC member and planning minister.
7 Staff Gen 'Adnan Khayrallah, RCC member and minister of defense.

On the Syrian side:

1 His Excellency President Hafiz al-Asad, president of the republic.
2 Muhammad 'Ali al-Halabi, prime minister.
3 'Abd al-Halim Khaddam, deputy prime minister and foreign minister.
4 Jamil Shayya, deputy prime minister for economic affairs.
5 Fahmi al-Yusufi, deputy prime minister for services.
6 Gen Mustafa Talas, defense minister.
7 Zuhayr Mashariqah, education minister.

Third, the committee will meet every 3 months or whenever the need arises, and alternately in the two capitals of the two countries.

Fourth, a number of central subcommittees[3] stem from this committee, as follows:

1 The subcommittee of political, information and cultural affairs headed on the Iraqi side by Tariq 'Aziz, member of the RCC, and on the Syrian side by 'Abd al-Halim Khaddam, deputy prime minister and foreign minister. This subcommittee will propose joint policies and supervise coordination, integration and cooperation between the two countries in the political, information and cultural fields.
2 The subcommittee of economic affairs and technical cooperation headed on the Iraqi side by 'Adnan Husayn, member of the RCC and planning minister, and on the Syrian side by Jamil Shayya, deputy prime minister for economic affairs. This subcommittee is entrusted with bringing about coordination, integration and cooperation between the two countries in the various economic and technical fields, and with strengthening and developing relations in the fields of agriculture, industry, irrigation, trade, planning and transport and the various economic and technical fields.
3 The subcommittee of military cooperation. On the Iraqi side, this subcommittee is composed of:

A Staff Gen 'Adnan Khayrallah, minister of defense.
B Dr Sa'dun Hammadi, foreign minister.
C Staff Gen 'Abd al-Jabbar Shanshal, chief of the general staff of the armed forces.

On the Syrian side, this subcommittee is composed of:

A  'Abd al-Halim Khaddam, deputy prime minister and foreign minister.
B  Gen Mustafa Talas, minister of defense.
C  Gen Hikmat ash-Shihabi, chief of the general staff of the army and armed forces.

This subcommittee shall undertake the formulation of a joint defense pact providing the groundwork for complete military unity between the two countries.

4  The subcommittee for education, higher education and scientific research headed on the Iraqi side by Taha Yasin Ramadan, member of the RCC and minister of housing and reconstruction; and on the Syrian side by Zuhayr Mashariqah, minister of education. The subcommittee shall undertake the standardization curriculum in education, and bring about coordination and cooperation in scientific research.

Each of these subcommittees can add to its membership a number of specialists as the need arises. The dates of the meetings of these central subcommittees will be set in agreement between their co-chairmen. Each subcommittee should submit a report on the progress of its work to the joint higher political committee at least 2 weeks before the date of the meeting of the higher committee. Decisions taken by the subcommittees are subject to ratification by the higher committee. The higher committee authorizes the subcommittees to adopt and implement those decisions which the higher committee believes need not be referred to it.

Signed: Hafiz al-Asad, President of the Syrian Arab Republic; Ahmad Hasan al-Bakr, chairman of the RCC and president of the Republic of Iraq. Baghdad in 25 Dhi al-Qi 'dah 1398 Hegirah corresponding to 26 October 1978.

# Notes

## Introduction

1 In the more recent conceptual debate this Weberian definition of conflict (Weber, 1947; 1978) is advocated by Dahrendorf, 1959, p. 135; Galtung, 1978a; p. 434; and Galtung, 1978b, p. 486.

2 Constitution, General Principles (*Dustur, Mabadi' 'amma*), 6, 2 and 7; translation according to Haim, 1976, pp. 235 and 236.

3 Dates for Transjordan, Lebanon and Iraq according to Batatu, 1978, 743; dates for Saudi Arabia, Libya and Yemen according to Carré, 1980, p. 187; see also Dandachli, 1975, pp. 224–37.

4 Where no misunderstandings can occur, in the present text the term 'region' will also be used in its general English, i.e. non-Ba'thi, meaning.

5 For further details of the party's organizational structure and the rights and privileges of its different instances, cf. Batatu, 1978, pp. 744–5; Devlin, 1976, pp. 15–22; Mahr, 1971, pp. 123–9, 185.

6 It goes beyond the scope of the present work to enter into the detailed history of Arab nationalism and the political projects to which it gave rise; cf. e.g. Antonius 1969; Balfour-Paul, 1982; Dawn, 1973; Hourani, 1983, esp. pp. 260–323, 341–73; Khalidi, 1977; Khoury, 1983, 53–74; Porath, 1986; Simon, 1974; Tibi, 1987, translated in Tibi, 1981; Zeine, 1960; Zeine, 1966; and their further bibliographies. For documents see Hurewitz, 1956; Khairallah, 1919; Khalil, 1962; Rossi, 1944.

7 See definition of ethnic, pp. 18ff.

8 Rossi, 1944, pp. 2–3.

9 Khairallah, 1919, pp. 32–3; Rossi, pp. 9–10, 194.

10 Khairallah, 1919, pp. 47–56; Rossi, 1944, pp. 11–15.

11 Arnold, 1974; Sourdel, 1978, p. 946.

12 Dawn, 1973, p. 41.

13 Enayat, 1982, pp. 69–83; Hourani, 1983, pp. 298–304.

14 Cf. e.g. Braune, 1944, p. 434; Chejne, 1957; Hourani, 1983; Steppat, 1956, esp. p. 258; Tibi, 1987, translated in Tibi, 1981.

15 Tibi, 1987, p. 98, translated in Tibi, 1981.

16 Tibi, 1987, pp. 167–80, translated in Tibi, 1981.

17 Cf. Gomaa, 1977, pp. 36ff.; also Seale, 1965, pp. 16–23.

18 Antonius, 1969, pp. 82–4; more cautious are Dawn, 1973; Zeine, 1966.

19 Hourani, 1983, esp. pp. 274–6, 285–6; Tibi, 1987, pp. 59–112, 167–88, translated in Tibi, 1981.

20 As to cleavages between Syrians, Iraqis and Palestinians, cf. Atiyya, 1973, pp. 290ff.; Khoury, 1981, pp. 442ff.; Khoury, 1983, pp. 85–8; Khoury, 1983, p. 88, moreover insists on the largely Damascene character of Arab nationalism in Syria at that time while Dawn, 1973, pp. 158f. claims that during the second world war it

replaced Ottomanism as the dominant ideology throughout Syria.

21 Documents in Rossi, 1944, pp. 74–6, 95–8; see also Qasimiyya, 1971.

22 Kirkbride, 1956, p. 18; see also Morris, 1959; Seale, 1965, pp. 5–16; Wilson, 1987.

23 See e.g. Balfour-Paul, 1982; Seale, 1965, pp. 5–16; Wilson, 1987.

24 See e.g. Antonius, 1969, p. 213; Kedourie, 1976, pp. 144–6; Morris, 1958; Mousa, 1978.

25 Dawn, 1973, p. 47 note 127.

26 Dawn, 1973, pp. 40–9.

27 Dawn, 1973, pp. 48–9.

28 See e.g. Tibi, 1987, pp. 101–2, translated in Tibi, 1981; Sayigh, 1966.

29 See e.g. Balfour-Paul, 1982; Wilson, 1987.

30 Husri, 1975; Kedouri, 1987, pp. 181–93 insinuates that Faysal already pursued this goal while he was still in Damascus.

31 For the mandates see e.g. Antonius, 1969; Hourani, 1946, pp. 41–58; Longrigg, 1958; Monroe, 1963, pp. 11–70; Nevakivi, 1969; Tibawi, 1969, pp. 209–337; Yapp, 1987; Zeine, 1960.

32 See also Hourani, 1983, pp. 291ff.; Khoury, 1987, p. 6.

33 Khoury, 1983, p. 88.

34 For the mandates see note 31.

35 See e.g. Hourani 1946, 163–179; Khoury 1987; Raymond 1980

36 See e.g. Hourani, 1983, p. 295.

37 See e.g. Muslih, 1988, pp. 146–74; Porath, 1974.

38 See e.g. Buheiry, 1981; Buheiry, n.d., pp. 3f, 7, 20; Hourani, 1946, pp. 183, 198; Hourani, 1981, pp. 149–78; Shehadi, 1987, pp. 8–10; Yamak, 1966, pp. 43–52.

39 See e.g. Farouk-Sluglett and Sluglett, 1987, pp. 16–23.

40 Khoury, 1987, p. 146.

41 Yamak, 1966; see also Hourani, 1983, pp. 317ff.; Seale, 1965, pp. 64–73; Tibi, 1987, pp. 180–8, translated in Tibi, 1981.

42 Balfour-Paul, 1982, referring to Dawn, 1948.

43 Hourani, 1983, p. 293.

44 See e.g. Balfour-Paul, 1982, esp. p. 14; Dawn, 1948; Porath, 1984a; Porath, 1986; Seale, 1965, pp. 5–16; Simon, 1974; Wilson, 1987, pp. 129–67.

45 See e.g. Balfour-Paul, 1982; Hurewitz, 1956, II, pp. 236–7; Porath, 1984b; Porath, 1986; Seale, 1965, pp. 5–16; Sa'id, 1943; Simon, 1974.

46 See e.g. Balfour-Paul, 1982, p. 20; Louis, 1984, p. 313; Seale, 1965, esp. p. 8; Wilson, 1987.

47 Shlaim, 1988; Wilson, 1987, pp. 103–28.

48 For the history of the Arab League see Gomaa, 1977.

49 Bakdash, 1944, in Abdel-Malek, 1970, pp. 84ff.

50 For a detailed account see e.g. Balfour-Paul, 1982; Büren, 1987; Kerr, 1971; Porath, 1984a; Porath, 1984b; Porath, 1986; Seale, 1965; Simon, 1974.

51 European translators seem persistently to mistranslate this party's name: as Parti populaire syrien at first, and later after the inclusion of 'social' as the Syrian Social Nationalist Party.

52 Yamak, 1966; see also Hourani, 1983, p. 318; Seale, 1965, pp. 64–73.

53 See e.g. Balfour-Paul, 1982; Louis, 1984, pp. 350–4; Porath, 1984a; Porath, 1986; Seale, 1965, p. 11; Simon, 1974; Wilson, 1987, pp. 129–67.

54 See e.g. Balfour-Paul, 1982; Porath, 1984b; Porath, 1986; Seale, 1965; Simon, 1974, pp. 218ff.

55 Seale, 1965, pp. 138, 169f., 267–73.

56 Balfour-Paul, 1982, p. 20; Seale, 1965, p. 139.

57 For details see Balfour-Paul, 1982; Seale, 1965; Simon, 1974.

58 Seale, 1965, p. 49.

59 Seale, 1965, pp. 75–83.

60 Seale, 1965, p. 2.

61 As to Iraqi motives see Balfour-Paul, 1982; Seale, 1965; Simon, 1974.

62 See e.g. Seale, 1965, pp. 186–238.

63 Seale, 1965, pp. 78–81, 311.

64 Khalil Kallas became Minister of Economy and Salah al-Din Bitar became Minister of Foreign Affairs, see Seale, 1965, p. 258.

65 For details see Seale, 1965, pp. 164–326; Kerr, 1971, pp. 1–16.

66 See also Devlin, 1976, p. 197.

67 For the *infisal* see Dandachli, 1975, pp. 361–94; Kerr, 1971, pp. 21–37; Picard, 1980a, p. 157.

68 Dann, 1968, pp. 348–9; Kerr, 1971, pp. 27–43.

69 For details see van Dam, 1973; van Dam, 1978; van Dam, 1979a; Dandachli, 1975, pp. 395–442; Devlin, 1976, pp. 231–53, 281–307; Mahr, 1971, pp. 61–81; Picard, 1980a, pp. 157–64; Rabinovich, 1972, pp. 26–108; see also Abu Jaber, 1966, pp. 75–96.

70 For details see Batatu, 1978, pp. 1003–26; Devlin, 1976, pp. 255–279; Rabinovich, 1972, pp. 75–108; also Abu Jaber, 1966, pp. 67–96; Mahr, 1971, pp. 61–81.

71 For details cf Kerr, 1971, pp. 44–77; Mahr, 1971, pp. 68–81; also Devlin, 1976; Rabinovich, 1972.

72 For details see Kerr, 1971, pp. 48–92.

73 For details see Kerr, 1971, pp. 92–4.

74 For details see Batatu, 1978, pp. 1003–26; Devlin, 1976, pp. 255–79; Kerr, 1971, pp. 94–5; Rabinovich, 1972, pp. 75–108.

75 See also Kerr, 1971, pp. 120–1.

76 Ajami 1978/9 who still mentions several other factors for the 'retreat' of 'pan-Arabism'; Büttner and Scholz, 1983, esp. pp. 235–9. Nobody has illustrated this defeat of Arab socialism, intimately connected with a certain concept of Arab unity, more sharply than 'Azm, 1968; 'Azm's criticism must not be confused with the mainstream analysis of the military defeat that resulted in a selective revival of Islam, but it illustrates the defeat of the ideology of Arab socialism in the eyes of the secular left.

77 Ibrahim, 1980, p. 13, my translation; Ibrahim is supported by Nafaa, 1987.

78 Kerr, 1971, pp. 7–11; Seale, 1965, pp. 316–17.

79 As to the problem of the territorial state, see also Korany, 1987, and his further bibliography; Salamé, 1987, esp. pp. 69ff.; Tarabishi, 1982

80 Anderson, 1983, esp. p. 15

81 as to language see Abuhamdia, 1988; Tarabishi, 1982, pp. 107ff.; as to social structure see Barakat, 1984.

82 Barth, 1969.

83 Anderson, 1983, esp. pp. 15.

84 Despres, 1975; Glazer and Moynihan, 1975; Horowitz, 1975.

85 To be distinguished from what may be called the primordialist approach, see Scheffler, 1985, pp. 30 – 33. The latter of the two goes back to Geertz, 1963, and Shils, 1957. However, as also pointed out by Scheffler, this approach does not posit the primordiality of primordial relationships based on criteria like kinship, race, religion, etc.; instead it posits that these criteria are considered as primordial by the actors who apply them and refer to them. Hence the possibility to reconcile this approach with the instrumentalist one.

86 For such processes in an Indian context see Horowitz, 1975.

87 Refer to note 85.

88 In the original, '*introuvable*', Seurat, 1980, p. 116.

89 Touraine, 1973, p. 278.

90 Seurat, 1980, p. 89.

91 Wittfogel, 1957, pp. 301–68

92 Wittfogel, 1957; for criticism of Wittfogel see e.g. Leach, 1959; Scheffler, 1983, pp. 138f.

93 Katouzian, 1983.

94 See e.g. Korany, 1987.

95 See e.g. Harik, 1987.

96 Gellner, 1983.

97 E.g. Nairn, 1977, pp. 96ff.; Tilly, 1975, p. 79; Wallerstein, 1984, p. 129.

98 Especially al-Hafiz, 1979; Vieille, 1984a, pp. 12–13; for an English summary and discussion of Vieille, 1984a, see Zubaida, 1989, pp. 140ff.; Vieille, 1984b; Katouzian, 1983, pp. 274ff.

99 Davis, 1987, pp. 15ff.

100 See Abdel-Fadil, 1988; Beblawi, 1988; Luciani, 1988; Mahdavy, 1970. See also the literature about the 'New Arab Order': Ibrahim, 1982; Kerr, Leites and Wolf, 1978; Kerr, 1981; Kerr and Yassin, 1982.

101 See e.g. Leca, 1988; Seurat, 1980, p. 124; Vieille, 1984a, pp. 1ff., for an English summary of this text see Zubaida, 1989, pp. 140ff.

102 See e.g. Leca, 1988.

103 See e.g. Leca, 1988; Vieille, 1984a, for an English summary of this text see Zubaida, 1989, pp. 140ff.

104 E.g. Amin, 1976, pp. 67ff.; al-Hafiz, 1965; Halliday, 1974, pp 21ff.; Tibi, 1969, pp. 26ff., 31ff.

105 Salamé, 1987, esp. pp. 115ff., 213ff.

106 Seurat, 1980, pp. 124, 128; Leca, 1988, pp. 197f.; Farouk-Sluglett and Sluglett, 1987, pp. 227–54; Vieille, 1984a, for an English summary of this text see Zubaida, 1989, pp. 140ff.

107 See also Leca, 1988, p. 197f.

108 Seurat, 1980, pp. 120ff.; Vieille, 1984a, p. 8.

109 Touraine, 1973, p. 260.

110 More vividly than in most academic texts this process is described and analysed in the novels *Mazar al-Dubb* and *Dayr al-Jasur* by the writer Michel Kilu (Tunis, forthcoming).

111 See also Seurat, 1980, p. 122:

Ainsi au terme d'un long processus de 'mise au pas' de la société civile par l'État, cette effervescence politique qu'a connue la Syrie dans les années 1950 a fait place à une léthargie des masses populaires lesquelles ne sont plus que l'instrument de l'État qui les 'fait parler' quand bon lui semble, en fonction des circonstances et de ses intérêts propres.

112 Illustrated by Baram, 1983a; 1983b for Iraq.

113 Michaud, 1984, 190–1, p. 195.

114 Michaud, 1984; Seurat, 1985.

115 Ibn Khaldun, 1958; Ibn Khaldun, 1967; Ibn Khaldun, 1971 (*Muqaddima*, chapter 2).

116 Seurat, 1985, p. 58: 'L'État moderne au Machreq, quand il existe réellement et non pas seulement comme une idée, est une *'asabiyya* qui a réussi.'

117 Michaud, 1981, p. 121.

118 See also Leca, 1988, esp. pp. 196–200.

119 See also Leca, 1988, pp. 197f.

120 Owen, 1983, p. 20.

121 Seale, 1965.

122 Kerr, 1971.

123 E.g. Amin, 1970; Frank, 1967; Galtung, 1971; Galtung, 1980; Wallerstein, 1974; Wallerstein, 1984; Wilber, 1978.

124 E.g. Hoffmann, 1960, p. 180, who, though considering 'transnational movements' as actors or rather – more timidly – as forces in international relations, fails to conclude explicitly that there is a non-distinction between internal and external at least amongst the members of these movements, illustrated for instance by the Internationales. Though making the step from 'transnational society', as formulated by Aron (1962, p. 113), to 'transnational politics' Kaiser (1969) also stops short of discussing the implications for the traditional distinctions between internal and externa affairs. The same deficiency characterizes Field's concept of the New Tribe; see Field (1970).

125 Rosenau, 1966,p. 65 defined a 'penetrated political system' as 'one in which non-members of a national society participate directly and authoritatively, through actions taken jointly with the society's members, in either the allocation of its values or the mobilization of support on behalf of its goals'. On the same page he comes close to the definition of the interior given above: 'Just as a society's shortages lead non-members to participate in its politics, so does the existence of plenitude serve to attract participation by non-members who wish to obtain either financial aid or political support'; in this context see also Deutsch 1966 on 'linkage groups'.

126 Rosenau, 1969, pp. 45f.

127 Ibid.

128 Within the limitations of a more conventional terminology this is described by Laroui, 1977, p.317.

129 E.g. Dessouki and Matar, 1980; Korany, 1983; Noble, 1971; Noble, 1984; the Arab system must not be confused with the Middle Eastern system dealt with by Binder, 1958; Brecher, 1969.

130 E.g. Evron and Bar-Siman-Tov, 1976.

131 Evans-Pritchard and Fortes, 1940.

132 Ajami, 1978/9; Ajami, 1981; Farah, 1978; Farah, 1982; Farah, 1988.

133 Ajami, 1981, pp. 12–13, 50–75, 126; Büttner and Scholz, 1983, pp. 235–9; Dekmejian, 1985, esp. pp. 28–9; Farah, 1988; Piscatori, 1986, pp. 22–239.

134 al-Hafiz, 1979; Michaud, 1984.

135 Seurat, 1985, p. 59: 'Au Machreq le politique se pense et se joue au niveau de la région tout entière. Et dans ce qui pourrait donc être défini comme un *système politique arabe global* les différentes *'asabiyyat* peuvent donner toute la mesure de leur génie manœuvrier.'

136 The term 'narrow conflict of interest' is meant to designate conflicts of interest over limited, well-defined resources; it designates them more precisely than the term 'conflict of interest' as such which, correctly understood, must also include unlimited conflicts of interest such as conflicts over mutual domination or over the very existence of one of the conflict parties.

137 Picard, 1979c; Rokach, 1979; Turquié, 1979. Others, though worthwhile reading, were overtaken by events or disproved by later information: Bolz and Koszinowski, 1979; Chabry and Chabry, 1980; Tarbush, 1978.

138 Bari, 1977.

139 Dessouki and Korany, 1984; Farouk-Sluglett, 1984, pp. 3, 12; Farouk-Sluglett and Sluglett, 1987, pp. 90, 144, 201ff.; Krämer 1987a, pp. 21–291; Petran, 1972, pp. 203, 241; Seale, 1988, pp. 354ff.; articles on Syria, Iraq and inter-Arab relations in *Middle East Record*, subsequently abbreviated as *MER*, 1967, 1968, 1969/70, and in *Middle East Contemporary Survey*, subsequently abbreviated as *MECS*, I, II, III, etc.

140 Baram, 1986.

141 Anonymous, in *Cahiers de l'Orient*, 1987.

142 Ahmad, 1984; Baram, 1980, pp. 132–4; Guerreau and Guerreau-Jalabert, 1978; Helms, 1984; Hinnebusch, 1984, though otherwise extremely lucid; Kaminsky and Kruk, 1987; Khadduri, 1978; Marr, 1985; Mughissudin, McLaurin and Wagner, 1977, pp. 248–9, are completely erroneous as far as Syro-Iraqi relations are concerned; Nyrop, 1979; Nyrop, 1980; P. Rondot, 1979a; P. Rondot, 1979b; Ph. Rondot 1978; Ph. Rondot 1979; Ph. Rondot 1987.

# 1 The consolidation conflict, 1968–1972

1 This chapter is the revised version of a previous publication (Kienle, 1985).

2 It is beyond the scope of this analysis to give a detailed and systematic account of the history of the Ba'th Party in general or for the period under review. The most reliable publications dealing with this subject are: Batatu, 1978; Ben-Tsur, 1968; van Dam, 1973, 1978, 1979a; Dandachli, 1975; Devlin, 1976, 1979; Farouk-Sluglett and Sluglett, 1987; Kerr, 1971; Picard, 1979b, 1980a; Rabinovich, 1972; see also Abu Jaber, 1966; Mahr, 1971; before reading Olson, 1982, refer to the book review by van Dam in *MEJ*, 1983, p. 691; esp. for the Asad–Jadid rivalry see also Kiwan, 1983, pp. 190–229. Relevant memoirs are al-Jundi, 1969; al-Razzaz, 1979; 'Umran, 1970.

3 van Dam, 1979, p. 49 note 51.

4 To distinguish between them and the 'old guard', Ben-Tsur coined the term 'Neo-Ba'th', see Ben-Tsur, 1968.

5 The slogan of the Arab Socialist Ba'th Party reads *Unity, Freedom, Socialism*.

6 According to Batatu, 1978, p. 1220, who appears to be most knowledgeable; other authors give slightly different information.

7 For a detailed account and analysis of the July coups of 1968, see Batatu, 1978, pp. 1073–110; Farouk-Sluglett and Sluglett, 1987, p. 107–22; *MER*, 1968, pp. 516–521.

8 Razzaz had been elected Secretary General in April 1965 after 'Aflaq, increasingly resentful of the Ba'thi offiers' bid for power, had refused to stand for re-election. 'Aflaq nonetheless remained the central figure of the 'old guard' see Devlin, 1976, pp. 281–307; Rabinovich, 1972, pp. 154–7.

9 van Dam, 1979a, pp. 67–9.

10 For a detailed account of 'Aflaq's grievances see *MER*, 1969/70, p. 711.

11 After his first visit which began on 25 May 1969 he returned in early August 1969 and apparently again in October 1969; see *MER*, 1969/70, p. 711.

12 *al-Hayat*, Beirut, 16 November 1970.

13 van Dam, 1979a, pp. 51–66.

14 van Dam, 1979a, esp. pp. 42–50, 53 note 51; see also Devlin, 1976, pp. 187–308; Rabinovich, 1972.

15 van Dam, 1979a, pp. 62–63, 67–71.

16 van Dam, 1979a, pp. 69–75.

17 van Dam, 1979a, pp. 71–5.

18 van Dam, 1979a, pp. 77–8.

19 Interviews, Syria, 1984, 1985.

20 Interviews, Syria, Beirut, 1984, 1985.

21 Interviews, Syria, 1985. 'Umran nonetheless pursued a policy aiming at 'Alawi domination within Syria; see van Dam, 1979a, 52–6, even though this may have slightly changed in the late sixties and early seventies; interviews, Damascus, Paris 1985, 1987.

22 Interviews, Damascus, 1985.

23 For the October session: *al-Hayat*, Beirut, and *al-Nahar*, Beirut, 13 October 1968, confirmed by interviews, Damascus, 1985; for the March session: Lebanese and Western press of 23–5 March 1969, e.g *al-Nahar*, *L'Orient*, Beirut, etc.

24 As to supra- and sub-state loyalties in Syria, see van Dusen, 1972; Ma'oz, 1972; Ma'ot, 1973; Sevrat, 1980. Interviews, Damascus, 1985; Beirut, 1985.

25 This is also reflected in the official cultural policy of the regime. See Baram, 1983a; Baram, 1983b. Confirmed by interviews, Damascus, 1985; Lebanon, 1985.

26 As to later 'Syrian connections' of the 'Ammashs, see p. 158.

27 *al-Ba'th*, Damascus, 18 July 1968.

28 *al-Ba'th*, Damascus, 19–30 July 1968; *BBC/SWB*. 19–30 July 1968.

29 Cf. e.g. *al-Hayat*, Beirut 21 July 1968 (for Syro-Iraqi relations *al-Hayat* can be considered impartial); also *al-Jumhuriyya*, Beirut, 23 July 1968.

30 Ibid.

31 *al-Muharrir*, Beirut, 24 July 1968.

32 *al-Ba'th*, Damascus, 28 July 1968.

33 *al-Ba'th*, Damascus, 31 July 1968.

34 After 1 August 1968 the Syrian media again returned to silence; cf. *al-Ba'th*, Damascus; *al-Thawra*, Damascus; *BBC/SWB*; *FBIS/DR*.

35 *al-Ba'th*, Damascus, 19 November 1968.

36 Interview with *al-Jumhuriyya*, Cairo, 23 July 1968;

37 E.g. *Kull Shay*, Beirut, 27 July 1968.

38 *al-Jumhuriyya*, Baghdad, 4 September 1968.

39 Asad imposed military censorship over the Syrian media in his confrontation with Jadid in March 1969 but this was abandoned again when they had reached compromise.

40 E.g. *al-Thawra*, Damascus, 12 October 1969.

41 E.g. *al-Thawra*, Damascus, 12 October 1969.

42 E.g. report on the Syrian commemoration of the 8 February 1963 'revolution' in Iraq, Radio Damascus, Home Service, 8 February 1969, as quoted by *BBC/SWB*, 11 February 1969.

43 Chairman of the Trade Union Federation of Syria in his speech at the mass rally in Damascus on 8 February 1969, commemorating the first Ba'thi 'revolution' in Iraq, Radio Damascus, Home Service, 8 February 1969 as quoted by *BBC/SWB*, 11 February 1969.

44 Press Review, Radio Damascus, Home Service, 13 February 1969, as quoted by *BBC/SWB*, 14 February 1969.

45 *MER* 1969/70, 631; *Akhbar al-yawm*, Beirut, 24 October 1970.

46 E.g. *al-Thawra*, Damascus, 17 November 1969; slightly different *al-Thawra*, Damascus, 3 February 1969 or Radio Damascus, Home Service 9 February 1970 as quoted by *BBC/SWB*, 11 February 1970.

47 E.g. Syrian President Nur al-Din al-Atasi in his speech on 18 November 1968, commemorating the overthrow of Iraq's first Ba'thi government, *al-Ba'th*, Damascus, 19 November 1970; also *al-Thawra*, Damascus, 3 February 1969.

48 Radio Damascus, Home Service, 7 February 1969, quoted according to *BBC/SWB*, 10 February 1969.

49 *al-Ba'th*, Damascus, 17 November 1970.

50 *al-Ba'th*, Damascus, 18 November 1970.

51 Cf. Iraqi press reports of that period.

52 E.g *al-Thawra al-'arabiyya*, Baghdad, nos 9–12, vol. II, 1969, pp. 679–81, as quoted by Baram 1983, p. 190.

53 E.g. *al-Thawra al-'arabiyya*, Baghdad, nos 7–12, vol. II, 1969, pp. 123–4, 145, 135–9, 571–82, 681, as quoted by Baram 1983, p. 190.

54 In an interview with *al-Jumhuriyya*, Cairo, 23 July 1968, quoted above.

55 On Radio Baghdad, Home Service, 7 February 1969, in *BBC/SWB*, 10 February 1969. Interview with the *Guardian*, London, 6 August 1970.

56 INA dispatch (from Baghdad), 23 February 1969, quoted according to *BBC/SWB*, 28 February 1969.

57 In an interview with *L'Orient–Le Jour*, Beirut, 18 May 1971.

58 Transmitted by Radio Baghdad, Home Service, 14 March 1971, in *FBIS/DR*, 15 March 1971.

59 According to some reports and rumours, however, 'Aflaq not too long afterwards again left Iraq, apparently due to a disagreement over the regime's policies; see e.g. *ARR*, 1974, p. 249, although an absence of four years as alleged by this source can be disproved.

60 Cf. conclusion, note 1.

61 See e.g. Chatelus, 1980, p. 258; Longuenesse, 1978, esp. pp. 34–7.

62 See also Jarry, 1984; Sadowski, 1986.

63 See also Chatelus, 1980, pp. 225–72, esp. pp. 248–50; Longuenesse, 1978, pp. 23–42, esp. pp. 31–42; Picard, 1978, 1979b, pp. 49–62; *ARR*, 1974, p. 112; *ARR*, 1975, p. 148.

64 Cf. conclusion, note 1.

65 Interviews, Syria, 1984, 1985, 1986.

66 See also al-Khafaji, 1984; al-Khafaji, 1986.

67 Interviews, Damascus, 1985.

68 Picard, 1979b; interviews, Beirut, Damascus, 1985.

69 See e.g. Farouk-Sluglett and Sluglett, 1987, pp. 92, 108, 109, 119.

70 For details, see Amin, 1982; Bolz, 1979; Chatelus, 1980; Farouk-Sluglett, 1982; Farouk-Sluglett and Sluglett, 1987; Khadduri, 1978; Longuenesse, 1978, 1979; Niblock, 1982; Picard, 1979b, 1980a; Samarbaksh, 1978, pp. 199–262.

71 The issue has been dealt with in a number of studies, e.g. Ben-Tsur, 1968; Carré, 1980; Saab, 1968; Schmucker, 1973/4; for details see speeches and communiqués of the period 1966–70 as published by the Damascus press.

72 The constitution – *Dustur al-hizb* – is available in numerous booklets and other party publications almost regularly published or reprinted in different languages by the Syrian and the Iraqi party. Translations are also given by Haim, 1962. pp. 233–41 (reprinted in Devlin, 1976, pp. 345–52), and many other books on Arab nationalism or the history of Syria.

73 Interviews, Syria, 1985.

74 Interview, Damascus, 1985.

75 Interview, Damascus, 1985.

76 Interview, Syria, 1985.

77 Interviews, Damascus, 1985.

78 Interviews, Paris, 1984; Beirut and Damascus, 1985.

79 Among the better known of those arrested in early 1970 were 'Akl Kurban and Yusuf Nasir; see also Kutschera, 1983, p.12 note 5.

80 Interviews, Damascus, 1985.

81 Interviews, Damascus, 1985.

82 Interviews, Damascus and Beirut, 1985.

83 Interviews, Damascus, 1985.

84 Farouk-Sluglett and Sluglett, 1987, p. 118; also *al-Hawadith*, Beirut, 11 October 1968; *al-Sayyad*, Beirut, 10 and 24 October 1968 which report the participation of pro-Syrian Ba'this in an abortive coup attempt by former Free Officers, apparently staged on 18 September 1968.

85 *al-Hawadith*, Beirut, 28 November 1969.

86 *al-Hayat*, Beirut, 4 March 1970.

87 *al-Hayat*, Beirut, 16 July 1968; *al-Anwar*, Beirut, 19 July 1969.

88 Talabani and his supporters had left the KDP in 1968 or 1969; in the early seventies they then rejoined the KDP before in 1975 they separated again.

89 Interviews, Damascus, 1985; Berlin, 1987, 1988.

90 Ibn Khaldun, 1958; Ibn Khaldun, 1967; Ibn Khaldun, 1971.

91 See Batatu, 1981; van Dam, 1978; van Dam, 1980; Dawisha, 1978; Drysdale, 1981: Drysdale, 1985; Ma'oz, 1976; Michaud, 1981; Michaud, 1982; Rabinovich, 1972; Seale, 1988, pp. 8ff.

92 See Anonymous 1987/8; Batatu, 1978, pp. 1073–110, 1216–30; van Dam, 1980. Confirmed by Baram, 1989, despite his attempts to redefine these criteria, e.g. p. 457.

93 See van Dam, 1978; van Dam, 1979a; Drysdale, 1981; Ma'oz, 1976; Rabinovich, 1972.

94 A feature reminiscent of Hourani's concept of a 'compact minority' (1947, pp. 22, 123).

95 This statement is perhaps somewhat too general as it does not sufficiently take into account the integrationist current in 'Alawi politics. As, however, 'Alawi politics have been mostly dominated by the 'separatist' current in the tradition of Ibrahim al-Kinj, the first president of the Assembly of the French-created 'État des Alaouites', and Hafiz al-Asad's father, who both contributed to the elaboration of the memorandum of 1934 calling for a fully independent 'Alawi state, it is at least correct in its main current. For details, see Khoury, 1987, pp. 466, 523ff.; Méouchy, 1989; Seale, 1988, pp. 18ff.

96 These are seemingly crude ethnic or 'sectarian' arithmetics, but they are confirmed by interviews, Damascus and Beirut, 1985. Asad in the 1970s, obtained from Shi'i authorities of Lebanon recognition of the 'Alawis as true Shi'is (see Ma'oz, 1987, p. 7; Carré and Michaud, 1983, p. 183; Seale, 1988, 352) but this remained largely academic and did not affect popular opinion.

97 al-Ba'th, Damascus, 18 November 1970.

98 al-Ba'th, Damascus, 2 November 1970.

99 Malik al-Amin, member of the Syrian Ba'th National Command resuming the 'comprehensive report' approved by the Tenth (Syrian) Extraordinary National Congress, Radio Damascus, Home Service, 8 November 1970, as quoted by BBC/SWB, 10 November 1970.

100 E.g. the interview with an anonymous Syrian Ba'th leader, al-Muharrir, Beirut, 24 July 1968.

101 E.g. al-Ba'th Damascus, 7 and February 1969 reprinting a statement published by the Syrian Ba'th National Command.

102 Statement ascribed to the RC of the pro-Syrian Ba'th Party in Iraq, published in al-Thawra, Damascus, 12 October 1969.

103 E.g. statement by the Syrian Ba'th National Command of 7 January 1969.

104 MER 1969/70, p. 712, quoting several sources.

105 See note 102.

106 Statement by the Syrian NC, 7 February 1969; although this statement was issued shortly after Col. Nasrat's assassination, the term 'assassination' does not specifically reflect this event.

107 Syrian Foreign ministry statement reported by Radio Damascus, Home Service, 25 May 1969, as quoted by BBC/SWB, 28 May 1969.

108 Such reproaches frequently recurred in 1969 and 1970, e.g. editorial in al-Ba'th, Damascus, 6 February 1970.

109 E.g al-Ba'th, Damascus, 26 October 1970, which calls the Iraqi leaders 'professionals of verbal revolution' who are plotting against the Palestinian resistance.

110 al-Ba'th, Damascus, 27–30 November 1970, 17 April 1971 and p.q.

111 For some time after the second July coup of 1968 the Iraqi regime continued to be classified as a 'progressive' one; the term 'reactionary' only later became one of its standard attributes; cf. MER, 1969/70, p. 142.

112  Statement ascribed to the RC of the pro-Syrian and Syrian-based Ba'th Party in Iraq, published in *al-Thawra*, Damascus, 12 October 1969.

113  E.g. *al-Thawra*, Damascus, 3 February 1969 or *al-Ba'th*, Damascus, 5 February 1969.

114  E.g. statement by the RC of the pro-Syrian and Syrian-based Ba'th in Iraq broadcast by Radio Damascus, Home Service, 19 November 1969, quoted according to *BBC/CWB*, 20 November 1969.

115  Communiqué of the Eleventh National Congress of the Syrian Ba'th, released in Damascus, 5 September 1971.

116  *MER*, 1969/70, p. 633, quoting *al-Thawra*, Baghdad, 5 May 1970.

117  E.g. Iraqi Foreign Minister Abd al-Karim al-Shaykhli in his press conference on 8 August 1968, *al-Jumhuriyya*, Baghdad, 9 and 12 August 1968.

118  Iraq's Arab policy of that period is best described by Baram 1983.

119  Statement by Iraqi General Workers Union, according to *al-Hayat*, Beirut, 4 May 1970, as quoted by *MER*, 1969/70, p. 633.

120  Proclamation no. 1, 17 July 1968, according to Radio Baghdad, Home Service, same date, in *FBIS/DR*, 17 July 1968.

121 E.g. INA 21 July 1969, as quoted by the *New York Times*, 22 July 1969.

122  E.g. *al-Thawra*, Baghdad, 17 April 1970, according to Radio Baghdad, Home Service, same date as quoted by *BBC/SWB*, 10 April 1970. Similar charges recur frequently, especially between January and August 1970.

123  A late but eloquent illustration of the Iraqi point of view is given by Defence Minister Hammad Shihab in his letter to his Egyptian counterpart Muhammad Fawzi, published by *al-Thawra*, Baghdad, 20 December 1970.

124  Radio Baghdad, Home Service, 20 March 1971, in *BBC/SWB*, 23 March 1971.

125  *al-Thawra*, Baghdad, 20 August 1971.

126  *MER*, 1969/70, pp 714, 719. A pro-Syrian coup attempt reported by *al-Hawadith*, Beirut, 11 October 1968 and *al-Sayyad*, Beirut, 10 and 24 October 1968, was never confirmed by Iraq.

127  Cf. previously quoted statement by anonymous Syrian Ba'th leader in *al-Muharrir*, Beirut, 24 July 1968; also Prime Minister Zu'ayyin in his speech in Tartus, 17 July 1968.

128  *Jerusalem Post*, Jerusalem, 14 January 1969, referring to Syrian sources.

129  *al-Ba'th*, Damascus, 22 July 1969.

130  *al-Thawra*, Damascus, 17 November 1969.

131  *ARR*, 1971, pp. 38, 419, 608.

132  van Dusen, 1972; Ma'oz, 1972; Michaud, 1984; Seurat, 1980.

133  Regarding the difficulties of internal legitimacy, see also Hinnebusch, 1982; Koszinowski, 1985; Picard, 1979b; for their impact on foreign policy, Bar-Siman-Tov, 1983.

134  After unsuccessful negotiations to increase the government's say in Iraqi oil production as well as its share in the sales revenue Law no. 80 decreed on 11 December 1961 dispossessed the Western-owned Iraq Petroleum Company (IPC) of 99.5 per cent of its concession territory, thus allowing it only to exploit the oilfields already tapped.

135  O'Ballance, 1973, p. 157; in 1969 this war absorbed some 30 per cent of the Iraqi budget.

136  Baram, 1983, pp. 194–5.

137 Indeed Libya made a gift of US $10 million to Syria immediately after Asad's take-over but the payment of some further US $38 million then promised may well have depended on some Syrian concessions to Libya. Of course, the initial US $10 million may already have been part of such a wider deal; as to the figures, see Kerr, 1973, pp. 701–2.

138 Kerr, 1973, p. 702.

139 Indeed, there is no evidence to confirm Baram, (1986, p. 128), who claims that Syro-Iraqi co-operation in this period 'was particularly marked' not only for the exportation of Iraqi oil via Syria, but also in the 'commitment to the radicalization and unification of the Arab world and the war against Israel'.

140 Interview, Damascus, 1985.

141 Interviews, Damascus, 1985.

142 *MER*, 1969/70, p. 563, quoting *al-Ahram*, Cairo, 16 and 17 March 1969, *al-Hayat*, Beirut, 16 March 1969 and 10 April 1969, and others.

143 *al-Hayat* and *al-Nahar*, Beirut, 25 August 1968.

## 2   From regime consolidation to regional competition, 1972–1975

1 In this context see also the insights of a politician who frequently had to deal with Asad: Pakradouni, 1984, pp. 76–8, 80.

2 *L'Orient–Le Jour*, Beirut, 27 May 1974.

3 Interviews, Damascus, 1985; Paris, 1987.

4 See Asad's toast at the official banquet for Nixon in the *Nadi al-Sharq* in Damascus, 15 June 1974, in *BBC/SWB*, 18 June 1974.

5 Not to be confused with the later Treaty of Friendship and Co-operation.

6 For details, see Baram, 1983, pp. 194–5.

7 This dispute has been dealt with extensively by a number of authors especially Brown, 1979; Farouk-Sluglett and Sluglett, 1987, pp. 145–8, 154–6; Penrose and Penrose, 1978, pp. 405–20; Whittleton, 1986; also Marr, 1985, pp. 223–4; Khadduri, 1978, pp. 123–9.

8 Penrose and Penrose, 1978, pp. 390–4.

9 Farouk-Sluglett and Sluglett, 1985, p. 18 note 71; Farouk-Sluglett and Sluglett, 1987, p. 147 note 123.

10 Penrose and Penrose, 1978, pp. 441ff.

11 Penrose and Penrose, 1978, p. 442.

12 As to the financial strength of the IPC see the *Financial Times*, London, 31 August 1966.

13 Brown, 1979, pp. 118–20; Marr, 1985, pp. 223–4.

14 Brown, 1979, p. 114.

15 Sayigh, 1978, p. 37, based on British Petroleum (BP), *Statistical Review*, London.

16 *Financial Times*, London, 2 June 1972.

17 In March and April 1972 the IPC dropped its production in the Kirkuk area from 1.23 million barrels a day to 694,000 barrels a day, using previous months as a base, *Financial Times*, London, 3 June 1972.

18 Whittleton, 1986, p. 64.

19 *Financial Times*, London, 1 June 1972: 'In the short and medium term it is difficult to see how Iraq can market IPC oil in any quantity.'

20 *Financial Times*, London, 6 June 1972; the bank was the Union de Banques arabes et françaises in which the government-controlled Crédit lyonnais held a 40 per cent stake.

21 *The Economist*, 1 July 1972.

22 Brown, 1979, pp. 122–3.

23 Brown, 1979, p. 123; Farouk-Sluglett and Sluglett, 1987, p. 154.

24 Marketing successes in spring can be inferred from an Iraqi statement of March 1973 excluding the possibility of further barter deals, see *MEES* 31 May 1973, p. 155.

25 Penrose and Penrose, 1978, pp. 414, 439–41.

26 Farouk-Sluglett and Sluglett, 1987, pp. 154–5.

27 *ARR*, 1972, p. 475.

28 *ARR*, 1972, p. 475.

29 *ARR*, 1973, p. 17.

30 *L'Orient–Le Jour*, Beirut, 19 and 23 January 1973; *The Times*, London, 19 January 1973, p. 31; ARR 1973, 31; Penrose and Penrose, 1978, p. 443.

31 Penrose and Penrose, 1978, p. 443.

32 See *Financial Times*, London, 19 January 1977: 'The rates decreed by the Syrians would have considerably harmed Iraq's efforts to market the nationalized oil at anything like the current market price.'

33 *ARR*, 1976, p. 73; Penrose and Penrose, 1978, p. 443.

34 *MEES* 26 April 1976, p. 7.

35 *ARR*, 1973, pp. 30–1; *MEES*, 2 January 1976, p. 3.

36 *Financial Times*, London, 14 October 1972; the amount for 1971 was relatively low due to the production cuts decided by the IPC; see *supra*.

37 Calculated from figures given by Chatelus, 1980, pp. 268, 271; the amount of US $443.14 million is obtained by an internal revenue of 1,686 million Syrian pounds at a rate of 3.82 pounds equalling US $1 for 1971. In 1970 9.6 per cent of Syrian government revenue came from transit dues, including royalties from the Saudi-Arabia–Sidon TAP-line which, however, represented only 3.3 per cent of the total amount of US $53.9 million of transit dues received in that year, see Desoutier, 1974, pp. 38f; this means that in 1970, which was a 'better' year than 1971, some 9.25 per cent of Syrian budget revenues came from transit fees on Iraqi oil exports.

38 Penrose and Penrose, 1978, pp. 441–2.

39 Penrose and Penrose, 1978, pp. 443–4; *MEES*, 7 March 1977, p. 5.

40 *ARR*, 1973, p. 7.

41 *L'Orient–Le Jour*, Beirut, 14 June 1973; *MEES*, 6 July 1973, p. 4; *ARR*, 1973, p. 249; Penrose and Penrose, 1978, pp. 443–4.

42 *L'Orient–Le Jour*, Beirut, p. 27 and 30 August 1973.

43 *MEES*, 4 May 1973, p. 2.

44 *MEES*, 18 May 1973, p. 9; *MEES*, 13 June 1977, p. 5.

45 *L'Orient–Le Jour*, Beirut, 29 December 1975.

46 *ARR*, 1973, p. 492.

47 *MEED*, 5 March 1976, p. 13.
48 *MEES*, 2 January 1976, p. 1; *MEED*, 2 January, p. 13.
49 Radio Damascus 16 August 1975, according to *ARR*, 1975, p. 476.
50 *al-Thawra*, Baghdad, 13 June 1974.
51 *al-Thawra*, Baghdad, 26 February 1973.
52 Farouk-Sluglett and Sluglett, 1987, p. 122; Ramazani, 1975, p. 418.
53 Farouk-Sluglett and Sluglett, 1987, pp. 122, 129.
54 For details, see Kutschera, 1979, pp. 267–76.
55 For details, see Chubin and Zabih, 1974, pp. 185–91; *MER*, 1969/70, pp. 652–9.
56 For details, see *MER*, 1969/70, pp. 652–9; Ramazani, 1975, p. 418.
57 Farouk-Sluglett and Sluglett, 1987, p. 122.
58 Then still part of the Trucial States; the United Arab Emirates were formed about a month later, in December 1971.
59 Farouk-Sluglett and Sluglett, 1987, pp. 167–8; Ismael, 1982, p. 20; Ramazani, 1975, 436–8.
60 For details see e.g. Marr, 1985, pp. 232–3; Kutschera, 1979, p. 283; Farouk-Sluglett and Sluglett, 1987, pp. 164–7; also Ismael, 1982.
61 Farouk-Sluglett and Sluglett, 1987, pp. 159, 164–5; McDowall, 1985, pp. 20–2; Kutschera, 1979, pp. 282–93; Vanly, 1978, p. 255.
62 Farouk-Sluglett and Sluglett, 1987, pp. 164–7; Kutschera, 1979, pp. 289–93.
63 Ismael, 1982, p. 20; Niblock, 1982, p. 141; the clashes between Iraq and Iran culminated in February 1974, cf. Farouk-Sluglett and Sluglett, 1987, p. 168.
64 O'Ballance, 1978, p. 171.
65 See Farouk-Sluglett and Sluglett, 1987, pp. 167–70; McDowall, 1985, pp. 22–4; Kutschera, 1979, pp. 300–19; Vanly, 1978, pp. 268–71.
66 *ARR*, 1973, p. 432 and *MEJ*, 1974, p. 35.
67 *ARR*, 1973, p. 432 and *MEJ*, 1975, p. 35.
68 O'Ballance, 1978, pp. 170–1, and *ARR*, 1974, pp. 432–4.
69 O'Ballance, 1978, p. 171.
70 O'Ballance, 1978, pp. 171f.; *ARR*, 1973, p. 434.
71 O'Ballance, 1978, p. 172.
72 O'Ballance, 1978, p. 195.
73 O'Ballance, 1978, p. 195.
74 O'Ballance, 1978, p. 215.
75 O'Ballance, 1978, p. 195, also pp. 196–9; this is confirmed by my own interviews in Syria, 1984, 1985.
76 O'Ballance, 1978, p. 217; confirmed by interviews, Syria, 1984, 1985; and from the Israeli point of view by Baram, 1986, p. 131.
77 *ARR*, 1973, pp. 432–46, 467–87.
78 *al-Thawra*, Baghdad, 30 October 1973.
79 See e.g. initial Syrian statement accepting the cease-fire, broadcast in the early morning of 24 October 1973 over Radio Damascus, Home Service, in *BBC/SWB*, 25 October 1973; cf. *al-Ba'th*, Damascus, 25 October 1973.
80 *al-Ba'th*, Damascus, 8 March 1972; see also notes on subsequent pages.
81 *al-Ba'th*, Damascus, 9 March 1972; see also notes on subsequent pages.
82 *al-Ba'th*, Damascus, 15 November 1973.

83 Interview granted to *al-Sayyad*, Beirut, 6 March 1974; speech as reproduced in *al-Ba'th*, Damascus, 9 March 1974 and in *al-Ba'th*, Damascus, 8 April 1974.

84 E.g. *al-Ba'th*, Damascus, 7 March 1974.

85 E.g. *al-Ba'th*, Damascus, 15 November 1974.

86 *al-Anwar*, Beirut, 11 August 1972.

87 *al-Ra'y al-'amm*, Kuwait, 31 January 1973.

88 Radio Damascus, Home Service, 7 April 1972, quoted according to *FBIS/DR*, 10 April 1972.

89 Radio Damascus, Home Service, 22 February 1973, in *FBIS/DR*, 22 February 1973.

90 *al-Hayat*, Beirut, 25 October 1972.

91 Indeed, the Iraqi regime had not actually asked for membership of this existing federation but rather to set up a union comprising itself together with Egypt and Syria; the Iraqi project remained mute about what should become of Libya and of the existing federation.

92 *al-Hayat*, Beirut, 25 October 1972.

93 Interviews, Syria, 1984, 1985.

94 E.g. Foreign Ministry spokesman on 17 October 1972, cf. *OM*, 1972, p. 641.

95 *al-Ba'th*, Damascus, 27 September 1973.

96 Statement of the National Command of the Syrian Ba'th Party, 7 March 1974, in *BBC/SWB*, 9 March 1974.

97 Cf. quote on p. 75.

98 E.g. SANA dispatch (from Damascus), 25 September 1973, referring to a statement allegedly issued by the (pro-Syrian) Iraqi National Grouping (more correctly translated as Iraqi National Gathering), *BBC/SWB*, 27 September 1973.

99 See Batatu, 1978, pp. 1085–93.

100 As to internal legitimacy difficulties of the Syrian regime in the years 1972 to 1975, see Hinnebusch, 1982a; Hinnebusch, 1982b; Koszinowski, 1985; Picard, 1980b.

101 *al-Jumhuriyya*, Baghdad; *al-Thawra*, Baghdad 8 April 1972.

102 *al-Jumhuriyya*, Baghdad, 18 July 1972, 17 July 1973; a further example is Bakr's address on the anniversary of the party in 1973, see *al-Jumhuriyya*, Baghdad 8 April 1973.

103 INA dispatch, 19 July 1973, in *FBIS/DR*, 20 July 1973.

104 For instance Saddam Husayn in his press conference of July 1973, cf. INA dispatch 19 July 1973, in *FBIS/DR*, 20 July 1973; or Information Minister Hamid al-Juburi to *al-Nahar*, Beirut, 3 October 1973.

105 Radio Baghdad, Home Service, 29 October 1973, quoted according to *FBIS/DR*, 30 October 1973. 'Homeland' in this translation renders the Arabic *watan*, pan-Arab the Arabic term *qawmi*.

106 *al-Jumhuriyya*, Baghdad, 2 March 1974; further examples are Bakr's speeches of 13 January 1974 and 17 July 1974.

107 See *al-Thawra*, Baghdad, 11 March 1972; *al-Thawra*, Baghdad, 19 February 1973.

108 E.g. *al-Thawra*, Baghdad, 7 January 1973.

109 *al-Thawra*, Baghdad, 12 November 1973, on the day after the Israeli–Egyptian agreement of 101 kilometre.

110 Statement of 11 November 1973, Radio Baghdad, Home Service, 12 November 1973, according to *FBIS/DR*, 13 November 1973.

111 *al-Jumhuriyya*, Baghdad 7 December 1973; 15 December 1973.

112 E.g. *al-Thawra*, Baghdad, 31 December 1973; *al-Thawra*, Baghdad, 14 January 1974.

113 *al-Thawra*, Baghdad, 13 June 1974.

114 Ibid.

115 *Newsweek*, New York, 3 March 1975; but according to *al-Ba'th*, Damascus, 25 February 1975, Asad's view was not correctly rendered by *Newsweek*.

116 *al-Thawra*, Baghdad, 3 March 1975.

117 *al-Thawra*, Baghdad, 7 January 1973.

118 E.g. *al-Thawra*, Baghdad, 3 November 1972; Saddam Husayn in an interview with *al-Nahar*, Beirut, 21 February 1975; *Bayrut*, Beirut, 26 February 1975.

119 Press Conference on 19 July 1973, quote according to *FBIS/DR*, 20 July 1973.

120 *al-Thawra al-'arabiyya*, Baghdad, nos 6–7, vol. IV, 1973, pp. 7, 15, quoted according to Baram, 1983, pp. 190–1.

121 *OM* 1972, p. 338.

122 At the same round of talks an agreement in principle was reached that Iraq could resume its oil exports in Syria interrupted for technical reasons after the nationalization of the IPC.

123 *ARR*, 1972, p. 460, referring to INA dispatch, 19 September 1972; *ARR*, 1972, p. 384.

124 *L'Orient–Le Jour*, Beirut, 31 January 1974.

125 *MEED*, 1 November 1974, p. 1322; *ARR*, 1974, p. 462; at least Iraq seemed to pursue the project of a rail link seriously as contracts for consultancy and specifications were awarded, cf. *MEED*, 16 August 1974, p. 944, and then consultants invited to submit studies and designs, cf. *MEED*, 25 October 1974, p. 1286.

126 When Saddam Husayn was in Damascus in March 1972 the Syrians demanded that Iraq should accept they take 40 per cent of the Euphrates waters. When Husayn offered even 45 per cent the Syrian delegation after consulting Asad retreated; a subsequent Iraqi offer of 50 per cent was equally rejected; interview Damascus, 1985.

127 *OM*, 1972, p. 388; *ARR*, 1972, p. 435; cf. *Jerusalem Post*, 20 November 1973;

128 *al-Watan*, Kuwait, 17 January 1974; *L'Orient–Le Jour*, Beirut, 18 January 1974.

129 *al-Hayat*, Beirut, 27 September 1972.

130 Seurat, 1980, 135.

131 For details, see Batatu, 1978, p. 1094; Marr, 1985, pp. 216f.; Farouk-Sluglett and Sluglett, 1987, pp. 160ff.

132 This applies to the arrest of Abd al-Khaliq al-Samarra'i in 1973; for details, see Batatu 1978, p. 1094; Farouk-Sluglett and Sluglett, 1987, pp. 161f.

133 Interview, Syria, 1985.

134 Interviews, Syria, 1984, 1985.

135 Interview, Damascus, 1985; interview, Berlin, 1989.

136 A communiqué informing about the establishment of this grouping was issued in Beirut on 28 December 1971; see *MEJ*, 1972, p. 168.

137 Interviews, Syria, 1985; Paris, 1987.

## 3   Escalation and exacerbation of regional competition, 1975–1978

1 As to Iraq's quest for regional influence, see Ahmad, 1984; Baram, 1980; Chubin and Tripp, 1988; Dawisha, 1983; Farouk-Sluglett, 1984; Farouk-Sluglett and Sluglett, 1987; Rokach, 1979.

2 As to Syria's quest for regional influence, see Abdel Hamid, 1986; Dawisha, 1980; Hinnebusch, 1984; 1986; Harris, 1985; Krämer 1987a; 1987b; Kutschera, 1988; Michaud, 1984; Newmann 1983/4; Picard, 1987; Rabinovich, 1978, 1982, 1986; Rokach, 1979; Seale, 1988.

3 The text of the Algiers agreement is available in different publications, e.g. *OM*, 1975, p.118.

4 Rokach, 1979.

5 Pakradouni, 1984, p. 76.

6 Interview by Patrick Seale, *The Observer*, London 6 March 1977.

7 Evron, 1987, p. 29.

8 *al-Thawra*, Damascus, 30 August, 1976.

9 For details, see *MECS*, VIII, 540–48.

10 For details see Roussillon, 1983; *MEI*, London, issues of May, June, July 1983.

11 See interview by Patrick Seale, *The Observer*, London, 6 March 1977.

12 Radio Damascus, Home Service, 20 July 1976, quoted according to *FBIS/DR* 21 July 1976.

13 *al-Thawra*, 9 July 1981, quoted according to *BBC/SWB*, 11 July 1981.

14 *The Observer*, London, 6 March 1977.

15 As to Syro-Saudi relations see also Holden and Johns, 1982, pp. 298–9.

16 Kanovsky, 1986, pp. 294–5; *The Middle East*, London, December, 1978.

17 Rokach, 1979.

18 Quoted according to Ahmad, 1984, p. 159 and note 59.

19 *Alif-Ba'*, Baghad, 2 January 1980.

20 See also Holden and Johns, 1982, pp. 448–9.

21 Rokach, 1979.

22 In 1983 Kuwait helped with 130,000 barrels a day and Saudi Arabia with 200,000 barrels, according to the *Wall Street Journal*, New York, 24 October 1983. In the period 1985–7 both countries together still sold some 200,000–300,000 barrels a day of 'swap oil' for Iraq, see *MEES* 28 September 1987, p. 1.

23 *MECS*, III, p. 572.

24 For the history of the project and its realization, see chapter 2 and Bari, 1977.

25 *Syrie et monde arabe*, Damascus, 25 April 1982, p. 56.

26 *Office arabe de presse*, Damascus.

27 As reproduced by Ubell, 1971.

28 Associates for Middle East Research, 1987; for further sources see below.

29 Samman, 1980, pp. 23–5; *Syrie et monde arabe*, Damascus, 11 July 1982; *al-Thawra*, Damascus, 21 March 1982; *Tishrin*, Damascus, 3 February 1985 and Nyrop, 1979, pp. 114–19, give the figure 12,000 million cu.m.

30 There is some indication, at least, that in July 1975 the water-level of the lake was higher than 290 m above sea level; cf. p. 100.

31 *Tishrin*, Damascus, 3 February 1985.

32 Ibid.; *Syrie et monde arabe*, Damascus, 25 April 1982, p. 56; Samman, 1980, pp. 23–5.

33 According to some sources filling was only completed in 1978; see Nyrop, 1979, pp. 114–19.

34 Clawson, Landberg and Alexander, 1971.

35 Ubell, 1971; the Syrian figure mentioned earlier does not appear to be realistic in normal years.

36 *Financial Times*, London, 2 May 1975.

37 Statistisches Bundesamt, 1978, 15 referring to Iraq, Minster of Planning, *Annual Abstract of Statistics*, 1975; no figures for the years after 1975 are available except for 1978 when, according to al-Hadithi, 1979, 26,900 million cu.m flowed into Iraq.

38 Interview, Syria, 1985; for further evidence, see *Financial Times*, London, 2 May 1975.

39 According to Bari, 1977, p. 239 note 35; earlier Syrian sources had given lower figures, cf. *ARR*, 1979, p. 289.

40 Bari, 1977, p. 235.

41 al-Hadithi, 1979.

42 Associates for Middle East Research 1987; this report postdates the Syro–Iraqi row over the sharing of the Euphrates waters in 1975, but it can be assumed that similar calculations were made in Baghdad at that time.

43 Ubell, 1971, puts the consumption for this section at 17, 213 million cu.m annually for the years 1960–9. The figure of 12,700 million cu.m is obtained by subtracting from Ubell's figure some 4,500 million cu.m that were diverted into the Hawr Abu Dibis depression as a flood protection measure but not used for any other purpose; information according to a communication by J. Fischer, Freie Universität, Berlin.

44 United Nations, 1982, p. 70.

45 Hannoyer, 1985, p. 29.

46 As to Iraq's attitude to Turkish claims on the Euphrates water, see Bari, 1977, p. 242.

47 In the 1970s Syria and Iraq held that they had no difference with Turkey, although Turkey also increased its use of the Euphrates waters. As to Turkey's role and relations with Syria and Iraq, see Bari, 1977.

48 Cf. interview with Nur al-Din al-Rifa'i, former Syrian Minster of Industry, in *al-Nahar*, Beirut, 17 May 1977.

49 Iraq, Ministry of Information, n.d.

50 Nur al-Din al-Rifa'i in *al-Nahar*, Beirut, 17 May 1975.

51 Iraq, Ministry of Information, n.d.

52 Iraq, Ministry of Information, n.d.

53 al-Rifa'i in *al-Nahar*, 17 May 1975.

54 See Bari, 1977, and Iraq, Ministry of Information, n.d.

55 *L'Orient–Le Jour*, Beirut 8 April 1975; *Financial Times*, London, 2 May 1975.

56 Cf. e.g. *ARR,* 1975, p. 276; *OM* 1975, p. 108.

57 E.g. *ARR,* 1975, p. 289.

58 Interview, Damascus, 1985.

59 For a detailed account of events, see e.g. *ARR*, 1975, pp. 748, 276, 289, 308, 319, 335, 345; *OM*, 1975, pp. 107ff., 330 ff., 354f.

60 *ARR*, 1975, p. 345, referring to Radio Damascus, 3 June 1975; see also *al-Hawadith*, Beirut, 24 July 1975

61 *ARR*, 1975, p. 355; *L'Orient–Le Jour*, Beirut, 10 June 1975.

62 *al-Ba'th*, Damascus, 13 August 1975.

63 Foreign Minister Khaddam on Radio Damascus 18 April 1975, in *FBIS/DR*, 18 April 1975

64 *al-Ba'th*, Damascus, 9 April 1975.

65 AFP dispatch, 7 April; 1975; *al-Nahar* and *al-Safir*, Beirut, 8 April 1975.

66 *L'Orient–Le Jour*, Beirut, 16 April 1975.

67 *al-Ba'th*, Damascus, 21 April 1975, quoted according to *FBIS/DR*, 28 April 1975; a similar statement was released at the end of the Twelfth National Congress of the Syrian Ba'th Party in *al-Ba'th*, Damascus, 4 August 1975. Another example of the irrelevance of the theme of Ba'thi legitimacy is Asad's speech on 8 March 1975; see *Tishrin*, Damascus, 9 March 1975.

68 E.g. *al-Ba'th*, Damascus, 7 and 8 May 1975; 20 May 1975.

69 E.g. *al-Ba'th*, Damascus, 30 May 1975 and afterwards.

70 E.g. SANA dispatch, 7 June 1975.

71 *al-Ba'th*, Damascus, 29 June 1975.

72 Interview, 1985.

73 See Picard, 1979a; Picard, 1980a; Chatelus, 1980; Kerr, 1973; Firro, 1986.

74 Firro, 1986, p. 59.

75 Radio Baghdad, Home Service, 27 March 1975, paraphrasing speech by Jazrawi in Arbil on 26 March 1975, quoted according to *BBC/SWB*, 2 April 1975.

76 Radio Baghdad, Home Service, 4 April 1975, reporting on a speech by Haddad to a student rally at Lake Habbaniyya, on the same day, quoted according to *BBC/SWB*, 7 April 1975.

77 Cf. Farouk-Sluglett and Sluglett, 1986; Farouk-Sluglett and Sluglett, 1987; al-Khafaji, 1984, 1986.

78 E.g. Radio Baghdad, Home Service, 27 March 1975, paraphrasing a speech by Jazrawi in Arbil on 26 March 1975, in *BBC/SWB*, 2 April 1975.

79 Speech by President Bakr, Radio Baghdad, Home Service, 17 July 1975, in *FBIS/DR*, 18 July 1975.

80 INA dispatch 13 August 1975.

81 E.g. statement by the National Command of the Syrian Ba'th Party at the end of the Twelfth National Congress, Damascus; Radio Damascus, Home Service, 4 August 1975, in *FBIS/DR*, 5 August 1975; also article by Rif'at al-Asad in *al-Ba'th*, Damascus, 27 July 1975.

82 Radio Damascus 16 August 1975, according to *ARR*, 1975, p. 476.

83 *al-Thawra*, Baghdad, 3 September 1975.

84 *ARR*, 1975, pp. 496–7; *al-Thawra*, Baghdad, 5 September 1975.

85 Some signs of Syrian willingness to ease tension with Iraq appeared already in late August and in September 1975.

86 *Financial Times*, London, 15 November 1975.

87 The decision was heavily criticized by Iraq; cf. *ARR*, 1975, p. 658; *al-Thawra*, Baghdad, 26 November 1975.

88 *al-Thawra*, Baghdad, 26 November 1975.

89 *L'Orient-Le Jour*, Beirut, 14 and 15 May 1975, 13 June 1975.

90 *Baghdad Observer*, Baghdad, 29 August 1975.

91 *ARR*, 1975, p. 508.

92 *ARR*, 1975, p. 587; the *Guardian*, London, 22 October 1975.

93 *ARR*, 1975, pp. 587, 588.

94 ARR, 1975, p. 616.

95 *MECS*, I, p. 161.

96 Interview, Damascus, 1975.

97 The *Sunday Times*, London, 25 May 1975.

98 *ARR*, 1975, pp. 385, 396; *OM*, 1975, p. 332.

99 Information according to which the PUK was founded on 1 July 1975 are incorrect; interviews, Damascus, 1984, Berlin 1988.

100 Interview, Berlin, 1987; Talabani had first been expelled from the KDP in 1964 and then led his own organization till in 1970 he merged it again with Barzani's KDP.

101 According to the *Financial Times*, London, 23 June 1975, referred to by *ARR*, 1975, p. 359, Syria had offered 'the Kurds' support 'in every respect' if they would resume fighting in northern Iraq. A similar offer had been made as early as March 1975.

102 Interviews, Syria, Lebanon, 1984, 1985. The *Guardian*, London, 10 April 1975; events reported by most Lebanese and important European newspapers; in its annual report for 1974–5 Amnesty International claimed to know the names of 69 persons arrested in the purge.

103 *ARR*, 1975, p. 308

104 *ARR*, 1975, pp. 385, 396; *OM*, 1975, p. 332.

105 *ARR*, 1976, p. 230; Radio Damascus Home Service, 12 April 1976, in BBC/SWB 14 April 1976.

106 *ARR*, 1976, p. 315; *ARR*, 1976, pp. 328; confirmed by Bakr himself in his letter to some Arab kings and heads of state written on 29 November 1977, as published by INA on 1 February 1978, in *BBC/SWB,* 3 February 1978, Beirut Inter-Press Service 31 May 1976.

107 *ARR*, 1976, p. 394.

108 MENA, Cairo, 14 April 1976.

109 *al-Siyasa*, Kuwait, 21 April 1976.

110 E.g. the statement made by the Syrian government on 1 April 1976, broadcast on Radio Damascus, Home Service, on the same day, in *BBC/SWB*, 2 April 1976; also, Asad's speech of 12 April 1976, broadcast on the same day by the above station, in BBC/SWB 14 April 1976.

111 E.g. *al-Ba'th*, Damascus, 17–21 April 1976.

112 E.g. *al-Ba'th*, Damascus, 22 and 24 June 1976.

113 E.g *al-Ba'th*, Damascus 22 June 1976.

114 UPI dispatch, 22 August 1976.

115 See *ARR*, 1976, p. 522. On 17 August another explosive charge reportedly heavily damaged the oil pipeline near the Homs refinery. The attack was claimed by the Organization of Syrian Revolutionaries, cf. AFP dispatch, 26 August 1976.

116 Syria accused Iraq of planning, supporting or carrying out acts of physical aggression in yet other cases which, however, are more easily substantiated by the facts; see pp. 114ff.

117 See e.g. *ARR*, 1976, pp.231, 329; *International Herald Tribune*, 3 and 4 April 1976.

118 *ARR*, 1976, p. 231; van Dam, 1979a, pp. 78, 95 note 22, 96 note 35.

119 MENA, 29 August 1976.

120 *ARR*, 1976, p. 73.

121 *MEES*, 19 December 1975, 2; *MEED*, 2 January 1976, p. 13.

122 *MEED*, 5 March 1976, p.13: US $11.60 per barrel as opposed to US $11.85–11.95 per barrel.

123 *MEES*, 5 April 1976, p. 1.

124 If calculated on an average transit charge of US $0.35 (US $0.30 for oil lifted at Tripoli and $0.41 for oil lifted at Banyas).

125 *MEED*, 20 February 1976; *ARR*, 1976, pp. 73 and 113.

126 *MEED*, 16 February 1976, p. 24; *ARR*, 1976, p. 216.

127 *MEES*, 26 April 1976, p. 7; in March Iraq already channelled some 500,000 barrels a day through its new North–South pipeline, *MEES*, 5 April 1976, p. 1.

128 *MEES*, 5 April 1976, p. 1; *MEED*, 5 March 1976, p. 13. At a later stage this capacity was to reach some 48–50 million tons a year or 1 million barrels a day, see 26 April 1976, p. 7; Penrose and Penrose, 1978, p. 446; *MEES*, 2 January 1976, p. 1.

129 *MEES*, 7 June 1976, p. 6; see also Penrose and Penrose, 1978, p. 446.

130 *MEES*, 19 April 1976, p. iii; in some months, however, average throughput of the trans-Syrian pipeline amounted to 1,050,000 barrels a day.

131 *MEES*, 7 June 1976, p. 6.

132 MEES, 6 July 1973, p. 4; *MEES*, 26 April 1976, p. 7, which also gives the figure of 1.1 million barrels a day for the regular throughput of this pipeline, thus contradicting *MEES*, 19 April 1976, p. iii, which, however, appears more founded.

133 Arab Petroleum Research Centre, 1983, p. 131.

134 *MEED*, 7 May 1976, p. 26; *ARR*, 1976, p. 265; Penrose and Penrose, 1978, p. 445, however, estimate the net loss to Syria at only US $188 million, which corresponds to some 4.1 per cent of the budget. Both percentage figures are obtained on the assumption that the absolute figures correspond to the loss incurred in 1976 which, however, is not entirely clear from the sources. In case the absolute figures reflect an annual loss starting in April 1976, the percentage figures obviously have to be revised.

135 *MEED*, 7 May 1976, p. 26; as to ensuing budget costs, see also *ARR*, 1976, p. 329; however, cf. note 134 above.

136 *al-Thawra*, Baghdad, 22–30 April 1976.

137 *al-Ba'th*, Tishrin, Damascus, same dates and throughout May 1976.

138 For definition, see Introduction.

139 Interviews, Damascus, 1984, 1985, Berlin, 1987.

140 Interviews, Syria, 1984, 1985.

141 *al-Jumhuriyya*, Cairo, 27 April 1976.

142 Carré, 1980, p. 196.

143 Interviews, Damascus, 1984, 1985; *MECS*, I, p. 161.

144 *ARR*, 1976, p. 347, President Bakr made a similar statement later (*MECS*, I, p. 161), and on 9 June 1976 review troops were supposed to leave for Syria (*ARR*, 1976, p. 347).

145 *ARR*, 1976, p. 347.

146 Radio Baghdad, Home Service, 17 June 1976, in *ARR*, 1976, p. 378.

147 Radio Damascus, Home Service, 22 June 1976, in *ARR*, 1976, p. 378.
148 Ibid.
149 Interviews, Damascus, 1984, 1985.
150 Interviews, Damascus, 1984, 1985.
151 *Daily Telegraph*, London, 14 June 1976.
152 Interviews, Damascus, 1984, 1985.
153 *al-Nahar*, 27 September 1976.
154 Precise accounts of these events are in Michaud, 1983; *MECS*, I, p. 606; *MECS*, II, pp. 226, 729–30; *MECS*, III, p. 803.
155 Precise accounts of these events are in Michaud, 1983; *MECS*, I, p. 606; *MECS*, II, pp. 226, 729–30; *MECS*, III, p. 803.
156 Interviews, Damascus, 1985; Cairo Radio, Home Service, 26 September 1976, in BBC/SWB 28 September 1976.
157 E.g. Bakr's statement to the Iraqi magazine *Hurras al-Watan*, Baghdad, 10 July 1977, on the occasion of the anniversary of the July revolution. In contrast, however, Bakr abstained from anti-Syrian remarks in his interview with INA on 5 April 1977, in BBC/SWB 7 April 1977.
158 E.g. Bakr's statement mentioned in note 157 above; articles published by *al-Thawra*, Baghad on 6 and 7 February 1978.
159 *MECS*, I, p. 162; according to *BBC/SWB*, 16 October 1978, the *Sawt Syria al-'arabiyya* was broadcasting at least from 31 October 1976.
160 *MECS*, I, p. 162; similar calls were also transmitted through different channels, e.g. statement by the RC of the pro-Iraqi Ba'th Party in Syria of 4 February 1978, distributed by INA 4 February 1978, according to *BBC/SWB*, 7 February 1978.
161 E.g. Radio Baghdad, Home Service, 6 October 1976, in *FBIS/DR*, 7 October 1976; Radio Baghdad, Home Service, 2 December 1976, in *BBC/SWB*, 4 December 1976.
162 INA dispatch, 4 October 1976, quoted according to *BBC/SWB*, 6 October 1976.
163 *Financial Times*, London, 16 December 1976.
164 *al-Thawra*, Baghdad, 11 February 1977; *MECS*, I, pp. 405–6.
165 Cf. e.g. Iraqi Youth Minister Karim al-Mulla, in his interview with *Arbeiter–Zeitung*, Wien, 30 April 1977; INA dispatch, 11 May 1977, in *BBC/SWB*, 13 May 1977; *MECS*, II, p. 226; *al-Thawra*, Baghad, 6 and 7 February 1978.
166 *al-Thawra*, Baghdad, 6 and 7 February 1978.
167 E.g. Radio Baghdad, Home Service, 9 February 1977, in *BBC/SWB*.
168 E.g. Radio Baghdad, Home Service, 11 February 1977, in *BBC/SWB*, 14 February 1977.
169 INA dispatch, 28 March 1977, quoted according to *FBIS/DR*, 30 March 1977.
170 Voice of Arab Syria, Baghdad, 30 January 1977, according to *FBIS/DR*, 1 February 1977.
171 INA dispatch, 17 March 1977, according to *BBC/SWB*, 19 March 1977.
172 Statement by Bakr, published by *Hurras al-Watan*, Baghdad, 10 July 1977.
173 Radio Baghdad, Home Service, 6 September 1977, quoted according to *FRIS/DR*, 7 September 1977. For March 1977 see Radio Baghdad, Home Service, 3 March 1977, in *FBIS/DR*, 3 March 1977.
174 E.g. Radio Baghdad, Home Service, 11 July 1977, quoted according to *FRIS/DR*, 11 July 1977.

175 E.g. INA dispatch (From Baghdad), 4 February 1978, in *BBC/SWB*, 7 February 1978.

176 *al-Thawra*, Baghdad, 23 November 1977.

177 *al-Thawra*, Baghdad, 6 February 1978.

178 DPA dispatch from Cairo, 16 February 1978, in *FBIS/DR*, 17 February 1978.

179 E.g. Radio Baghdad, Home Service, 8 May 1977, in *FBIS/DR*, 10 May 1977.

180 E.g. Radio Baghdad, Home Service, 19 August 1977, in *BBC/SWB*, 20 August 1977.

181 E.g. INA dispatch 23 June 1977 in *BBC/SWB*, 25 June 1977, on inner-regime differences over how to tackle the economic crisis.

182 E.g. Voice of Arab Syria, Baghdad, 24 August 1978, in *BBC/SWB*, 26 August 1978.

183 Radio Baghdad, Home Service, 30 August 1978, in *BBC/SWB*, 1 September 1978.

184 Ibid.

185 Interview with Radio Damascus, Home Service, 6 May 1977, in *FBIS/DR*, 8 May 1977.

186 SANA dispatch 6 January 1977, in *FBIS/DR*, 6 January 1979.

187 Cf. e.g. Radio Damascus, Home Service, 28 March 1977, in *FBIS/DR*, 30 March 1977; *MECS*, I, p. 609; *OM*, 1977, p. 323; Radio Damascus, 2 June 1977, in *FBIS/DR*, 3 June 1977.

188 *al-Ba'th*, Damascus 23 and 24 February 1977.

189 Interviews, Syria 1984, 1985; Carre, 1980, p. 196, but gives incorrect date of assassination.

190 *al-Thawra*, Damascus, 22 March 1977.

191 *Le Monde*, Paris, 27 October 1977; official Syrian Press commentary in *al-Ba'th*, Damascus, 26 October 1977; Radio Damascus, Home Service, 26 October 1977, in *FBIS/DR*, 26 October 1977.

192 *MECS* II, p. 729.

193 *Tishrin*, Damascus, 18 September 1978.

194 See e.g. Radio Damascus, Home Service, 26 September 1976, in *BBC/SWB*, 28 September 1976; *al-Ba'th*, Damascus, 27 September 1976; *al-Ba'th* and *Tishrin*, Damascus, 2 and 3 December 1976; Radio Damascus, Home Service, 4 July 1977, in *BBC/SWB*, 6 July 1977.

195 Radio Damascus, Home Service, 13 July 1977, quoted according to *BBC/SWB*, 15 July 1977.

196 Interviews, Syria 1984, 1985, Berlin, 1988.

197 Interviews, Syria, 1984, 1985, *MECS*, II, p. 226.

198 E.g. Radio Damascus, Home Service, 27 October 1977, quoted according to *FBIS/DR*, 28 October 1977.

199 E.g. Radio Damascus, Home Service, 28 October 1978, in *BBC/SWB*, 29 July 1978.

200 Letter from the executive office of the Syrian General Federation of Labour Unions to the president of the Iraqi Confederation of Trade Unions, quoted by Radio Damascus, Home Service, 3 April 1978, according to *BBC/SWB*, 6 April 1978.

201 Radio Damascus, Home Service, 29 October 1976, quoted according to *BBC/SWB*, 1 November 1976.

202 Radio Damascus, Home Service, 5 January 1977, quoted according to *BBC/SWB*, 7 January 1977.

203 E.g. Radio Damascus, Home Service, 13 March 1977, in *BBC/SWB*, 15 July 1977, but extremely recurrent.

204 Cf. Radio Damascus, Home Service, 2 November 1976, quoted according to *BBC/SWB*, 4 November 1976.

205 E.g. Radio Damascus, Home Service, 13 March 1977, quoted according to *BBC/SWB*, 15 July 1977.

206 E.g. SANA dispatch, 12 July 1977, quoted according to *BBC/SWB*, 13 July 1977.

207 Constitution of the Arab Socialist Ba'th Party, Damascus, 1947, part III, article 2 (my translation).

208 E.g. Radio Damascus, Home Service, 13 July 1977, in *BBC/SWB*, 14 July 1977; also Radio Damascus, Home Service, 28 May 1978, in *FBIS/DR*, 30 May 1978.

209 *MECS*, I, p. 408; also SANA dispatch (from Baghdad), 12 February 1977, in *BBC/SWB*, 14 February 1977.

210 SANA dispatch (from Damascus), 13 February 1977, quoted according to *FBIS/DR*, 14 February 1977.

211 Radio Damascus, Home Service, 17 February 1977, quoted according to *BBC/SWB*, 19 February 1977.

212 Radio Damascus, Home Service, 23 February 1977, quoted according to *FBIS/DR*, 25 February 1977.

213 Radio Damascus, Home Service, 28 March 1977, in *FBIS/DR* 30 March 1977.

214 *al-Ba'th*, Damascus, 21 June 1978; in August opposition within the army was reported to heavily intensify, Radio Damascus, Home Service, 21 August 1978, in *BBC/SWB*, 22 August 1978.

215 Again in Radio Damascus, Home Service, 27 June 1978, in *BBC/SWB*, 29 June 1978.

216 Ibid.; also: Radio Damascus, Home Service, 5 August 1978.

217 *Tishrin*, Damascus, 28 July 1978.

218 Radio Damascus, Home Service, 21 August 1978, quoted according to *BBC/SWB*, 22 August 1978; as to declarations on the occasion of regime anniversaries see also statement of the NC of the Syrian Ba'th Party, 7 March 1977, in *BBC/SWB*, 9 March 1977, though Asad in his speech on 8 March 1977 still ignored the Syro–Iraqi conflict, cf. *BBC/SWB*, 10 March 1977.

219 Radio Damascus, Home Service, 20 July 1976, in *FBIS/DR*, 21 July 1976; see also *ARR*, 1976, 463–4.

220 Chatelus, 1980; Firro, 1986; Kanovsky, 1986, esp. pp. 280–5.

221 Firro, 1986, p. 59.

222 Kanovsky, 1986, p. 283.

223 Batatu, 1982; Lawson, 1982.

224 As to the dwindling internal legitimacy of the Syrian regime in this period, see Anonymous in *Studia Diplomatica*, 1980; Batatu, 1982; Hinnebusch, 1982; Hudson, 1983; Michaud, 1983; Picard, 1979b; Picard, 1979c.

225 Picard, 1980a, p. 181; see also Kanovsky, 1986, p. 283; as to further costs, see Kanovsky, 1986, p. 283.

226 Kanovsky, 1986, p. 301.

227 Eftekhari, 1987; Farouk-Sluglett, 1982; Marr, 1985, pp. 240–70; Niblock, 1982, esp. p. 32; Whittleton, 1986; cf. Batatu, 1978, pp. 1095–6.

228 E.g. Farouk-Sluglett/Sluglett, 1987; Hudson, 1983; Khafaji, 1986.

229 *MECS*, II, p. 226, seems to overstate its relavance for this period.

230 E.g. statement of the RC of the pro-Iraqi Syrian Ba'th Party in Syria, INA dispatch, 4 February 1978, in *FBIS/DR*, 7 February 1978.

231 *al-Thawra*, Baghdad, 6 February 1978.

232 INA dispatch (from Baghdad), 5 April 1977, in *BBC/SWB*, 7 April 1977.

233 Radio Damascus, Home Service, 22 February 1977, quoted according to *BBC/SWB* 24 February 1977.

234 *MEES*, 7 March 1977, p. 5; *MEES*, 4 April 1977, p. 1; *MEES*, 25 April 1977, p. 6; *MEES*, 13 June 1977, p. 5.

235 *MEES*, 24 January 1977, p. 7.

236 *MEES*, 13 June 1977, p. 5.

237 *MEES*, 4 April 1977, p. 1.

238 *MEES*, 7 March 1977, p. 5.

239 *MEED*, 1 January 1977, p. 28.

240 It was reopened only on 15 June 1978 for 'partial traffic', and completely on 22 October 1978.

241 *ARR*, 1977, p. 941; *MECS* II, p. 226.

242 AFP dispatch, 6 February 1978, in *FBIS/DR*, 7 February 1978; INA dispatch, 21 February 1978, in *BBC/SWB*, 23 February 1978; Arabia and the Gulf, 6 March 1978.

243 *L'Orient–Le Jour*, Beirut, 26 February 1977.

244 *MECS*, I, p. 160.

245 According to INA 21 December 1976, in *FBIS/DR*, 22 December 1976, the papers concerned were the following ones: *al-Muharrir, Bayrut, al-Dustur, al-Yawm, al-Safir, al-Nahar, L'Orient–Le Jour, al-Hurriyya,* and *al-Nida'*; cf. *MECS*, I, p. 509.

246 *MECS*, I, p. 414.

247 *MECS*, I, p. 162; interviews, Syria, Lebanon, 1984, 1985.

248 *ARR*, 1976, p. 674.

249 *ARR*, 1977, p. 829.

250 The *Guardian*, London, 25 November 1977. That the initiative was Syrian is confirmed by the letter which Bakr according to Iraqi sources on 29 November 1977 sent to several Arab heads of state; for this letter see pp. 131ff.

251 The *Guardian*, London, 25 November 1977.

252 Reportedly other countries also attempted to mediate between Syria and Iraq at that time; cf. an anonymous and otherwise not always precise and commendable article in *Les cahiers de l'Orient*, 2e trimestre 1987, no. 6, p. 220.

253 INA dispatch (from Baghdad), 1 February 1978, quoted according to *BBC/SWB*, 3 February 1978.

254 *al-Thawra*, Baghdad, 30 November 1977; INA dispatch 30 November 1977, in *BBC/SWB*, 1 December 1977.

255 *al-Thawra*, Baghdad, 5 February 1978.

256 See INA dispatch (from Baghdad), 3 February 1978, in *BBC/SWB*, 6 February 1978, *al-Thawra*, Baghdad, 3 February 1978.

257 INA dispatch (from Baghdad), 3 February 1978, in *FBIS/DR*, 7 February 1978.
258 *MECS*, II, pp. 219, 736.
259 *al-Manar*, London, 7 January 1978.
260 *MECS*, II, p. 226.
261 Arabia and the Gulf, 9 January 1978; *Financial Times*, London, 11 January 1978.
262 AFP dispatch, 29 January 1978 in *FBIS/DR*, 30 January 1978.
263 *al-Thawra*, Baghdad, 7 February 1978.

## 4  The rapprochement in 1978–1979

1 Interview, Tariq 'Aziz in *al-Ba'th*, Damascus, 19 January 1979.
2 Rokach, 1979, p. 35.
3 INA dispatch (from Baghdad), 2 November 1978, in *FBIS/DR* 3 October 1978.
4 Interview of Information Minister Ahmad Iskandar Ahmad with *Tishrin*, Damascus, 25 November 1978; Interview of Foreign Minister Khaddam with *al-Mustaqbal*, Paris, 30 December 1978; and National Command statement, Radio Damascus Home Service, 5 October 1978, in *FBIS/DR*, 6 October 1978.
5 INA dispatch (from Baghdad), 3 October 1978, in *FBIS/DR*, 3 October 1978.
6 INA dispatches (from Baghdad), 7 October 1978, in *FBIS/DR*, 10 October 1978.
7 See *Doha QNA*, 7 October 1978, in *FRIS/DR*, 10 October 1978.
8 Rokach, 1979, p. 36.
9 *BBC/SWB*, 16 October 1978.
10 Interviews, Damascus, 1984, 1985, Archiv der Gegenwart 1978, 22 January 1975, referring to Reuters.
11 Interviews, Damascus, 1984, 1985.
12 Interviews, Damascus, 1984, 1985.
13 In Iraq the Charter was ratified by the RCC still on the same day, cf. Radio Baghdad, Home Service, 30 October 1975, in *BBC/SWB*, 1 November 1978.
14 INA dispatch (from Baghdad), 26 October 1978, in *FBIS/DR*, 27 October 1978.
15 For the composition of these committees, see Charter in appendix.
16 Radio Damascus, Home Service, 16 January 1979, in *FBIS/DR*, 17 January 1979.
17 Baghdad Voice of the Masses 1 October 1978, in *BBC/SWB*, 3 October 1978; see also *The Economist*, London, 4 November 1978, p. 58.
18 Interview, Paris, 1987.
19 Radio Damascus, Home Service, 7 January 1979, quoted according to *FBIS/DR*, 8 January 1979.

20 Interview, Syria, 1985.

21 *MECS*, III, p. 807.

22 Interviews, Damascus, 1984, 1985.

23 *MECS*, III, p. 807; interviews, Damascus, 1984, 1985.

24 *al-Akhbar*, Amman, 5 November 1978.

25 van Dam, 1979b, pp. 7–8.

26 Radio Damascus, Home Service, 6 November 1978, quoted according to *FBIS/DR*, 7 November 1978.

27 INA dispatch (from Baghdad), 26 November 1978, quoted according to *FBIS/DR*, 28 November 1978.

28 Interviews, Damascus, 1985.

29 See e.g. *The Times*, London, 24 October 1978; *New York Times*, 24 November 1978; *Financial Times*, 4 January 1979; *Middle East International*, London 2 March 1979; *al-Hawadith*, Beirut, 16 March 1979; numerous interviews, Syria, Lebanon, 1984–5.

30 See *MECS*, III, p. 816.

31 INA dispatch (from Baghdad), 28 October 1978, in *FBIS/DR*, 31 October 1978; *The Economist*, London, 4 November 1978.

32 Interviews, Damascus, 1985.

33 SANA dispatch (from Damascus), 29 October 1978, in *BBC/SWB*, 3 October 1978.

34 Radio Damascus, Home Service 8 November 1978, in *FBIS/DR*, 8 November 1978.

35 Radio Damascus, Home Service, 8 November 1978, in *FBIS/DR*, 8 November 1978.

36 According to *The Economist*, 4 November 1978, p. 58, this happened slightly earlier.

37 Radio Damascus, Home Service, 13 November 1978, in *FBIS/DR*, 14 November 1978.

38 Interviews, Syria, 1984, 1985.

39 Radio Damascus, Home Service, 16 December 1978, *FBIS/DR*, 19 December 1978.

40 INA dispatch (from Baghdad), 6 December 1978, in *BBC/SWB*, 8 December 1978; INA dispatch 7 December 1978 (from Baghdad as well), in *BBC/SWB*, 9 December 1978; INA dispatch (from Baghdad) 8 December 1978, in *FBIS/DR*, 11 December 1978.

41 *al-Watan*, Kuwait, 26 December 1978.

42 INA dispatch (from Damascus), 4 January 1979, in *BBC/SWB*, 6 January 1979.

43 INA dispatch (from Damascus), 15 January 1979, in *BBC/SWB*, 16 January 1979.

44 INA dispatch, 23 January 1979, in *BBC/SWB*, 26 January 1979.

45 *al-Watan al-'arabi*, Paris, 15 January 1979.

46 *al-Thawra*, Baghdad, 22 January 1979.

47 INA dispatch (from Baghdad), 28 January 1979, quoted according to *FBIS/DR*, 29 January 1979. Iraqi pressure is moreover confirmed by Turquié, 1979, p. 9.

48 *The Middle East* London, December 1978, p. 38.

49 Baram, 1980; Baram, 1983.

50 Curiously, some authors take Bakr's nationalist rethoric at face value but not Husayn's: Baram, 1983; Batatu, 1978, 1079–84; Seale, 1988, 354ff.

51 Batatu, 1978, p. 1079; Farouk-Sluglett and Sluglett, 1987, p. 206.

52 Baram, 1983; Farouk-Sluglett and Sluglett, 1987.

53 Batatu, 1978, pp. 1079–84.

54 Batatu, 1978, pp. 1073–110, especially pp. 1084–93.

55 Radio Damascus, Home Service, 30 January 1979, quoted according to *BBC/SWB*, 1 February 1979. Increased Iraqi pressure is also confirmed by interviews conducted in Syria and Europe in 1984 and 1985 as well as by the well-informed Selim Turquié (1979, p. 9).

56 Baghdad Voice of the Masses, 30 January 1979, in *FBIS/DR*, 31 January 1979.

57 *Jerusalem Post,* 24 February 1979; Turquié, 1979, p. 9.

58 INA dispatch, 28 May 1979, in *FBIS/DR*, 31 May 1979.

59 INA dispatch (from Baghdad), 12 April 1979, in *FBIS/DR*, 13 April 1979.

60 INA dispatch (from Baghdad), 5 May 1979, in *FBIS/DR*, 7 May 1975; INA dispatch (from Baghdad) 7 May 1975, in *FBIS/DR*, 8 May 1975.

61 Muhammad Haydar is not related to the head of Special Forces (*Quwat khassa*), the 'Alawi general 'Ali Haydar.

62 *al-Hawadith*, Beirut, 16 March 1979.

63 Foreign Report, London, 6 June 1979.

64 Interviews, Syria, Lebanon, 1984, 1985.

65 For details see *MECS*, III, p. 808.

66 Interview, Damascus, 1985. Regarding the cruel fate of some pro-Iraqi Ba'this see Turquié, 1979, p. 9.

67 INA dispatches (from Baghdad), 19 June 1979, in *FBIS/DR*, 20 June 1979, and in *BBC/SWB*, 21 June 1979; *al-Thawra*, Baghdad, 20 June 1979; *al-Ba'th*, Damascus, 20 June 1979.

68 INA dispatch (from Baghdad), 19 June 1979, quoted according to *BBC/SWB*, 21 June 1979.

69 INA dispatch (from Baghdad), 19 June 1979, in *BBC/SWB*, 21 June 1979.

70 See June *MECS*, III, pp. 559–67.

71 See the anonymous article in *Les Cahiers de l'Orient*, 2e trimestre 1987, no. 6, p. 225. The second version of Syrian involvement is presented by Seale, 1988, 354ff.

72 INA dispatch (from Baghdad), 28 July 1979, in *FBIS/DR*, 30 July 1979.

73 See Chabry and Chabry, 1980, pp. 7–8.

74 This theory can be confirmed by a report in *al-Safir*, Beirut, 31 July 1979, according to which some of those arrested in connection with the plot, foremost among them Mashhadi, had demanded an open debate within the party before choosing Bakr's successor.

75 Chabry and Chabry, 1980, pp. 7–8, referring to informed sources insist that there actually was a conspiracy. For further details and theories concerning this plot, see *MECS*, III, 559–67.

76 *OM*, 1979, p. 786, and *Le Monde*, Paris, 31 July 1979, referring to *al-Nahar* and *al-Safir*, Beirut, without giving dates of issues.

77 Cf. however Chabry and Chabry, 1980, pp. 7–8, referring to the confession made by a 'plotter' on Iraqi television.

78 *al-Nahar*, Beirut, 20 August 1979.

79 *Der Spiegel*, Hamburg, 27 August 1979, citation in the translation given in *MECS*, III, 816.

80 *MECS*, III, p. 803.

81 Carré and Michaud, 1983, pp. 135–6.

82 Interviews, Damascus, 1984, 1985; Paris 1987.

83 Foreign Report, London, 28 February 1979.

84 Interview, Damascus, 1985.

85 For tension between the Soviet Union on the one side and Syria or Iraq on the other, see Rokach, 1979, p. 39, and Turquié, 1979, p. 9; confirmed by interviews, Damascus, 1986; Paris, 1987.

86 Salamé, 1980; Seale, 1965; interview, Beirut, 1985.

## 5   The period after 1979

1 There were, of course, some exceptions, see p. 154.

2 Interviews, Damascus 1985, 1986.

3 For details see Chatelus, 1980; Firro, 1986; Kanovsky, 1986; irregular but frequent reports and notes in *MEED, MEES, MECS, MEI*.

4 Cf. Picard, 1986; Batatu, 1982; Lawson, 1982; Longuenesse, 1978; Longuenesse, 1979.

5 As to internal unrest in Syria after the *rapprochement* of 1978–9, cf. Batatu, 1982 Carré and Michaud, 1983; Carré and Seurat, 1982; Drysdale, 1982, Hottinger, 1983; Koszinowski, 1985; Maler, 1989; Michaud, 1983; *MECS*, IV, pp. 759–64.

6 See e.g. Farouk-Sluglett and Sluglett, 1986; Farouk-Sluglett and Sluglett, 1987, pp. 227–68; al-Khafaji, 1984; al-Khafaji, 1986; Marr, 1985, pp. 229–305; Muhsin, 1986, 236–42; casual reports in *MEI, MEED, MEES*.

7 For details see *MECS*, III, p. 803; *MECS*, IV, p. 765; confirmed by interviews, Syria, 1984, 1985.

8 *al-Ahrar*, Beirut, 2 July 1980.

9 *MECS*, 111, pp. 519 f.; *MECS*, IV, pp. 760f., 767; interviews, Damascus, 1984, 1985; *Le Monde*, Paris, 16 September 1982; Batatu, 1982.

10 *al-Ra'y al-'amm*, Kuwait, 17 May 1980.

11 Anonymous article in *Studia Diplomatica*, Bruxelles, 1980, p. 107.

12 E.g. Tariq 'Aziz in an interview with *Kifah al-'arabi*, Beirut, 24 March 1980; a similar statement had been made by the Iraqi Foreign Minister Hammadi in an interview with *al-Nahar*, Beirut, 2 October 1979.

13 INA dispatch (from Baghdad), 27 March 1980, in *FBIS/DR*, 28 March 1980; *Le Monde*, Paris, 26 July 1980.

14 *Le Monde*, Paris, 26 July 1980.

15 INA dispatch 21 July 1980, in *BBC/SWB*, 23 July 1980; *Le Monde*, Paris, 26 July 1980.

16 E.g. Baghdad Home Service 18 June 1980, in *BBC/SWB*, 20 June 1980.

17 *FBIS/DR*, 14 January 1981 and 11 March 1981.

18 For the regimes' regional ambitions, cf. *supra*; for problems of legitimacy in Syria

see Batatu, 1982; Hinnebusch, 1982; Hudson, 1983; Koszinowski, 1985; Lawson, 1982 and *infra*; or the internal legitimacy of the Iraqi regime see Farouk-Sluglett and Sluglett, 1987; Chubin and Tripp, 1988.

19 E.g. *al-Thawra*, Baghdad, 7 October 1980; Voice of Arab Syria, Baghdad, 7 March 1981, in *FBIS/DR*, 11 March 1981; Radio Damascus, Home Service, 7 March 1982, in *FBIS/DR*, 8 March 1982.

20 E.g. *Le Monde*, Paris, 26 July 1980 and 10 October 1980; Voice of Arab Syria quoted in note 368; *al-Thawra*, Baghdad, 28–30 June 1980 and throughout February 1982; Radio Damascus, Home Service, 7 March 1982, in *FBIS/DR*, 8 March 1982.

21 E.g. *Tishrin*, Damascus, 17 November 1981.

22 E.g. Ghassan Haddad, Syrian exile, according to INA dispatch of _7 August 1980, in *BBC/SWB*, 29 August 1980; *Le Monde*, Paris, 10 October 1983; *Neue Zürcher Zeitung*, Zürich, 3 July 1986.

23 *FBIS/Dr*, 1 July 1982; *MECS*, VI, 615–28; *al-Jumhuriyya*, Baghdad, 28 June 1982.

24 INA dispatch 18 August 1980, in *BBC/SWB*, 20 August 1980.

25 *al-Watan al-'arabi*, Paris, 21 December 1981; *al-Thawra*, Baghdad, 20 and 21 December 1981; *Le Monde*, Paris, 24 April 1982, 21 June 1983; *Frankfurter Allgemeine Zeitung*, Frankfurt, 28 November 1986.

26 Interviews, Damascus, 1984, 1985.

27 Interviews, Berlin, 1987.

28 The subsequent account is based on primary and secondary sources; it largely differs from information given by Hudson 1983, p. 91.

29 *MECS*, V, p. 586; however, partly contradicted by *MECS*, VI, p. 598; Interview, Damascus, 1986; *Tishrin*, Damascus 13 November 1980; *FBIS/DR*, 14 January 1981.

30 Radio Damascus, Home Service, 14 October 1980, in *BBC/SWB*, 16 October 1980.

31 Interviews, Damascus, 1986; Paris, 1987.

32 MECS, V, 586; *Tishrin*, Damascus, 13 November 1980 Interview, Damascus, 1986

33 Interviews, Damascus, 1986; Paris, 1987; *MECS*, V, p. 586.

34 *MECS*, V, p. 586, partly contradicted by *MECS*, VI, p. 598.

35 *MECS*, V, p. 586.

36 Hudson, 1983, p. 91, who however used this appellation for a previous period before it had currency.

37 *MECS*, V, p. 586.

38 *MECS*, VI, p. 596.

39 *MECS*, VI, p. 596.

40 Radio Damascus, Home Service, 14 February 1982, in *BBC/SWB*, 16 February 1982.

41 *MECS*, VI, p. 600.

42 Interview, Berlin, 1988.

43 Interview, Berlin, 1988.

44 Interviews, Syria, 1986; Paris 1987;

45 *MECS*, V, p. 589.

46 *MECS*, V, p. 796.

47 Interviews, Syria, 1984, 1985.

48 E.g. Voice of Arab Syria, Baghdad, 7 March 1981, in *FBIS/DR*, 11 March

1981.

49  Ibid.

50  Radio Baghdad, 18 June 1980, in *BBC/SWB*, 20 June 1980.

51  E.g.Statement of the RC of the pro-Iraqi Ba'th in Syria, 22 January 1981; INA dispatch (from Baghdad), 2 February 1981, in *FBIS/DR*, 3 February 1981; also *al-Tahrir*, organ of the pro-Iraqi Syrian Ba'th Party, Baghdad, 28 February 1981.

52  Baghdad Voice of the Masses, Baghdad, 8 November 1980, in *BBC/SWB*, 11 November 1980

53  *al-Thawra*, Baghdad, 19 November 1980

54  *Le Monde*, Paris, 12 and 13 October 1980.

55  Baghdad Voice of the Masses, Baghdad, 17 October 1980, in *FBIS/DR*, 22 October 1980.

56  E.g. INA dispatch 7 April 1981, in *FBIS/DR*, 8 April 1981; INA dispatch 21 May 1981, referring to an incident that allegedly occurred on 13 April 1981.

57  For the complete statement see *FBIS/DR*, 1 July 1982; *MECS*, VI, pp. 615–28; *al-Jumhuriyya*, Baghdad, 28 June 1982.

58  Interviews, Paris, 1986.

59  Carré and Michaud, 1983, p. 158.

60  This is not the place to go into the details of the still largely obscure history of the Muslim movements of Syria. For the years under review see Batatu, 1982; Kutschera, 1983; Péroncel–Hugoz, 1982; Carré and Michaud, 1983, pp. 156–9; and the corresponding entries of *MECS*. The reader will realize that there is no unanimity as to the many aspects of this history.

61  Interviews, Paris, 1986, 1988.

62  *al-Ra'id*, Aachen, No. 53, April 1981.

63  *MECS*, VI, pp. 850f.

64  For details see *MECS*, VI, pp. 850–5; Carré and Michaud, 1983, pp. 159–61; Kutschera, 1987.

65  Radio Damascus, Home Service, 7 March 1982, in *FBIS/DR*, 8 March 1982.

66  *Tishrin*, Damascus, 41 April 1982.

67  *al-Watan*, Kuwait, 16/9/1980

68  Interviews, Paris, 1984, 1985, 1987; Kutschera, 1983, pp. 12–13.

69  For partly incorrect details cf. Kutschera, 1983, pp. 12–13; *MECS*, VI, p. 764.

70  Composition according to interviews, Damascus, 1984, 1985, 1986; Paris, 1987; Kutschera, 1983, pp. 12–13; *MECS*, VI, p. 854; Interviews, Damascus, 1986: Paris, 1987.

71  Kutschera, 1983, pp. 12–13.

72  Interviews, Paris, 1984, 1985, 1987; *al-Watan al-'arabi*, Paris, 26 February 1982.

73  *FBIS/DR*, 11 March 1981.

74  Kutschera, 1987; interviews, Damascus, 1986; *Le Monde*, Paris, 18 April 1986, 20 April 1986; 2 May 1986; 7 May 1986; 9 May 1986.

75  Interviews, Syria, 1985.

76  Interviews, Syria, 1986.

77  *al-Watan al-'arabi*, Paris, 15 February 1982; Kutschera, 1983, p. 13; Interviews, Damascus, 1985, 1986; Paris, 1987; see also *MECS*, VI, p. 849.

78  Radio Damascus, Home Service, 7 March 1982, in *FBIS/DR*, 8 March 1982.

79  Radio Damascus, Home Service, 26 October 1980, quoted according to *FBIS/DR,* 28 October 1980.

80  Radio Damascus, Home Service, 7 March 1982, quoted according to *FBIS/DR*, 8 March 1982.

81  E.g. Radio Damascus, Home Service, 25 October 1980, quoted according to *FBIS/DR*, 28 October 1980; Radio Damascus, Home Service, 26 October 1980, in *FBIS/DR*, 28 October 1980.

82  E.g. *Frankfurter Allgemeine Zeitung*, Frankfurt, 14 June 1986.

83  *Le Monde*, Paris, 13 April 1982; *New York Times*, 15 April 1982.

84  *Le Monde*, Paris, 2 June 1983, referring to a declaration by the then Syrian ambassador to France, Yusuf Shakur.

85  *Le Monde*, Paris, 13 April 1982.

86  Hirschfeld, 1986, p. 108, who refers to al-Nahar Arab Report and Memo, Beirut, April 1982.

87  Interview, Paris, 1986.

88  *Tishrin*, Damascus, 4 April 1982; *Le Monde*, Paris, 10 April 1982.

89  *Le Monde*, Paris, 25 November 1983.

90  Radio Cairo, Home Service, 20 October 1983, in *Deutsche Welle, Monitor-Dienst*, Köln, 24 October 1983; *Middle East Review*, 1986, Saffron Walden, 1985, p. 116, gives the slightly smaller figure of 500,000–600,000 barrels a day.

91  *Middle East Review*, 1986, Saffron Walden, 1985, p. 116.

92  *Kuwait Times*, Kuwait, 29 November 1983.

93  *Middle East Review*, 1986, Saffron Walden, 1985, p. 116; contrary to some sources this pipeline link according to *MEES*, 28 September 1987, p. 1, is functioning at its maximum capacity.

94  *MEES*, 28 September 1987; *MEES*, 15 January 1990.

95  *al-Jumhuriyya*, Baghdad, 7 December 1983, quoting the Iraqi Oil Minister Qasim Ahmad Taki; *MECS*, VIII, p. 490, confirms the planned rise in the pipeline's capacity but only for summer 1987.

96  Interviews, Syria, 1986.

97  Interviews, Syria, 1986.

98  *Le Monde*, Paris, 6 November 1980; interviews, Damascus, 1984, 1985; Seale, 1988, p. 358.

99  E.g. *New York Times*, 25 May 1982.

100  Interviews, Syria, 1984, 1985, 1986.

101  *Le Monde*, Paris, 6 December 1980; 11 December 1980.

102  Seurat, 1982, p. 66.

103  Voice of Lebanon 4 May 1982, according to *MECS*, VI, p. 866.

104  *New York Times*, 14 April 1982; *FBIS/DR*, 18 July 1985.

105  *New York Times*, 7 June 1982.

106  *Le Monde*, Paris, 25 February 1982.

107  *Le Monde*, Paris, 12–13 October 1980.

108  *al-Ra'y al-'amm*, Kuwait, 10 September 1982.

109  Muir, 1986b.

110  Muir, 1986c.

111  Interview, Damascus, 1986.

112  *Le Monde*, Paris, 29 May 1986.

113  *Le Monde*, Paris, 5 June 1986.

114  *FBIS/DR*, 29 May 1986.

115  *New York Times*, 7 June 1986.

116  *Le Monde*, Paris, 12 June 1986.

117 Arab News, Jidda, 14 June 1986; *Le Monde*, Paris, 15 and 16 June 1986.
118 Muir, June 1986a.
119 *MEES*, 20 May 1986.
120 Jansen, 1987, p. 7.
121 Muir, 1986c.
122 Ibid.; *Washington Post*, Washington, DC 18 June 1986.
123 Haeri, 1986, p. 6.
124 *Maghreb-Machrek*, Paris, no. 114, Octobre–Décembre, 1986, p. 57; *Le Monde*, Paris, 8 July 1986.
125 Jansen, 1987, p. 7.
126 Interviews, Paris, 1987, 1988.
127 Confirmed by Jordanian Prime Minister Zayd al-Rifa'i; cf. Muir, 1987, p. 6–7.
128 IRNA 25 April 1987.
129 Jansen, 1987, p. 7.
130 Interviews, Paris, 1987.

## Conclusion

1    Syrian and Iraqi per capita GNP in market prices and current US dollars for the period concerned.

|       | 1969 | 1970 | 1971 | 1972 | 1973 | 1974 | 1975 |
| ----- | ---- | ---- | ---- | ---- | ---- | ---- | ---- |
| Syria | 250  | 261  | 295  | 314  | ?    | 547  | 676  |
| Iraq  | 278  | 300  | 344  | 393  | 483  | 951  | 1159 |

*Source*:    United Nations, Statistical Yearbooks 1973, 1974, 1975, 1976, 1977, 1978.

## Appendix

1    Text as translated by *FBIS/DR*, 27 October 1978; footnotes added.
2    This is *qawm* in the original; the present author prefers to render *qawmi* as '(Arab) national'.
3    The term *lijan* (sing. *lajna*) used in the original should rather be translated as 'committee(s)'.

# Abbreviations

| | |
|---|---|
| AFP | Agence France Presse |
| *ARR* | *Arab Report and Record* |
| *BBC/SWB* | *British Broadcasting Corporation: Summary of World Broadcasts,* *Part 4: The Middle East and Africa* |
| CARDRI | Committee Against Repression and for Democratic Rights in Iraq |
| DPA | Deutsche Presse Agentur |
| *FBIS/DR* | *Foreign Broadcasting Information Service: Daily* *Report, The Middle East and Africa* |
| INA | Iraqi News Agency |
| IRNA | Islamic Revolution News Agency (Tehran) |
| *MECS* | *Middle East Contemporary Survey* |
| *MEED* | *Middle East Economic Digest* |
| *MEES* | *Middle East Economic Survey* |
| *MEI* | *Middle East International* |
| *MEJ* | *Middle East Journal* |
| MENA | Middle East News Agency (Cairo) |
| *MER* | *Middle East Record* |
| *OM* | *Oriente Moderno* |
| QNA | Qatari News Agency |
| SANA | Syrian Arab News Agency |
| UPI | United Press International |
| WAFA | Palestine News Agency |

# Bibliography

Abdel-Fadil, M. (1988). 'The macro-behaviour of oil-rentier states in the Arab region', in H. Beblawi and G. Luciani (eds), *The Rentier State* (London).

Abdel Hamid, A. (1986). 'Die jordanisch-syrischen Beziehungen in den Jahren 1946 bis 1976', unpublished Ph.D. thesis (Universität Hamburg).

Abdel-Malek, A. (1970). *La Pensée politique arabe contemporaine* (Paris).

Abuhamdia, Z. (1988). 'Speech diversity and language unity: Arabic as an integrating factor', in G. Luciani and Gh. Salamé. *The Politics of Arab Integration* (London).

Abu Jaber, K. S. (1966). *The Arab Ba'th Socialist Party* (Syracuse, NY).

Ahmad, A. Y. (1984). 'The dialectics of domestic environment and role performance: the foreign policy of Iraq', in A. E. H. Dessouki and B. Korany, *The Foreign Policy of Arab States* (Boulder, Co.)

Ajami, F. (1978/9). 'The end of pan-Arabism', in *Foreign Affairs*, LVII, 2, 355–73.

Ajami, F. (1981). *The Arab Predicament: Arab Political Thought and Practice Since 1967* (Cambridge and New York).

Amin, S. (1970). *L'Accumulation a l'échelle mondiale* (Paris and Dakar).

Amin, S. (1976). *La Nation arabe: nationalisme et luttes de classe* (Paris).

Amin, S. (1982). *Irak et Syrie 1960–1980* (Paris).

Anderson, B. (1983). *Imagined Communities: Reflections on the Origin and Spread of Nationalism* (London and New York).

Anonymous (1980). 'La Syrie en 1979' in *Studia diplomatica* (Bruxelles), XXXIII, 1/2, 99–116.

Anonymous (1987). 'Les Relations syro-irakiennes: quarante ans de rivalité', in *Les Cahiers de l'Orient*, no. 6, 2e trimestre 1987, 201–32.

Anonymous (1987/8). 'La Nomenklatura irakienne ou l'organisation du pouvoir en Irak', in *Les Cahiers de l'Orient*, nos 8/9, 4e trimestre 1987/1er trimestre 1988, 341–51.

Antonius, G. (1969). *The Arab Awakening: the Story of the Arab National Movement* (Beirut, 1st edn 1938).

Arab Petroleum Research Centre (ed.) (1983). *Arab Oil and Gas Directory* (Paris).

Arab Political Documents *al-Watha'iq al-'arabiyya*, 1963–, published by the American University of Beirut. Arabic edition 1963–; English edition 1963–6.

Archiv der Gegenwart (annual) (Bonn).

Arnold, T. W. (1974). 'Khalifa', in H. A. R. Gibb and J. H. Kramers (eds), *Shorter Encyclopaedia of Islam* (Leiden).

Aron, R. (1962). *Paix et guerre entre les nations* (Paris).

Associates for Middle East Research (1987). 'Water Issues in the Middle East: the Euphrates Basin', Philadelphia, unpublished report, forthcoming as book by its main author, J. Colars.

Atiyya, Gh. R. (1973). *Iraq 1908–1921: a Political Study* (Beirut).

Attali, J. (1972). *Les Modèles politiques* (Paris).

Aubert, V. (1963). 'Competition and dissensus: two types of conflict resolution', in *Journal of Conflict Resolution*, VII, 26–42.

Al-Azm, S. J. (1968). *Al-Naqd al-dhati ba'da al-hazima* (Beirut).

Bakdash, Kh. (1944). *Al-Hizb al-shuyu'i fi al-nidal li-ajl al-istiqlal wa al-siyada al-wataniyya* (Beirut).

Barakat, H. (1984). *Al-Mujtama' al-'arabi al-mu'asir* (Beirut).

Baram, A. (1980). 'Saddam Hussein: a Political Profile', in *The Jerusalem Quarterly*, no. 17 (autumn), 115–144.

Baram, A. (1983a). 'Culture in the service of Wataniyya: the treatment of Mesopatamian-inspired art in Ba'thi Iraq', in *Asian and African Studies*, XVII, 265–313.

Baram, A. (1983b). 'Mesopatamian identity in Ba'thy Iraq', in *Middle Eastern Studies*, XIX, 4, 416–55.

Baram, A. (1983c). 'Qawmiyya and Wataniyya in Ba'thi Iraq: the Search for a new balance', in *Middle Eastern Studies*, XIX, 2, 188–200.

Baram, A. (1986). 'Ideology and power politics in Syrian-Iraqi relations 1968–1984', in M. Ma'oz and A. Yaniv, *Syria under Assad* (London).

Baram, A. (1989). 'The ruling political elite in Ba'thi Iraq, 1968–1986: the changing features of a collective profile', in *International Journal of Middle East Studies*, XXI, 4, 447–93.

Bari, Z. (1977). 'The Syrian-Iraqi dispute over the Euphrates waters', in *International Studies* (New Delhi), XVI, 2, 227–44.

Bar-Siman-Tov, Y. (1983). *Linkage Politics in the Middle East: Syria between Domestic and External Conflict 1961–1970* (Boulder, Co.)

Barth, F. (1969). Introduction, in F. Barth (ed.), *Ethnic Groups and Boundaries* (Boston, Mass.)

Batatu, H. (1978, 1982). *The Old Social Classes and the Revolutionary Movements of Iraq: a Study of Iraq's Old Landed and Commercial Classes and of its Communists, Ba'thists and Free Officers* (Princeton, NJ).

Batatu, H. (1981). 'Some observations on the social roots of Syria's ruling military group and the causes for its dominance', in *Middle East Journal*, XXXV, 3, 331–4.

Batatu, H. (1982). 'Syria's Muslim brethren', in *MERIP-Report*, XII, 9 (no. 110), 12–21.

Beblawi, H. (1988). 'The Rentier State in the Arab world', in H. Beblawi and G. Luciani (eds), *The Rentier State* (London).

Beblawi, H. and Luciani, G. (eds) (1988). *The Rentier State* (London).

Bengio, O. (1981). 'Saddam Husayn's quest for power and survival', in *Asian and African Studies*, XV, 3, 323–41.

Ben-Tsur, A. (1968). 'The Neo-Ba'th-Party of Syria', in *Journal of Contemporary History*, III, 3, 161–81.

Binder, L. (1957/8). 'The Middle East as a subordinate international system', in *World Politics*, X, 3, 408–29.

Bolz, R. (1979). 'Die Entwicklungspolitik im Irak nach 1968 und ihre bisherigen Ergebnisse', in *Orient*, XIX, 1, 68–89.

Bolz, R. and Koszinowski, T. (1979). 'Die syrisch-irakischen Einigungsbestrebungen: Hintergründe, Grenzen und Auswirkungen', in *Orient*, XIX, 3, 63–86.

Braune, W. (1944). 'Die Entwicklung des Nationalismus bei den Arabern', in R. Hartmann (ed.), *Beiträge zur Arabistik, Semitistik und Islamwissenschaft* (Leipzig).

Brecher, M. (1969). 'The Middle East subordinate system', in *International Studies Quarterly*, XV, 2, 117–39.

Brown, M. E. (1979). 'The nationalization of the Iraqi Petroleum Company', in *International Journal of Middle East Studies*, X, 107–24.

Buheiry, M. (1981). 'Bulus Nujaym and the Grand Liban ideal 1908–1919', in M. Buheiry (ed.), *Intellectual Life in the Arab East 1890–1939* (Beirut).

Buheiry, M. (n.d.) *Beirut's Role in the Political Economy of the French Mandate 1919–1939* (Oxford).

Büren, R. (1987). *Aufzeichnungen zur Rationalität arabischer Politik: Die Dialektik der Machterhaltung und der Primat der Innenpolitik* (Ebenhausen).

Burton, J. W. (1968). *Systems, States, Diplomacy and Rules*, (Cambridge and London).

Burton, J. W. (1972). *World Society* (Cambridge).

Büttner, F. and Scholz, F. (1983). 'Islamisch-orientalische Welt: Kulturtradition und Unterentwicklung', in N. Nohlen and F. Nuscheler (eds), *Handbuch der Dritten Welt*, Band 6 (Nordafrika und Naher Osten, Hamburg).

Carré, O. (1980). 'Le Mouvement idéologique ba'thiste', in A. Raymond (ed.), *La Syrie d'aujourd'hui* (Paris).

Carré, O. and Michaud, G. (1983). *Les Frères musulmans 1928–1982* (Paris).

Carré, O. and Seurat, M. (1982). 'L'Utopie islamiste au Moyen-Orient arabe et particulièrement en Egypte et en Syrie', in O. Carré (ed.), *L'Islam et l'État dans le monde d'aujourd'hui* (Paris).

Chabry, A. and Chabry, L. (1980). 'L'Irak et l'émergence de nouveaux rapports politiques intér-arabes', in *Maghreb-Machrek*, no. 88 (avril–juin), 5–24.

Chatelus, M. (1980). 'La Croissance économique: mutation des structures et dynamisme du déséquilibre', in A. Raymond (ed.), *La Syrie d'aujourd'hui* (Paris).

Chejne, A. G. (1957). 'Egyptian attitudes towards pan-Arabism', in *Middle East Journal*, XI, 253–67.

Chubin, S. and Tripp, Ch. (1988). *Iran and Iraq at War* (London).

Chubin, S. and Zabih, S. (1974). *The Foreign Relations of Iran: a Developing State in a Zone of Great-Power Conflict* (Berkeley, Calif.).

Clawson, M., Landberg, H. H. and Alexander, L. T. (1971). *The Agricultural Potential in the Middle East* (New York).

Cooley, J. K. (1986). 'Syria's fragile economy', in *Middle East International* (13 June), 3–4.

Czempiel, E. O. (1963). 'Der Primat der Auswärtigen Politik: Kritische Würdigung einer Staatsmaxime', in *Politische Vierteljahresschrift*, IV, 266–87.

Czempiel, E. O. (1969). 'Einleitung', in E. O. Czempiel (ed.), *Die anachronistische Souveränität: Zum Verhältnis zwischen Innen- und Aussenpolitik, Politische Vierteljahresschrift*, Sonderheft (special issue) 1, 7–10.

Czempiel, E. O. (1981). *Internationale Politik* (Paderborn).

Dahrendorf, R. (1959). *Class and Class Conflict in Industrial Society* (London and Stanford, Calif.)

van Dam, N. (1973). 'The struggle for power in Syria and the Ba'th Party 1958–1966', in *Orient*, XII, 1, 10–20.

van Dam, N. (1978). 'Sectarian and regional factionalism in the Syrian political elite', in *Middle East Journal*, XXXII, 2, 201–10.

van Dam, N. (1979a). *The Struggle for Power in Syria: Sectarianism, Regionalism and Tribalism in Politics 1961–1978*, (London).

van Dam, N. (1979b). 'Union in the Fertile Crescent', in *Middle East International* (20 July), 7–8.

van Dam, N. (1980). 'Middle Eastern political clichés: "Takriti" and "Sunni rule" in Iraq; "'Alawi rule" in Syria: a critical appraisal', in *Orient*, XX, 1, 42–57.

Dandachli, M. (1975). *Le Parti Baas arabe socialiste 1940–1963: aspects idéologiques et historiques, thèse de troisième cycle* (Université de Paris-I/Ecole pratique des hautes études, 6e section).

Dandachli, M. (Dandashli, M.) (1979). *Hizb al-ba'th al-'arabi al-ishtiraki 1940–1963: Musahama fi naqd al-haraka al-siyasiyya fi al-watan al-'arabi* (Saida).

Dann, U. (1968). *Iraq under Qassem* (New York).

Davis, J. (1987). *'Libyan Politics: Tribe and Revolution* (London).

Dawisha, A. I. (1976). *Egypt in the Arab World: the Elements of Foreign Policy* (London).

Dawisha, A. I. (1978a). 'Syria under Asad 1970–1978: the centres of power', in *Government and Opposition* XIII, 3, 341–54.

Dawisha, A. I. (1978b). 'The impact of external actors on Syria's intervention in Lebanon', in *Journal of South Asian and Middle Eastern Studies*, II, 1, 22–43.

Dawisha, A. I. (1980). *Syria and the Lebanese Crisis* (London).

Dawisha, A. I. (1983). 'Invoking the spirit of Arabism: Islam in the foreign policy of Saddam's Iraq', in A. I. Dawisha (ed.), *Islam in Foreign Policy* (Cambridge).

Dawn, E. (1948). 'The project of Greater Syria', unpublished Ph.D. thesis (Princeton University, NJ).

Dawn, C. E. (Dawn, E.) (1973). *From Ottomanism to Arabism: Essays on the Origins of Arab Nationalism*, (Urbana, Ill. and London).

Dekmejian, R. H. (1985). *Islam in Revolution: Fundamentalism in the Arab World* (Syracuse, NY).

Dencik, L. (1971). 'Plädoyer für eine revolutionäre Friedensforschung', in D. Senghaas (ed.), *Kritische Friedensforschung* (Frankfurt am Main).

Desoutier, B. (1974). 'Le Transport terrestre du pétrole: élement de la crise du Proche-Orient', in *Maghreb-Machrek*, no. 64 (mai–juin), 34–47.

Despres, L. A. (ed.) (1975). *Ethnicity and Resource Competition in Plural Societies* (Den Haag and Paris).

Dessouki, A.E.H. (Ali al-Din Hillal) and Matar, J. (1980, 1983). *Al-nizam al-iqlimi al-'arabi: dirasa fi al-'ilaqat al-siyasiyya al-'arabiyya* (Beirut).

Dessouki, A.E.H. and Korany, B. (1984). *Foreign Policies of Arab States* (Boulder, Co. and Cairo).

Deutsch, K. W. (1966). External influences on the internal behaviour of States', in F. B. Farrell (ed.), *Approaches to Comparative and International Politics* (Evanston, Ill.)

Deutsch, K. W. and Senghaas, D. (1971). 'Die brüchige Vernunft von Staaten', in D. Senghaas (ed.), *Kritische Friedensforchung* (Frankfurt am Main).

Devlin, J. F. (1976). *The Ba'th Party: a History from its Origins to 1966* (Stanford, Calif.)

Dishon, D. (1977). 'The web of inter-Arab relations', in *The Jerusalem Quarterly*, no. 2 (winter), 52–54.

Drysdale, A. (1981). 'The Syrian political elite 1966–1976: a spatial and social analysis', in *Middle Eastern Studies*, XVII, 1, 3–30.

Drysdale, A. (1982). 'The Asad regime and its troubles', in *MERIP-Report*, XII, 9 (no. 110), 3–11.

Drysdale, A. (1985). 'The succession question in Syria', in *Middle East Journal*, IXL, 2, 246–57.

van Dusen, M. H. (1972). 'Political integration and regionalism in Syria', in *Middle East Journal*, XXVI, 2, 123–36.

Eftekhari, M. (1987). 'Le Pétrole dans l'économie et la société irakiennes', in *Peuples méditerranéens*, no. 40 (juillet–septembre), 43–74.

Elsenhans, H. (ed.) (1974). *Erdöl für Europa* (Hamburg).

Enayat, H. (1982). *Modern Islamic Political Thought: the Response of the Shi'i and Sunni Muslims to the Twentieth Century* (London).

Evans-Pritchard, E. E. and Fortes, M. (1940). Introduction, in Evans-Pritchard and Fortes, *African Political Systems* (London).

Evron, Y. (1987). *War and Intervention in Lebanon: the Israeli-Syrian Deterrence Dialogue* (London).

Evron, Y. and Bar-Siman-Tov, Y. (1975). 'Coalitions in the Arab world', in *Jerusalem Journal of International Relations*, I, 2, 71–106.

Farah, T. (1978). 'Group Affiliations of university students in the Arab Middle East (Kuwait)', in *Journal of Social Psychology*, CVI, 161–5.

Farah, T. (1982). 'Politics and religion in Kuwait: two myths examined, in A. E. H. Dessouki (ed.), *Islamic Resurgence in the Arab World* (New York).

Farah, T. (1988). 'Attitudes to the nation and the state in Arab public opinion polls', in G. Luciani and Gh. Salamé (eds), *The Politics of Arab Integration* (London).

Farouk-Sluglett, M. (1982). '"Socialist" Iraq 1963–1978: towards a reappraisal', in *Orient*, XXIII, 2, 206–19.

Farouk-Sluglett, M. (1984). 'What price *'Uruba*? Aspects of Iraqi foreign policy since 1968', paper presented at the annual meeting of the British International Studies Association, Hatfield College, Durham University, 17–19 December.

Farouk-Sluglett, M. and Sluglett, P. (1978). 'Some reflections on the present state of Sunni/Shi'i relations in Iraq', in *Bulletin of the British Society for Middle Eastern Studies*, V, 79–87.

Farouk-Sluglett, M. and Sluglett, P. (1985). 'From gang to elite: the Iraqi Ba'th Party's consolidation of power 1968–1975', paper delivered at the conference of the International Political Studies Association, Paris, 15–20 July.

Farouk-Sluglett, M. and Sluglett, P. (1986). 'Iraqi Ba'thism: nationalism, socialism and National Socialism', in CARDRI (ed.), *Saddam's Iraq: Revolution or Reaction?* (London).

Farouk-Sluglett, M. and Sluglett, P. (1987). *Iraq since 1958: from Revolution to Dictatorship* (London).

Field, J. A. Jr (1970). 'Transnationalism and the new tribe', in R. O. Keohane and J. S. Nye Jr (eds), *Transnational Relations and World Politics* (Cambridge, Mass.)

Fink, C. F. (1968). 'Some conceptual difficulties in the theory of social conflict', in *Journal of Conflict Resolution*, XII, 412–60.

Firro, K. (1986). 'The Syrian economy under the Assad regime', in M. Ma'oz and A. Yaniv, *Syria under Assad* (London).

Frank, A. G. (1967). *Capitalism and Underdevelopment in Latin America* (New York).

Galtung, J. (1971). 'A structural theory of imperialism', in *Journal of Peace Research*, VIII, 1, 81–117.

Galtung, J. (1978a). 'Institutionalized conflict resolution: a theoretical paradigm', in J. Galtung, *Essays in Peace Research* (København [Copenhagen]), vol. III, 434–83; originally in *Journal of Peace Research*, IV (1965), 348–97.

Galtung, J. (1978b). 'Conflict as a way of life', in J. Galtung, *Essays in Peace Research* (København [Copenhagen]), vol. III, 484–507.

Galtung, J. (1980). *The True Worlds: a Transnational Perspective* (New York).

Geertz, C. (ed.) (1963). *Old Societies and New States: the Quest for Modernity in Asia and Africa*, (London and New York).

Gellner, E. (1983). *Nation and Nationalism* (Oxford).

Glazer, N. and Moynihan, D. P. (eds) (1975). *Ethnicity: Theory and Experience* (Cambridge, Mass.)

Gomaa, A. (1977). *The Foundation of the League of Arab States: Wartime Diplomacy and Inter-Arab Politics 1941 to 1945* (London).

Grimaud, N. (1984). *La Politique extérieure de l'Algérie 1962–1978* (Paris).

Guerreau, A. and Guerreau-Jalabert, A. (1978). *L'Irak: développement et contradictions* (Paris).

al-Hadithi, A. H. (1979). *Optimal Utilization of the Water Resources of the Euphrates River in Iraq* (Ann Arbor, Mich.)

Haeri, S. (1986). 'Sighs of relief', in *Middle East International*, (27 June), 6.

al-Hafiz, Y. (1965). *Hawla ba'du qadayat al-thawra al-'arabiyya* (Beirut).

al-Hafiz, Y. (1979). *Al-Hazima wa al-idiulujiyya al-mahzuma* (Beirut).

Haim, S. G. (ed.) (1976). *Arab Nationalism: an Anthology* (Berkeley, Calif. and Los Angeles, Calif.)

Halliday, F. (1974). *Arabia without Sultans* (Harmondsworth).

Hannoyer, J. (1985). 'Grand projets hydrauliques en Syrie', in *Maghreb-Machrek*, no. 109 (juillet–septembre), 24–42.

Harik, I. (1987). 'The origins of the Arab state system', in Gh. Salamé (ed.), *The Foundations of the Arab State* (London).

Harris, W. (1985). 'Syria in Lebanon', in *MERIP-Report*, XV, 6 (no. 134), 9–14.

Helms, C. M. (1984). *Iraq: Eastern Flank of the Arab World* (Washington DC).

Hinnebusch, R. A. (1982a). 'Syria under the Ba'th: State Formation in a Fragmented Society', in *Arab Studies Quarterly*, IV, 3, 177–99.

Hinnebusch, R. A. (1982b). 'The Islamic movement in Syria: sectarian conflict and urban rebellion in an authoritarian populist regime', in A. E. H. Dessouki (ed.), *Islamic Resurgence in the Arab World* (New York).

Hinnebusch, R. A. (1984). 'Revisionist dreams, realist strategies: the foreign policy of Syria', in A. E. H. Dessouki and B. Korany (eds), *The Foreign Policies of the Arab States* (Boulder, Co.)

Hinnebusch, R. A. (1986). 'Syrian policy in Lebanon and the Palestinians', in *Arab Studies Quarterly*, VIII, 1, 1–20.

Hirsch, F. (1977). *Social Limits to Growth* (London).

Hirschfeld, Y. (1986). 'The odd couple: Ba'thist Syria and Khomeini's Iran', in M. Ma'oz and A. Yaniv (eds), *Syria under Assad* (London).

Hoffmann, S. (1960). *Contemporary Theory in International Relations* (Englewood Cliffs, NJ).

Holden, D. and Johns, R. (1982). *The House of Saud* (New York).

Horowitz, D. L. (1975). 'Ethnic identity', in N. Glazer and D. P. Moynihan (eds), *Ethnicity: Theory and Experience* (Cambridge, Mass.)

Hottinger, A. (1983). 'One year after Hama', in *Swiss Review of World Affairs*, XXXIII, 4, 26–8.

Hourani, A. (1946). *Syria and Lebanon: a Political Essay* (Oxford).

Hourani, A. (1947). *Minorities in the Arab World* (London).

Hourani, A. (1981). *The Emergence of the Modern Middle East* (London).

Hourani, A. (1983). *Arabic Thought in the Liberal Age 1798–1939* (repr. of the 1962 edn with new preface) (Cambridge).

Hudson, M. C. (1983). 'The Islamic factor in Syrian and Iraqi politics', in J. Piscatori (ed.), *Islam in the Political Process* (Cambridge).

Hurewitz, J. C. (1956). *Diplomacy in the Near and Middle East: a Documentary Record 1517–1956*, 2 vols.

Husri, K. (1975). 'King Faysal I and Arab unity 1923–1933', in *Journal of Contemporary History*, X, 2, 323–40.

Ibn Khaldun (1958). *The Muqaddimah*, trans. F. Rosenthal (New York).

Ibn Khaldun (1967). *Discours sur l'histoire universelle*, trans. V. Monteil, (Paris).

Ibn Khaldun (1971). *Tarikh Ibn Khaldun al-musamma bi kitab al-'ibar wa diwan al-mubtada wa al-jabr, fi ayam al-'arab wa al-'ajam wa al-barbar wa min 'asrihum min dhawi al-sultan al-akbar* (Beirut).

Ibrahim, S. (1980). *Ittijahat al-ra'y al-'amm al-'arabi nahwa mas'alat al-wahda* (Beirut).

Ibrahim, S. (1982). *The New Arab Social Order: a Study in the Social Impact of Oil Wealth* (Boulder, Co. and Cairo).

Iraq, Ministry of Information (n. d.) *Azmat al-Furat: tarikh wa aqlam, Baghdad* (presumably published in 1975).

Ismael, T. (1982). *Iran and Iraq: Roots of Conflict* (Syracuse, NY).

Jansen, G. (1987). 'Syria and the USSR: under pressure', in *Middle East International* (15 May), 7.

Jarry, E. (1984). 'La Première entreprise de Syrie: milihouse n'a de militaire que son noms, in *Le Monde* (6 May).

al-Jundi, S. (1969). *Al-Ba'th, (Beirut)*.

Kaiser, K. (1969). 'Transnationale Politik: Zu einer Theorie der multinationalen Politik', in *Politische Vierteljahresschrift* (Sonderheft) (special issue) 1, 80–109.

Kaminsky, C. and Kruk, S. (1987). *La Syrie: politiques et stratégies de 1966 à nos jours* (Paris).

Kanovsky, E. (1986). 'What's behind Syria's current economic problems?', in *Middle East Contemporary Survey (MECS)*, VIII (Tel Aviv).

Katouzian, H. (1983). 'The aridisolatic society: a model of long-term social and economic development in Iran', in *International Journal of Middle East Studies*, XV, 259–81.

Kedourie, E. (1970). 'The Kingdom of Iraq: a retrospect', in E. Kedourie, *The Chatham House Version and Other Middle Eastern Studies* (London).

Kedourie, E. (1976). *In the Anglo-Arab Labyrinth: the McMahon-Husayn Correspondence and its Interpretation 1914–1939* (London and Cambridge).

Kedourie, E. (1987). *England and the Middle East: the destruction of the Ottoman Empire, 1914–1921*, 3rd edn (London).

Kelidar, A. (1975). *Iraq: the Search for Stability* (London).

Keohane, R. O. and Nye, J. S. Jr (eds) (1970). *Transnational Relations and World Politics* (Cambridge, Mass.)

Kerr, M. H. (1971). *The Arab Cold War: Gamal Abd al-Nasir and his Rivals 1958–1970* (London and Oxford).

Kerr, M. H. (1973). 'Hafiz al-Asad and the changing patterns of Syrian politics', in *International Journal* (Canadian Institute of International Affairs), XXVIII, 4, 689–706.

Kerr, M. H. (1981). 'Rich and poor in the new Arab order', in *Journal of Arab Affairs*, I, 1, 1–26.

Kerr, M. H. Leites, N. and Wolf, C. Jr (1978). *Inter-Arab Conflict Contingencies and the Gap between the Arab Rich and Poor* (Santa Monica, Calif.)

Kerr, M. H. and Yassin, El Sayed (eds) (1982). *Rich and Poor States in the Middle East* (Boulder, Co. and Cairo).

Khadduri, M. (1978). *Socialist Iraq: A Study in Iraqi Politics since 1968* (Washington, DC).

al-Khafaji, I. (al-Khafaji, 'I) (1984). *Al-Dawla wa al-tatawwur al-ra'smali fi al-'Iraq 1968–1979* (Cairo).

al-Khafaji, I. (1986). 'The parasitic base of the regime', in CARDRI (ed.), *Saddam's Iraq: Revolution or Reaction?* (London).

Khairallah, K. T. (1919). *Le Problème du Levant: les régions arabes libérées: Syrie–Irak–Liban: lettre ouverte à la Société des Nations* (Paris).

Khalidi, R. L. (1977). 'Arab nationalism in Syria: the formative years', in W. W. Haddad and W. Ochsenwald (eds), *Nationalism in a Non-National State: the Dissolution of the Ottoman Empire* (Columbus, Ohio).

Khalil, M. (1962). *The Arab States and the Arab League* (Beirut).

Khoury, Ph. (1981). 'Factionalism among Syrian nationalists during the French mandate', in *International Journal of Middle East Studies*, XIII, 441–69.

Khoury, Ph. (1983). *Urban Notables and Arab Nationalism: the Politics of Damascus 1800–1920* (Cambridge).

Khoury, Ph. (1987). *Syria and the French Mandate: the Politics of Arab Nationalism 1920–1945* (London).

Kienle, E. (1985). *The Conflict between the Baath Regimes of Syria and Iraq prior to their Consolidation: from Regime Survival to Regional Domination* (Berlin [West]).

Kienle, E. (1988). *Ethnizität und Machtonkurrenz in inter-arabischen Beziehungen: Der syrisch-irakische Konflikt unter den Ba'th-Regimen* (Berlin [West]).

Kienle, E. (1989). 'Ethnicity in inter-Arab relations: Syrian policies towards Iraq in the period of Ba'thi coexistence since 1968', paper presented at the international conference on Ethnicity and Inter-state Relations in the Middle East, Free University of Berlin.

Kilu, M. (forthcoming). *Dayr al-Jusur, Masar al-Dubb.*

Kirkbride, A. (1956). *A Crackle of Thorns* (London).

Kiwan, F. (1983). *La Tradition des coups d'État et la pérennisation d'une dictature* (Université de Paris-I), thèse d'État.

Korany, B. (1983). 'Structure et processus du système international arabe', in *Le Moyen-Orient: enjeux et perspective* (Québec).

Korany, B. (1987). 'Alien and besieged, yet here to stay: the contradictions of the Arab territorial state', in Gh. Salamé (ed.), *The Foundations of the Arab State* (London).

Koszinowski, T. (1985). 'Die Krise der Ba'th-Herrschaft und die Rolle Asads bei der Sicherung der Macht', in *Orient*, XXVI, 4, 549–71.

Krämer, G. (1987a). *Arabismus und Nationalstaatlichkeit: Syrien als nahöstliche Regionalmacht* (Ebenhausen).

Krämer, G. (1987b). 'Syriens Weg zu regionaler Hegemonie', in *Europa-Archiv*, XLII (25 November), 665–74.

Krippendorff, E. (1963). 'Ist Aussenpolitik *Aussen*politik? Ein Beitrag zur Theorie und der Versuch, eine unhaltbare Unterscheidung aufzuheben', in *Politische Vierteljahresschrift*, IV, 243–66.

Kutschera, C. (1979). *Le Mouvement national kurde* (Paris).

Kutschera, C. (1983). 'Syrie: l'opposition démocratique et la difficile intégration du mouvement islamique', in *Le Monde diplomatique* (mars), 12–13.

Kutschera, C. (1987). 'L'Éclipse des frères musulmans syriens', in *Les Cahiers de l'Orient*, no. 7, 3e trimestre, 121–33.

Kutschera, C. (1987/8). 'Damas–Téhéran: objectif Saddam Hussein', in *Les Cahiers de l'Orient*, nos 8–9, 4e trimestre 1987/1er trimestre 1988, 31–46.

Laqueur, W. (1968). *The Road to War 1967–68* (London).

Laroui, A. (1977). *L'Idéologie arabe contemporaine* (Paris).

Lawson, F. (1982). 'Social bases for the Hamah revolt', in *MERIP-Report*, XII, 9 (no. 110), 24–8.

Leach, E. R. (1959). 'Hydraulic society in Ceylon', in *Past and Present*, no. 15, 2–26.

Leca, J. (1988). 'Social structure and political stability: comparative evidence from the Algerian, Syrian and Iraqi cases', in A. I. Dawisha and I. W. Zartman (eds), *Beyond Coercion: the Durability of the Arab State* (London).

Light, M. and Groom, A. J. R. (1985). *International Relations: a Handbook of Current Theory* (London).

Longrigg, S. H. (1958). *Syria and Lebanon under the French Mandate* (London).

Longuenesse, E. (1978). 'Bourgeoisie, petite-bourgeoise et couches moyennes en Syrie: contribution à une analyse de la nature de classe de l'État', in *Peuples méditerranéens*, no. 4, juillet–septembre, 21–42.

Longuenesse, E. (1979). 'The class nature of the state in Syria: contribution to an analysis', in *MERIP-Report*, IX, 4 (no. 77), 3–11.

Louis, Wm. R. (1984). *The British Empire in the Middle East 1945–1951: Arab Nationalism, the United States and Postwar Imperialism* (Oxford).

Luciani, G. (1988). 'Allocation vs. production states: a theoretical framework', in H. Beblawi and G. Luciani (eds), *The Rentier State* (London).

Mahdavy, H. (1970). 'Patterns and problem of economic development in rentier states: the case of Iran', in M. A. Cook (ed.), *Studies in the Economic History of the Middle East from the Rise of Islam to the Present Day* (London).

Mahr, H. (1971). *Die Baath-Partei: Portrait einer pan-arabischen Bewegung* (München and Wien).

Maler, P. (1980). 'La Société syrienne contre son État', in *Le Monde diplomatique* (avril).

Mansour, C. (1982). 'Palestine and the Gulf: an Eastern perspective', in R. Khalidi and C. Mansour (eds), *Palestine and the Gulf* (Beirut).

Ma'oz, M. (1972). 'Attempts at creating a political community in modern Syria', in *Middle East Journal*, XXVI, 389–404.

Ma'oz, M. (1973). 'Society and state in modern Syria', in M. Milson (ed.), *Society and Political Structure in the Arab World*, (New York).

Ma'oz, M. (1975). *Syria under Hafez Assad: New Domestic and Foreign Policies*, (Jerusalem).

Ma'oz, M. (1976). 'Alawi officers in Syrian politics 1966–1974', in H. Z. Schiffrin (ed.), *Military and State in Modern Asia* (Jerusalem).

Marr, Ph. (1987). *The Modern History of Iraq* (Harlow).

McDowall, D. (1985). *The Kurds* (London).

Méouchy, N (1989). 'Les Formes de conscience politique et communautaire au Liban à l'époque du mandat francais 1920–1935', thèse de doctorat, Université de Paris-IV.

Michaud, G. (*nom de plume* of M. Seurat) (1981). 'Caste, confession et société en Syrie: Ibn Khaldun au chevet du "progressisme arabe"', in *Peuples méditerranéens*, no. 16 (juillet–septembre), 119–30.

Michaud G. (1982). 'The importance of bodyguards', in *MERIP-Report*, XII, 9 (no. 110), 29–31.

Michaud, G. (1983). 'La Syrie ou l'État de barbarie 1979–1982', in *Esprit*, no. 88 (novembre), 16–30.

Michaud, G. (1984). 'Terrorisme d'État, terrorisme contre l'État: le cas syrien', in *Esprit*, nos 94/5 (octobre–novembre), 188–201.

*Middle East Contemporary Survey (MECS)* (New York and London, except vol. VIII) vols I–VIII: vol. I (covering 1976–7), C. Legum and H. Shaked (eds) (1978); vol. II (covering 1977–8), D. Dishon, C. Legum and H. Shaked (eds) (1979); vol. III (covering 1978–9) D. Dishon, C. Legum and H. Shaked (eds) (1980); vol. IV (covering 1979–80), D. Dishon, C. Legum and H. Shaked (eds) (1981); vol. V (covering 1980–1), D. Dishon, C. Legum and H. Shaked (eds) (1982); vol. VI (covering 1981–2), D. Dishon, C. Legum and H. Shaked (eds) (1984); vol. VII (covering 1982–3), D. Dishon, C. Legum and H. Shaked (eds) (1985); vol. VIII (covering 1983–4), D. Dishon and H. Shaked (eds) (Tel Aviv, 1986).

*Middle East Record (MER)* (Jerusalem): 1967, D. Dishon (ed.) (1971); 1968, D. Dishon (ed.) (1973); 1969/70, D. Dishon (ed.) (1977), 2 vols.

Mitchell, C. R. (1981). *The Structure of Conflict* (London).

Monroe, E. (1963). *Britain's Moment in the Middle East 1914–1956* (London).

Morgenthau, H. J. (1973). *Politics among Nations*, 5th edn (New York, repr. of first edn of 1948).

Morris, J. (1959). *The Hashemite Kings* (London).

Mousa, S. (1978). 'A matter of principle: King Hussein of the Hijaz and the Arabs of Palestine', in *International Journal of Middle East Studies*, IX, 2, 183–94.

Mughissudin, M., McLaurin, R. D. and Wagner, A. R. (1977). *Foreign Policy Making in the Middle East: Domestic Influences on Policy in Egypt, Iraq, Israel, Syria* (New York).

Muhsin, J. (1986). 'The Gulf war', in CARDRI (ed.), *Saddam's Iraq: Revolution or Reaction?* (London).

Muir, J. (1986a). 'What is cooking?', in *Middle East International* (30 May), 5–6.

Muir, J. (1986b). 'The two-way pressure of Hafiz al-Asad', in *Middle East International* (13 June), 3.

Muir, J. (1986c). 'Why Asad backed out', in *Middle East International* (27 June), 4–5.

Muir, J. (1987). 'The US and Syria: playing a shrewd game', in *Middle East International* (11 July), 6–7.

Muslih, M.Y. (1988). *The Origins of Palestinian Nationalism* (New York).

Nafaa, H. (1987). 'Arab nationalism: a response to Ajami's thesis on the "End of Pan-Arabism"', in T. Farah (ed.), *Pan-Arabism and Arab Nationalism: the Continuing Debate* (Boulder, Co. and London).

Nairn, T. (1981). *The Break-up of Britain: Crisis and Neo-Nationalism*, 2nd edn (London).

Nasr, M. (1981). *Tasawwur al-qawmi al-'arabi fi fikr Jamal 'Abd al-Nasir 1952–1970* (Beirut).

Neumann, R. G. (1983/4). 'Assad and the future of the Middle East', in *Foreign Affairs*, LXII, 2, 237–57.

Nevakivi, J. (1969). *Britain, France and the Arab Middle East 1914–1920* (London).

Niblock, T. (ed.) (1982). *Iraq: the Contemporary State* (New York).

Noble, P. C. (1971). 'Regionalism and conflict management: the case of the Arab system, unpublished Ph. D. thesis (Montreal, McGill University).

Noble, P. C. (1984). 'The Arab system: opportunities, constraints and pressures', in A. E. H. Dessouki and B. Korany (eds), *The Foreign Policies of Arab States* (Boulder, Co.)

Nyrop, R. F. (ed.) (1979). *Iraq: a Country Study* (Washington, DC).

Nyrop, R. F. (ed.) (1980). *Syria: a Country Study* (Washington, DC).

O'Ballance, E. (1973). *The Kurdish Revolt 1961–1970* (London).

O'Ballance, E. (1978). *No Victor, No Vanquished: the Yom Kippur War* (San Rafael, Calif. and London).

Olson, R. W. (1982). *The Ba'th and Syria 1947 to 1982: the Evolution of Ideology, Party and State: from the French Mandate to the Era of Hafiz al-Asad* (Princeton, NJ).

Owen, R. (1983). 'Arab nationalism, Arab unity and Arab solidarity', in T. Asad and R. Owen (eds), *Sociology of 'Developing Societies': the Middle East* (London).

Pakradouni, K. (1984). *La Paix manquée au Liban: le mandat d'Elias Sarkis 1976–1982* (repr. of first edn of 1983) (Beirut).

Palazzoli, C. (1977). *La Syrie: le rêve et la rupture* (Paris).

Penrose, E. and Penrose, E. F. (1978). *Iraq: International Relations and National Development* (Boulder, Co. and London).

Péroncel-Hugoz, J.P. (1982). 'Les Frères musulmans sont autant affaiblis par leurs divisions que par la répression' in *Le Monde* (16 September).

Petran, T. (1972). *Syria* (London).

Picard, E. (1978). 'La Syrie des militaires', in *Le Monde diplomatique* (avril).

Picard, E. (1979a). 'Ouverture économique et renforcement militaire en Syrie', in *Oriente moderno*, LIX (luglio–dicembre), 663–76.

Picard, E. (1979b). 'Clans militaires et pouvoir ba'thiste en Syrie', in *Orient*, XX, 3, 49–62.

Picard, E. (1979c). 'Le Rapprochement syro-irakien: vers une nouvelle donne des alliances au Proche-Orient', in *Maghreb-Machrek*, no. 83 (janvier–mars), 9–11.

Picard, E. (1980a). 'La Syrie de 1946 à 1979', in A. Raymond (ed.), *La Syrie d'aujourd'hui* (Paris).

Picard, E. (1980b). 'Y a-t-il un problème communautaire en Syrie?', in *Maghreb-Machrek*, no. 87 (janvier–mars), 7–22.

Picard, E. (1985). 'Les appareils de la dictature: le parti Ba'th au service des régimes militaires de Syrie et d'Iraq: discours du pouvoir et réponses des sociétés', paper delivered at the symposion 'Les appareils de la dictature', Universite de Paris-I (5–6 December).

Picard, E. (1987). 'La Politique de la Syrie au Liban', in *Maghreb-Machrek*, no. 116 (avril–juin), 5–34.

Piscatori, J. (1986). *Islam in a World of Nation-States* (Cambridge).

Porath, Y. (1974). *The Emergence of the Palestine-Arab National Movement 1918–1929* (London).

Porath, Y. (1984a). 'Abdallah's Greater Syria Programme', in *Middle Eastern Studies*, XX, 2, 172–89.

Porath, Y. (1984b). 'Nuri al-Sa'id's Arab unity programme', in *Middle Eastern Studies*, XX, 4, 76–98.

Porath, Y. (1986). *In Search of Arab Unity 1930–1945* (London).

Qasimiyya, Kh. (1971). *Al-hukuma al-'arabiyya fi Dimashq* (Cairo).

Rabinovich, I. (1972). *Syria under the Ba'th 1963–1966: the Army–Party Symbiosis* (New York and Tel Aviv).

Rabinovich, I. (1978). 'Syria, Israel and the Palestine question 1945–1977', in *Wiener Library Bulletin*, XXXI, New Series, 47–48, 135–41.

Rabinovich, I. (1982). 'The foreign policy of Syria: goals, capabilities, constraints and options', in *Survival*, XXIV, 4, 175–83.

Rabinovich, I. (1986). 'The changing prism: Syrian policy in Lebanon as a mirror, an issue and an instrument', in M. Ma'oz and A. Yaniv (eds), *Syria under Assad* (London).

Ramazani, R. K. (1975). *Iran's Foreign Policy 1941–1973: a Study of Foreign Policy in Modernizing Nations* (Charlottsville, Va.)

Raymond, A. (1980). 'La Syrie du royame arabe à l'indépendence 1914–1946', in A. Raymond (ed.), *La Syrie d'aujourd'hui* (Paris).

al-Razzaz, M. (1967). *Al-Tajriba al-murra* (Beirut).

Rokach, L. (1979). 'I passi verso l'unificazione fra Iraq e Siria: un disegno politico che tende alla "restaurazione"', in *Politica Internazionale* (luglio).

Rondot, P. (1979a). 'Politique syrienne et destin arabe', in *Etudes*, no. 351 (août–septembre) 165–80.

Rondot, P. (1979b). 'Iraq–Syrie: divergences et réconciliation', in *Défense nationale*, XXXV (février), 49–52.

Rondot, Ph. (1978). *La Syrie* (Paris).

Rondot, Ph. (1979). *L'Irak* (Paris).

Rondot, Ph. (1987). 'Syrie–Irak: du face-à-face au tête-à-tête', in *Arabies*, no. 7/8 (juillet–août), 36–9.

Rosenau, J. N. (ed.) (1964). *International Aspects of Civil Strife* (Princeton, NJ).

Rosenau, J. N. (1966). 'Pre-theories and theories of foreign policy', in R. B. Farrell (ed.), *Approaches to Comparative and International Politics* (Evanston, Ill.)

Rosenau, J. N. (ed.) (1967). *Domestic Sources of Foreign Policy* (New York).

Rosenau, J. N. (ed.) (1969). *Linkage Politics* (New York).

Rossi, E. (1944). *Documenti sull'origine e gli sviluppi della questione araba 1875–1944* (Roma).

Rouleau, E. (1983). 'La Syrie ou le miroir aux alouettes', in *Le Monde* (29 June, 30 June, 1 July).

Roussillon, A. (1983). 'La Crise du Fath, crise de l'OLP, crise syro-palestinienne? Les enjeux de la présence armée palestinienne au Liban', in *Maghreb-Machrek*, no. 102 (octobre–decembre), 89–110.

Saab, E. (1968). *La Syrie ou la révolution dans la rancœur* (Paris).

Sadowski, Y.M. (1988). 'Ba'thist ethics and the spirit of state capitalism: patronage and the party in contemporary Syria', in P. J. Chelkowski and R. J. Pranger (eds), *Ideology and Power in the Middle East: Studies in Honour of George Lenczowski* (London).

al-Sa'id, N. (1943). *Istiqlal al-'arab wa wahdatuhum* (Baghdad).

Salamé, Gh. (Salamah, Gh.) (1980). *Al-Siyasa al-kharijiyya al-sa'udiyya mundhu 'am 1945: Dirasa fi al-'ilaqat al-duwaliyya* (Beirut).

Salamé, Gh. (Salamah, Gh.) (1987). *Al-Mujtama' wa al-dawla fi al-mashriq al-'arabi* (Beirut).

Samarbaksh, A. G. (1980). *Socialisme en Irak et en Syrie* (Paris and Dakar).

Samman, N. (1980). 'The Euphrates dam project in Syria', in *International Water Engineering*, XVII, 4, 23–5.

Sayigh, A. (1966). *Al-Hashimiyyun wa al-thawra al-'arabiyya al-kubra* (Beirut).

Sayigh, Y. A. (1978). *The Economies of the Arab World: Development Since 1945* (London).

Scheffler, T. (1983). 'Konflikt, Identität und Parteien: Zum Verstäendnis von Grenzen und Politik', in W. Efferding (ed.), *Marxismus und Theorie der Parteien* (Argument-Sonderband AS 91) (Berlin [West]).

Scheffler, T. (1985). *Ethnisch-religiöse Konflikte und gesellschaftliche Integration im Vorderen und Mittleren Orient: Literaturstudie* (Berlin [West]).

Schmucker, W. (1973, 1974). 'Studien zur Baath-Ideologie', in *Die Welt des Islam*, XIV, 47–80, and XV, 146–82.

Seale, P. (1965). *The Struggle for Syria: a Study in Post-War Arab Politics 1945–1958*, 2nd edn 1986 (London and Oxford).

Seale, P. (1988). *Asad of Syria: the Struggle for the Middle East* (London).

Seurat, M. (1980). 'Les Populations, l'État et la société', in A. Raymond (ed.), *La Syrie d'aujourd'hui* (Paris).

Seurat, M. (1982). 'État et industrialisation dans l'Orient arabe', in A. Bourgey and CERMOC (eds), *Industrialisation et changements sociaux dans le monde arabe* (Beirut and Lyon).

Seurat, M. (1985). 'Le Quartier de Bâb Tebbané à Tripoli (Liban): étude d'une 'asabiyya urbaine', in CERMOC (ed.), *Mouvements communautaires et espaces urbains au Machreq* (Beirut).

Shehadi, N. (1987). 'The Idea of Lebanon: Economy and State in the Cenacle Libanais 1946–1954' (Oxford).

Shils, E. (1957). 'Primordial, personal, sacred and civil ties', in *British Journal of Sociology*, VIII, 130–45.

Shlaim, A. (1988). *Collusion Across the Jordan: King Abdullah, the Zionist Movement and the Partition of Palestine* (Oxford).

Simmel, G. (1955). *Conflict. The Web of Group Affiliations* (Glencoe, Ill.)

Simmel, G. (1958). 'Der Streit', in G. Simmel, *Soziologie: Untersuchungen über die Formen der Vergesellschaftung, 4. Auflage,* (Berlin [West]).

Simon, R. S. (1974). 'The Hashemite 'Conspiracy': Hashemite unity attempts 1921–1958', in *International Journal of Middle East Studies,* V, 314–27.

Sourdel, D. (1978). 'Khalifa: (i)The history of the institution of the caliphate', in E. van Donzel, B. Lewis and Ch. Pellat, *Encyclopaedia of Islam,* new edn (Leiden).

Statistisches Bundesamt (1978). *Länderbericht Irak 1978* (Mainz and Stuttgart).

Steppat, F. (1956). 'Nationalismus und Islam bei Mustafa Kamil: Ein Beitrag zur Ideengeschichte des ägyptischen Nationalismus', in *Die Welt des Islam,* IV, 241–341.

Tarabishi, G. (Tarabishi, J.) (1982). *Al-Dawla al-qutriyya wa al-nazariyya al-qawmiyya* (Beirut).

Tarbush, S. (1978). 'Iraq/Syria: reconciliation could have economic roots', in *Middle East Economic Digest,* XXII, 44 (3 November), 7–8.

Tibawi, A. L. (1969). *A Modern History of Syria including Lebanon and Palestine* (London and New York).

Tibi, B. (1969). *Die arabische Linke* (Frankfurt am Main).

Tibi, B. (1981). *Arab Nationalism: a Critical Enquiry* (London) (trans. of B. Tibi, *Nationalismus in der Dritten Welt am arabischen Beispiel,* Frankfurt am Main, 1971, repr. with new preface as Tibi 1987).

Tibi, B. (1987). *Vom Gottesreich zum Nationalstaat: Islam und panarabischer Nationalismus* (Frankfurt am Main).

Tilly, Ch. (1975). 'Reflections on the history of European state-making', in Ch. Tilly (ed.), *The Formation of National States in Western Europe* (Princeton, NJ).

Touraine, A. (1973). *Production de la société* (Paris).

Turquié, S. (1979). 'Le Projet d'union entre la Syrie et l'Irak', in *Le Monde diplomatique* (avril), 9.

Ubell, K. (1971). 'Iraq's water resources', in *Nature and Resources,* VII, 2, 3–9.

'Umran, M. (1970). *Tajribati fi al-thawra* (Beirut).

United Nations, Department of Economic and Social Affairs (1982). *Syrian Arab Republic: Approximate Classification of Present Water Use and Projected Water Needs for 1985* (New York).

Vanly, I. C. (1978). 'Le Kurdistan d'Irak', in G. Chaliand (ed.), *Les Kurdes et le Kurdistan* (Paris).

Vielle, P. (1984a). 'L'État périphérique et son héritage', in *Peuples méditerranéens,* nos 27/8 (avril–septembre), 5–37.

Vielle, P. (1984b). 'Pétrole et société', in *Peuples méditerranéens,* no. 26 (janvier–mars).

Wallerstein, I. (1974). *The Modern World System I: Capitalist Agriculture and the Origins of the European World Economy in the Sixteenth Century* (London and New York).

Wallerstein, I. (1980). *The Modern World System II: Mercantilism and the Consolidation of the European World Economy 1600–1750* (London and New York).

Wallerstein, I. (1984). *The Politics of the World Economy* (Cambridge and Paris).

Wallerstein, I. (1989). *The Modern World System III: The Second Era of Great Expansion of the Capitalist World-Economy 1730–1840s* (London and San Diego, Calif.)

Weber, M. (1974) *Wirtschaft und Gesellschaft, 3. Auflage*, 2 vols (Tübingen).
Weber, M. (1978). *Economy and Society*, of Weber 1947, 2 vols (Berkeley, Calif.)
Whittleton, C. (1986). 'Oil and the Iraqi economy', in CARDRI (ed.), *Saddam's Iraq: Revolution or Reaction?* (London).
Wilber, C. K. (ed.) (1978). *The Political Economy of Development and Underdevelopment* (New York).
Wilson, M. C. (1987). *King Abdullah, Britain and the Making of Jordan* (Cambridge).
Wittfogel, K. (1957). *Oriental Despotism* (New Haven, Conn. and London).
Wolfers, A. (1962). 'The actors in world politics', in A. Wolfers (ed.), *Discord and Collaboration: Essays in International Politics* (Baltimore, Md.)
Yamak, L. Z. (1966). *The Syrian Social Nationalist Party: an Ideological Analysis*, (Cambridge, Mass.)
Yapp, M. E. (1987). *The Making of the Modern Middle East 1792–1923* (London).
Zeine, Z. N. (1960). *The Struggle for Arab Independence: Western Diplomacy and the Rise and Fall of Faisal's Kingdom in Syria* (Beirut).
Zeine, Z. N. (1986). *The Emergence of Arab Nationalism*, 2nd rev. edn (1st edn 1958) (Beirut).
Zubaida, S. (1989). *Islam, the People and the State: Essays in Political Ideas and Movements in the Middle East* (London and New York).

# Index